HISTORIC DRESS IN AMERICA

FIGURE 1.

REIGN OF JAMES II

1685

FRONTISPIECE (FIGURE 1).—This plate represents a soft brocade gown which was brought from England to the Barbadoes Colony in 1685 and has been lent to the writer by a direct descendant of the owner. It is looped back over a satin petticoat, originally white, but mellowed by time into a rich ivory tint, and trimmed with two flounces of lace. The sleeves of the low-cut bodice are short and finished with a fringed gimp of the prevailing soft red colour of the brocade. The stomacher is trimmed with graduated bows of ribbon in the fashion called "échelles." The undersleeves of fine lawn are finished with lace ruffles to correspond with the falling band or collar. The skirt of the gown is quite long in the back and is looped at the hips with knots of ribbon; it is laid in plaits around the waist and sewed to the bodice which is fitted close to the figure. At that period the hair was drawn back softly from the face and two curls hung down on the shoulders from the knot at the back.

HISTORIC DRESS IN AMERICA

1607–1800

WITH AN INTRODUCTORY CHAPTER ON DRESS IN THE SPANISH AND
FRENCH SETTLEMENTS IN FLORIDA AND LOUISIANA

BY

ELISABETH McCLELLAN

TRANSLATOR OF "SCHILLER AND HIS TIMES," ETC.

ILLUSTRATIONS IN COLOUR, PEN AND INK, AND HALF-TONE BY

SOPHIE B. STEEL

OF THE PENNSYLVANIA MUSEUM AND SCHOOL OF INDUSTRIAL ART

TOGETHER WITH REPRODUCTIONS FROM PHOTOGRAPHS OF RARE PORTRAITS,
ORIGINAL GARMENTS, ETC.

PHILADELPHIA
GEORGE W. JACOBS & COMPANY
PUBLISHERS

"Fashion wears out more apparel than the man," and happily for us some relics of by-gone days have been preserved intact and placed in our hands for the preparation of this book—veritable documents of history on the subject of Dress in America, which should teach you "the nice fashion of your country," and help you "to construe things after their fashion."

For these interesting old garments and also for the valuable portraits and family papers most generously entrusted to us for our work I take this opportunity to express, in behalf of Miss Steel and myself, our appreciation and sincere thanks.

ELISABETH McCLELLAN.

PHILADELPHIA, *October*, 1904.

5

Introduction to Present Edition

We all know there is much history in costume and yet at the time this work was begun there were many books to be had describing the furniture, silver, houses, churches, meeting-houses, school-buildings and even the coaching inns frequented by the people of colonial days in America, but of the dress of the colonists, little or nothing had been put into book form. Occasionally some contemporary biographer would describe the costumes worn at festivities in the larger towns of the colonies, and by their help we could easily picture to ourselves a lady of that time adjusting her lace ruffles before a Chippendale mirror, or a gentleman studying the graceful use of his snuff box with the aid of his reflection. But of the every day clothes of these same people worn during the busy hours of those stirring times, the dress of the merchants, the artisans, the farmers and their families, there was absolutely no book to be found on the shelves of the libraries. Before the Revolution many a ship load of immigrants, wearing the costume of the country of their birth, landed in our ports, lending a variety and contrast to the appearance of the people. Much research was necessary to collect the material for this book, but Miss Steel and I found that our interest grew as we worked. We are much gratified to know that a new edition has been called for, proving that the earlier one filled a demand and has been of use to authors, artists, playwrights and students of history, for whose benefit it was undertaken.

ELISABETH McCLELLAN.

June, 1917.

Contents

INTRODUCTORY CHAPTER

PAGE

The Spaniards in Florida and California, 1565–1764................. 25
The French Settlements in Louisiana and the Mississippi Valley, 1680–1764 32

PART I. THE SEVENTEENTH CENTURY

The English Colonies in Virginia, Maryland, the Barbadoes, and the Carolinas, 1607–1700.. 39
The English Colonies in Massachusetts, Connecticut, New Hampshire, Maine, and Rhode Island, 1620–1700 79
The Dutch and English in New York, Long Island, the Jerseys, Delaware, and Pennsylvania, 1621–1700 117

PART II. THE EIGHTEENTH CENTURY

Women's Dress, 1700–1800... 173
    Reign of Queen Anne... 181
    Reign of George I.. 190
    Reign of George II... 193
    Reign of George III 202
    After the Revolution... 255
Children's Garments, 1700–1800...................................... 279
Men's Apparel, 1700–1800 295
    Reigns of Queen Anne and George I.............................. 299
    Reign of George II... 307
    Reign of George III.. 316
    After the Revolution... 328
    Legal Dress in the Eighteenth Century.......................... 335
    Uniforms in America, 1775–1800................................. 340

GLOSSARY 381
INDEX 397
AUTHORITIES CONSULTED... 405

Illustrations

FIGURE   PAGE

1. (In colours) Gown of red brocade worn in the Barbadoes Colony about 1685. Lent by Mrs. Rachel St. Clair Miller.................*Frontispiece.*
2. (Initial) Spanish galleon 25
3. Spanish gentleman, end of sixteenth century.......................... 26
4. Spanish soldiers with rapiers and arquebuses, middle of sixteenth century 27
5. Fernando De Soto, in Spanish armour of the sixteenth century........... 29
6. Sieur de La Salle, in French costume of 1680.......................... 29
7. Pedro Menendez de Aviles, in Spanish dress, 1565..................... 29
8. Sir Francis Drake, in the dress of an English sea-captain, 1586.......... 29
9. French peasant women... 34
10. Jesuit missionaries 35
11. (Initial) Sir Walter Raleigh... 43
12. Captain John Smith, 1616... 44
13. Sir Edwyn Sandys, 1607.. 45
14. George Sandys, Secretary of the Virginia Colony, reign of Charles I...... 45
15. Sir Isaac Pennington, reign of Charles I.............................. 45
16. Sir John Pennington, reign of Charles I.............................. 45
17. A farthingale, 1607... 47
18. Ordinary dress of a boy, 1602–1676.................................. 47
19. Dress of a colonial governor, reign of Charles I...................... 49
20. Dress of a colonial lady, reign of Charles I.......................... 49
21. Costume of a planter's wife, reign of James I........................ 49
22. Costume of a gentleman planter, reign of James I..................... 49
23. Ordinary dress of a little girl, 1602–1676........................... 52
24. English mariner, 1650 and after..................................... 53
25. Countryman in doublet, 1660 and after................................ 54
26. Soldier in cuirass and morion, seventeenth century................... 55
27. Silver frontlet worn by the Queen of the Pamunkeys................... 57
28. Silver mace, used in the House of Burgesses, Virginia................ 57
29. George Percy, second governor of Virginia........................... 57
30. Steel vambrace dug up near Jamestown................................ 57
31. Doublet worn in the reign of James I................................ 59
32. Indoor dress of an English gentlewoman, reign of Charles I........... 65

FIGURE   PAGE

33. Outdoor summer costume of an English lady, reign of Charles I ... 65
34. Back view of outdoor dress, reign of Charles I ... 68
35. English lady in hood and apron, reign of Charles I ... 69
36. English gentlewoman in winter dress, furs and mask, reign of Charles I.. 69
37. A peddler, from an old print ... 73
37½. Monmouth cap ... 74
38. (In colours) Lady of quality in the fashionable dress of William and Mary's reign ... 75
39. (In colours) Typical dress of a child in the seventeenth century ... 75
40. (In colours) Outdoor dress of a tradeswoman, end of the seventeenth century ... 75
41. (In colours) Workingman, end of seventeenth century ... 75
42. (In colours) A gentleman in the reign of William and Mary ... 75
43. (Initial) A Puritan dame ... 83
44. Mandillion of black silk, 1620 and after ... 85
45. Photograph of a doublet, reign of Charles I ... 87
46. Photograph of a doublet, reign of James I ... 87
47. Typical winter costume of a lady, 1640 ... 90
48. Boy's doublet of white linen embroidered with gold silk, reign of Charles I 91
49. Bodice of white satin, reign of Charles I ... 91
50, 51, 52, 53, 54. Boots, 1595–1660 ... 94
55, 56, 57. Boots, 1660–1690 ... 95
58, 59, 60, 61, 62, 63, 64, 65. Shoes, 1610–1695 ... 96
66. Puritan colonist of the Massachusetts Bay Company ... 97
67. Puritan woman of the Massachusetts Bay Company ... 97
68. An English gentleman of about 1666 ... 97
69. A lady of the same date (1666) in walking hood and fur tippet ... 97
70, 71. Cannons or breeches fastenings, 1650 ... 99
72. Lady's glove with embroidered cuff, seventeenth century ... 101
73. Head, after Hollar, showing fashionable style of hair-dressing, reigns of Charles I and II ... 101
74, 75, 76, 77. Gloves worn in the seventeenth century ... 101
78. Man in buff coat and bandolier, 1620–1660 ... 103
79, 80. Points with aiglets, 1650–1660 ... 104
81. Samuel Sewall, Governor and Judge of Massachusetts Colony ... 105
82. Sir John Leverett, Governor of Massachusetts ... 105
83, 84, 85, 86, 87. Various forms of the buff coat ... 107
88, 89, 90. Gorgets, 1620–1645 ... 108
91. John Winthrop the second, 1640 ... 111
92. Sir John Leverett, about 1680 ... 111
93. John Winthrop, Governor of Massachusetts Colony in 1629 ... 111
94. Edward Winslow, Governor of Plymouth Colony, 1644 ... 111

FIGURE   PAGE

95. (Initial) Dutch colonist in New Amsterdam 121

96. Peter Stuyvesant, Governor of New York Colony, 1647 123

97. Sir Edmond Andros, Colonial Governor of New York, 1674–1681 123

98. Henry Hudson, 1609 123

99. Sir William Keith, Governor of the Province of Pennsylvania, 1717 ... 123

100. Dutch woman in working dress, seventeenth century 126

101. (In colours) Dutch lady of New Amsterdam, about 1640 127

102. (In colours) Patroon, about 1640 127

103. (In colours) Dutch lady, about 1660 127

104. (In colours) English gentleman, end of reign of Charles II 127

105. Dutchman in working dress, about 1650 129

106. Dutch girl in fur cap and fur-trimmed jacket, 1641 131

107. Dutch lady, hair arranged in puffs at the side, 1645 131

108. Little Dutch girl, middle of seventeenth century 131

109. Little Dutch boy, same period 131

110. Dutch lady in fur cap and mantle, 1644 131

111. Swedish lady in pointed fur cap and ruff, 1640 131

112, 113, 114, 115, 116, 117, 118, 119, 120. Hats, 1606–1692 135

121. Coif of a Dutch matron, late seventeenth century 136

122. Dress of an English gentlewoman, 1640 137

123. Swedish woman in clogs, 1640 137

124. Dutch lady in outdoor dress, 1640 137

125. English lady in house dress, 1640 137

126. Dutch lady in wide-brimmed hat and ruff, 1645 141

127. English lawyer, seventeenth century 141

128. English woman in silk hood and tippet, 1640 141

129. Dutch lady in fur tippet and hood, middle of seventeenth century 141

130. Boy in periwig, about 1680 141

131. English woman in coif and kerchief, 1640 141

132. Portrait of little girls in seventeenth century, reign of Charles I 145

133. Portrait of two Dutch boys, middle of seventeenth century 145

134. Periwig of Charles II, 1660 147

135. Periwig of William III, 1690 147

136. Campaign wig, 1684 147

137. Coat and full breeches of buff brocade, 1681 149

138. Coat and full breeches of dark red flowered silk, 1681 149

139. Coat and breeches of silk trimmed with fancy braid, reign of James II... 149

140. Jeremias Van Rensselaer, end of seventeenth century 153

141. Kiliaen Van Rensselaer, first patroon of New Amsterdam, 1695 153

142. Sergeant-at-law, reign of Charles II....: 156

143. Quaker gentleman, 1682 157

144. Quaker lady, 1682 157

FIGURE   PAGE

145. Huguenot lady, 1686 157
146. Huguenot gentleman, 1686.. 157
147. Sergeant-at-law, reign of James II................................... 159
148. Count Zinzendorf in preacher's robe............................... 161
149. Simon Bradstreet in judge's robe, about 1670..................... 161
150. Lady Fenwick, in widow's mourning, reign of William and Mary....... 161
151. Elisabeth Boehler, Moravian lady in Pennsylvania, 1787............. 161
152. Moravian coif 164
153. Reticule of white silk embroidered in crêpe flowers................. 165
154. Waistcoat of Count Lemcke, about 1798............................. 165
155, 156. White silk pocket cases embroidered in colours, about 1790........ 165
157, 158. Moravian cap of lawn worn over a coif........................... 167
159. Specimens of colonial silver, seventeenth century..................... 169
160. Specimens of pewter ware, carved knife boards, etc., seventeenth century 169
161. (Initial) Lady in sacque, early eighteenth century..................... 177
162. (In colours) Colonial costume of 1711, of buff chiné silk, from an original
    gown lent by Mrs. Rachel St. Clair Miller........................... 179
163. (In colours) Gentleman in costume of 1702–1720, reign of Queen Anne.. 179
164. (In colours) Colonial costume of reign of George I, from an original gown
    lent by Mrs. Samuel Chew... 179
165. (In colours) Man in dress of a gentleman in the reign of George I...... 179
166, 167. Colonial fashion baby, 1720..................................... 183
168, 169. Camlet hood, taken from an original garment of about 1702........ 185
170. Short sacque, early eighteenth century............................... 187
171. Colonial dress, worn in Pennsylvania in the reign of George I......... 191
172. White satin wedding gown, 1760................................... 191
173. Lutestring gown worn in Philadelphia in 1760...................... 191
174. Colonial dress of buff chiné silk worn in the Barbadoes Colony in reign
    of Queen Anne... 191
175. Lady in a cardinal, early eighteenth century......................... 194
176, 177, 178, 179, 180, 181. Caps, 1744–1745............................. 195
182. Man in a Roquelaure, reign of Queen Anne........................... 197
183. Back view of a yellow damask gown, reign of George I.............. 197
184. Green brocade gown, worn in Massachusetts Colony, reign of George I .. 197
185. Back view of gentleman's dress, reign of George I.................... 197
186, 187. Hooped petticoats, 1721–1750................................. 199
188. Pair of stays, about 1770. Lent by Miss Sarah Bache Hodge......... 200
189. Clog, eighteenth century.. 201
190. Patten, eighteenth century.. 201
191. Riding hat of fawn-coloured felt, reigns of George II and III........... 202
192. Colonial gown of kincob brocade, worn in Massachusetts about 1735.
    Lent by Miss Archie Newlin... 203

FIGURE   PAGE

193. Colonial gown worn in Virginia, about 1775 — 203

194. Riding mask, eighteenth century — 205

195. (In colours) Colonial gown of camlet, worn in the Massachusetts Colony, 1725. Lent by Mrs. Charles Hacker — 207

196. (In colours) Gown of kincob brocade, time of George II — 207

197. (In colours) Young gallant in full dress, 1740 — 207

198. (In colours) Colonial gown of green taffeta, worn by Mrs. Wilimina Weemys Moore, about 1740. Lent by Miss Sarah Brinton — 207

199. House-maid in sacque, apron and clogs, middle of eighteenth century — 209

200. Mrs. Catharine Van Rensselaer in the popular style of cap, about 1770 — 211

201. Mrs. Nathaniel Appleton in an every-day dress. From photograph lent by Mrs. Cutter — 211

202. Mrs. Nathaniel Appleton, Jr., showing a peculiar cap of 1784. From photograph lent by Mrs. Cutter — 211

203. Mrs. Mary Faneuil of Boston, about 1750 — 211

204. A Watteau gown of fawn-coloured silk brocaded with coloured flowers worn in Pennsylvania about 1752. Lent by Mrs. William Bacon Stevens — 215

205. Crimson brocade gown worn by Mrs. Faithful Hubbard of the Massachusetts Colony, 1750. From a photograph lent by Mrs. Cutter — 215

206. Another view of the green kincob gown over a white satin skirt with apron and stomacher of white silk embroidered in colours — 215

207. Back view of the kincob gown showing the Watteau plaits — 215

208. Lady's silk shoe, about 1775 — 217

209, 210, 211. Diagram of white satin gown worn by Mrs. St. Clair about 1760 — 218

212. (In colours) Wedding gown of a New England Quaker lady, about 1750. Lent by Mrs. Charles Hacker — 219

213. (In colours) Gown of rich brocade worn by Mrs. Michael Gratz about 1750. Lent by Miss Miriam Mordecai — 219

214. (In colours) Suit of uncut velvet worn by Robert Livingston of Clermont, reign of George II. Lent by Mrs. David E. Dallam — 219

215. (In colours) Back view of Watteau gown of fawn-coloured silk — 219

216. Beaver hat and short cloak, middle of eighteenth century — 221

217. Back view of suit of uncut velvet worn by Robert Livingston of Clermont. Lent by Miss Anna Griffith — 223

218. Back view of white satin wedding gown of Mrs. St. Clair — 223

219. Everyday costume of a young lady, flowered chintz over a quilted petticoat, about 1770 — 223

220. Elderly man of business in a coat of strong fustian over nankeen breeches, 1770–1790 From a coat lent by Miss Sallie Johnson — 223

221. Group of colonial garments, eighteenth century — 227

FIGURE   PAGE

222. Calashes, Quaker hats, Quaker bonnet, riding hat, etc., eighteenth
  century... 227

223. Lady in capuchin, with fur trimmings and muff, reign of George III.... 229

224. Mr. and Mrs. Ralph Izard, 1774.................................... 231

225. Portrait of the West family, 1799................................. 231

226, 227. Calashes, 1765 233

228. (In colours) Dress of blue lutestring worn by Mrs. St. Clair, 1760. Lent
  by Mrs. Rachel St. Clair Miller....................................... 235

229. (In colours) Suit of dark satin worn by Robert Livingston of Clermont.
  Lent by Miss Anna Griffith... 235

230. (In colours) White satin wedding gown of Mrs. St. Clair, 1760. Lent by
  Mrs. Rachel St. Clair Miller... 235

231. (In colours) Suit of uncut velvet, waistcoat of quilted satin, worn by
  Robert Livingston, of Clermont, reign of George III. Lent by Miss
  Anna Griffith.. 235

232. Quaker cape and cap, 1780....................................... 237

233. Embroidered reticule.. 239

234. Ladies gloves of doeskin, 1717. Lent by Mrs. William H. Dreer....... 239

235. Bead reticule and paste buckles. Lent by Mrs. John Biddle.......... 239

236. Bonnet of muslin made over reeds, 1780. Lent by Mrs. John Biddle... 239

237. Crêpe shawl with printed figures, late eighteenth century............. 239

238. Linen pocket embroidered in colours, 1752......................... 239

239. Colonial jewelry and snuff-box. Lent by Mrs. Howard Gardiner...... 239

240. Lady's slipper of green and white taffeta. Lent by Mrs. William H.
  Dreer.. 239

241. Fan painted by Gamble, 1771. Lent by Mrs. Charles Hodge.......... 239

242. Typical dress of a country girl, 1780.............................. 246

243. Night-rail, eighteenth century..................................... 252

244. Gown of mauve crêpe, end of eighteenth century. Lent by Miss Janethe 253

245. Front view of Watteau gown of fawn-coloured silk, brocaded in flowers.. 253

246. Gown of white embroidered muslin worn in 1790. Lent by Mrs. George
  Knorr.. 253

247. Calico short sacque, late eighteenth century........................ 253

248. Gown of glazed buff chintz, 1795. Lent by Mrs. Cooper Smith........ 253

249. Riding habit, about 1785.. 260

250. Mrs. Pennington in Quaker dress, 1780. From a portrait lent by Mrs.
  Howard Gardiner 261

251. Catharine Schuyler Van Rensselaer, 1795. Lent by Mrs. J. K. Van
  Rensselaer 261

252. Mrs. Morris in Quaker dress, 1785................................ 261

253. Dutch lady of the New York Colony, 1765. Lent by Mrs. J. K. Van
  Rensselaer 261

FIGURE   PAGE

254. Summer costume, 1790–1795... 264

255. (In colours) Suit worn at the court of France by William West, Esq., of
        Philadelphia, 1778. Lent by Mr. Hemsley 265

256. (In colours) Lady's costume of the prevailing French fashion, 1777–1779 265

257. (In colours) Gentleman's suit of drab cloth, 1786..................... 265

258. (In colours) Muslin gown with flowing skirt and long sleeved bodice,
        1790 265

259. Woman in typical working dress, 1790–1800.......................... 268

260. White satin wedding slippers, 1800. Lent by Mrs. Schaeffer.......... 269

261. Cups and saucers, owned by Robert Treat Paine. Lent by Mrs. William
        H. Dreer 269

262. Group of slippers, 1735–1780... 269

263. Blue brocade wedding slippers, 1771. Lent by Miss Helen Morton..... 269

264. Wine glasses and point lace belonging to Governor Wentworth, 1717–
        1730. Lent by Mrs. William H. Dreer............................... 269

265. Back of mauve crêpe shown in figure 341............................. 273

266. Silk pelisse with quilted border, 1797. Lent by Frank W. Taylor, Esq. 274

267, 268. Seventeenth century utensils...................................... 275

269. (Initial) Boy and girl after Sir Joshua Reynolds, late eighteenth century 283

270. (In colours) Girl in red stuff gown and muslin cap, about 1730......... 285

271. (In colours) Child in printed gown and embroidered cap, about 1710.... 285

272. (In colours) Child in gown of white damask linen, about 1720.......... 285

273. (In colours) Little boy in blue suit, about 1740....................... 285

274. (In colours) Boy in brown velvet suit and cocked hat, about 1760....... 285

275. (In colours) Boy in blue ribbed silk suit worn in Pennsylvania about
        1756 285

276. (In colours) Child in buff printed cambric dress, about 1760........... 285

277. (In colours) Child in sheer muslin gown, with cap to match, 1790...... 285

278. (In colours) Little girl in cloak, muff and hat, after Sir Joshua Reynolds,
        about 1780 285

279. (In colours) Young girl in muslin gown trimmed with embroidery, about
        1790 285

280, 281. Child's stays. Lent by Mrs. Gummere........................... 287

282. Portrait of young girl in Philadelphia, about 1760.................... 289

283. Miss Hill of Philadelphia, 1756....................................... 289

284. Portrait of a child in New York, about 1700. Lent by Mrs. J. K. Van
        Rensselaer 289

285. Christiana Ten Broeck, early eighteenth century...................... 289

286. Baby dress and cap, 1771. Lent by Mrs. George Knorr............... 291

287. Boy in ordinary dress, 1790.. 292

288, 289. Front and back views of a "flying Josie," late eighteenth century.
        Lent by Mrs. Schaeffer.. 293

FIGURE   PAGE

290. Suit of blue silk worn by a little boy about 1756........................ 293
291. Child's dress of buff chintz worn in Pennsylvania, 1710................ 293
292. White shift with plaited sleeves....................................... 293
293. Child's dress of damask linen worn about 1720 293
294. (Initial) Man in long trousers and riding boots, late eighteenth century.. 299
295. Kiliaen Van Rensselaer, reign of Queen Anne. Lent by Mrs. J. K. Van
        Rensselaer 301
296. Jan Baptist Van Rensselaer, reign of George I. Lent by Mrs. J. K.
        Van Rensselaer... 301
297. A genuine Roquelaure, middle of eighteenth century. Lent by Frank
        W. Taylor, Esq... 303
298, 299, 300. Wigs, 1700–1750... 304
301. William Penn, by Benjamin West..................................... 305
302. George Washington, by Gilbert Stuart, 1797 305
303. Back view of suit of dark satin worn by Robert Livingston............ 308
304. Rev. George Whitefield, latter half of eighteenth century.............. 309
305. Rev. Jacob Duché, D.D., late eighteenth century 309
306. Dr. Ezra Stiles, late eighteenth century 309
307. Rt. Rev. Richard Challoner, Vicar Apostolic of the English Colonies in
        America, 1756.. 309
308. Jonathan Edwards, second half of eighteenth century................. 309
309. Rt. Rev. Samuel Provoost, D.D., First Bishop of New York, late eight-
        eenth century 309
310. Back view of coat of light brown velvet, reign of George II.......... 313
311. Front view of same.. 313
312, 313. Front and back views of coat of brown twilled cotton jean, typical
        summer garment of a Friend.................................... 313
314. Gentleman in banyan and cap, middle of eighteenth century.......... 315
315. John Penn, in fur-trimmed coat.................................... 317
316. Thomas Penn as colonial governor................................. 317
317. Patrick Gordon as colonial governor............................... 317
318. James Hamilton, Lieutenant Governor of Pennsylvania, 1783.......... 317
319, 320, 321, 322. Boots, 1702–1784................................... 319
323. James Logan in judicial robe, 1745................................ 321
324. Fisher Ames, middle of eighteenth century......................... 321
325. John Jay in robe, as Chief Justice of the United States.............. 321
326. Nathaniel Appleton of Boston, by Copley 321
327. Henry Laurens, by Copley... 321
328. Man in working garb, 1750.. 323
329. John Hancock, Governor of the Massachusetts Colony, reign of George
        III 325
330. Samuel Shoemaker, Mayor of Philadelphia, and his son, 1789.......... 325

FIGURE   PAGE

331. Portrait showing the plain but handsome costume of a gentleman in Pennsylvania at the outbreak of the Revolution...................... 325

332. Portrait of a Quaker gentleman, 1774.................................. 325

333. Sporting dress, about 1733 327

334. Suit of velvet with raised figures, worn by Robert Livingston about 1770. Lent by Miss Anna Griffith................................ 329

335. Pistols with silver mounting, about 1765. Lent by Mrs. John Biddle.. 329

336. Cap worn by Governor Taylor of New York, 1730.................... 329

337. Silk waistcoat, 1780. Lent by Mrs. Krumbhaar.................... 329

338. Double-breasted waistcoat of figured silk, about 1790.................. 329

339. Working man, last half of eighteenth century.......................... 331

340. (In colours) Brown broadcloth suit worn by Mr. Johnson of Germantown, 1790. Lent by Miss Sallie Johnson........................ 333

341. (In colours) Mauve crêpe gown worn by Mrs. Sartori of San Domingo. Lent by Miss Janethe.. 333

342. (In colours) Dress of fine glazed buff cambric owned by Madame Chevaleir, end of eighteenth century. Lent by Mrs. Cooper Smith......... 333

343. (In colours) Man in short-waisted, high-collared coat and nankeen breeches, end of eighteenth century. Lent by Frank W. Taylor, Esq. 333

344. (In colours) Muslin dress trimmed with tambour embroidery worn in Philadelphia, 1797.. 333

345. Doctor of Civil Law, end of eighteenth century....................... 336

346. Summer coat of dark blue silk with nankeen breeches, late eighteenth century... 337

347. Back view of brown broadcloth coat worn by Mr. Johnson about 1790. Lent by Miss Sallie Johnson...................................... 337

348. Front view of same over nankeen waistcoat.......................... 337

349. Coat of brown twilled cotton, over white silk embroidered waistcoat and brown satin knee breeches, worn in Philadelphia about 1790. Lent by Mrs. John Biddle.. 337

350. Judge in scarlet robe, end of eighteenth century...................... 339

351. Dress of ordinary seaman, 1775..................................... 341

352. Portrait of Washington, drawn from life by Du Simitière............. 343

353. Henry Laurens, drawn from life by Du Simitière..................... 343

354. W. H. Drayton, Esq., drawn from life by Du Simitière................ 343

355. Gouverneur Morris, drawn from life by Du Simitière................. 343

356. Silhouette of John Randolph of Roanoke............................. 347

357. Silhouette of Washington, showing fine net over hair and queue......... 347

358. Silhouette of Bishop White, showing knickerbockers.................. 347

359. Silhouette of Alexander Hamilton.................................... 347

360. Silhouette of James McClellan, of Connecticut....................... 347

361. Uniform of Light Horse Troop of Philadelphia, 1775.................. 349

2

18   ILLUSTRATIONS

FIGURE   PAGE

362. Commodore Barry of the United States Navy........................ 351
363. Paul Jones of the United States Navy................................ 351
364. Camp at Valley Forge, showing military cloak and great coat......... 351
365. General Warren in dress of a minute-man............................ 355
366. General Daniel Morgan in buckskin coat of the Virginia Rangers...... 355
367. Comte De Rochambeau in dress of a French officer, 1791.............. 355
368. Uniform recommended by Washington in the early part of the Revolu-
      tion... 359
369. A minute-man... 359
370. Dress of First Company, Governor's Foot Guard, Connecticut......... 359
371. Dress of First Pennsylvania Infantry............................... 359
372. Dress of Second Pennsylvania Infantry............................. 359
373. Uniform directed by Minister of War, 1785......................... 359
374. Uniform of the Light Infantry, 1782............................... 359
375. Front view of uniform recommended by Minister of War, 1785........ 359
376. Major General Pinckney in uniform................................. 363
377. Major General St. Clair in uniform................................ 363
378. General O. H. Williams in uniform................................. 363
379. General Andrew Pickens in uniform................................ 363
380. General Montgomery in uniform................................... 367
381. General Francis Marion in uniform................................ 367
382. General Israel Putnam in uniform of a Continental trooper........... 367
383. General Philemon Dickinson in uniform........................... 367
384. General John Sullivan in uniform................................. 367
385. Uniform of an American officer, 1796.............................. 376

RULERS OF THE SETTLEMENTS AND COLONIES IN AMERICA

Spanish. Philip II...1556-1598
Philip III...1598-1621
Philip IV...1621-1665
Charles II..1665-1700
French. Louis XIII..1610-1643
Louis XIV..1643-1715
Swedish. Christina 1633-1654
Charles X..1654-1660
Charles XI 1660-1697
German. Frederick William, Elector of Brandenburg..................1640-1688
Frederick, Elector of Brandenburg, afterwards King Frederick
I of Prussia....................................1688-1713
Leopold I, Emperor of Germany.....................1658-1705
Dutch. Maurice, Stadtholder................................1587-1625
Frederick Henry...................................1625-1647
William II...1647-1650
United Provinces of the Netherlands 1650-1672
William of Orange, afterwards William III of England.......1672-1702
English. James I 1603-1625
Charles I 1625-1649
Commonwealth under Cromwell 1649-1653
Protectorate under Cromwell 1653-1660
Charles II 1660-1685
James II 1685-1689
William and Mary 1689-1702
Queen Anne 1702-1714
George I 1714-1727
George II 1727-1760
George III 1760-1820

PRESIDENTS OF THE UNITED STATES

George Washington..................................1789-1797
John Adams..1797-1801

DATES OF THE SPANISH, FRENCH, SWEDISH, AND GERMAN SETTLEMENTS

Florida ....1565............Spanish
Acadia ....1605............French
Quebec.....................................1608............French
Louisiana..................................1680............French
Texas (afterwards a part of the Spanish
    Province of Mexico)..................1692............Spanish
Mississippi Valley.........................1699............French
California ....1769............Spanish
Banks of the Delaware.....................1637............Swedish
Pennsylvania ....1683............German

---

DATES OF THE ENGLISH AND DUTCH COLONIES

Virginia ....1607............English
Massachusetts ....1620............English
{ New Amsterdam ....1621............Dutch }
{ New York.................................1664............English }
New Hampshire..............................1623............English
Barbadoes ....1625............English
Maryland...................................1633............English
Connecticut ....1635............English
Rhode Island ....1636............English
The Carolinas..............................1655............English
New Jersey ....1664............English
Pennsylvania ....1682............English
Delaware ....1682............English
Georgia ....1732............English

INTRODUCTORY CHAPTER

ON DRESS IN THE

SPANISH AND FRENCH SETTLEMENTS

UNDER

PHILIP II AND LOUIS XIV

The Spaniards in Florida and California
1565–1764

"Those were the days of dreams and legends,
Continents were new."

FIGURE 2.
A Spanish Galleon.

THE first settlement in North America was the Spanish post of St. Augustine in Florida, founded by Pedro Menendez de Aviles in August, 1565. Unsuccessful attempts had been made to colonize Florida both by the French and the Spaniards from very early in the sixteenth century, but the hostility of the native Indians had prevented the founding of anything like a colony. Menendez (Figure 7) found a small Huguenot mission when he landed, which he immediately destroyed, putting the people and Jean Ribaut, their leader, to death in the most heartless manner. Horribly cruel, deplorably superstitious, and very short-sighted in their policy were these early Spanish settlers, but their costumes, as represented by the great contemporary painters, Vargas, Roelas, Velasquez, Murillo, Moro and others, must have been strikingly picturesque.

Parkman says: "Month after month, and year after year the adventurers came, a procession of priests and cavaliers, crossbowmen and arquebusiers (Figure 4), and Indian guides laden with baggage." *

They came in search of fabulous riches which, according to some

* Pioneers of France in the New World, by Francis Parkman.

25

Spanish Munchausen, the soil of the interior contained, and also to bathe in the waters of a river of perpetual youth, a fable in which even their leaders believed.

The dress of a Spanish gentleman of this period consisted of a doublet and slashed breeches, with long silken hose and shoes of Cordovan leather slashed on the toe, a ruff of lace at the neck, and a silk hat with high soft crown and narrow brim. The dress of a Spanish soldier is shown in detail in Figure 4.

FIGURE 3.
A Spanish Gentleman, End of Sixteenth Century.

Sir Francis Drake (Figure 8), in 1586, stopped at St. Augustine on his way from the West Indies to join Sir Walter Raleigh in Virginia (Figure 11), and made a reconnoissance of the harbour, but the Spaniards fled at his approach. He destroyed a few houses and outposts in order probably to inspire the inhabitants with a wholesome respect for the English navy, and went on his way rejoicing in the capture of a pay-chest containing £2,000. St. Augustine at that time is described as "a prosperous settlement with a council house, church and handsome gardens." Some traces of the Spanish occupation are yet to be seen and the old castle or fortress built in 1620 is still standing.

It was never the policy of Spain to make her colonies self-supporting; they were not allowed to raise or manufacture even the necessaries of life, everything must be imported from the mother country.

Later in the seventeenth century, settlements were also made in California, where the Spaniards established missionary and military stations in 1698, and Spain had for a time two flourishing colonies in the territory now embraced within the limits of the United States.

In Spain and France, as well as in England and the Low Countries, the prevailing types of costume during the seventeenth century were very much alike, and the people in all the Colonies of America, following the fashions of their time, wore doublets, farthingales, ruffs, bands, hoods, riding-masks, etc., full descriptions of which are given in the glossary and throughout Part I, with many illustrations.

FIGURE 4.

Spanish Soldiers of the Middle of the Sixteenth Century, with Rapiers and Arquebuses
(from a Contemporary Print).

During the reign of Charles II of Spain his kingdom was continually at war with England. The Spanish population of St. Augustine numbered about three hundred people and fifty Franciscan friars in 1665, when Captain John Davis, the notorious English buccaneer, landed and destroyed the town. After this the Spanish Government established a fort at Pensacola to protect its interests in Florida, but finally the two kings, Charles II of England and Charles II of Spain, made a treaty for the suppression of buccaneering, causing a marked decline in that lawless but romantic profession which has furnished plots for many an exciting tale. In "The Buccaneers of America"* a portrait of Sir Henry Morgan shows a very rich costume of slashed doublet and embroidered baldrick. Francis Lolonais, a fierce-looking buccaneer of French extraction, is portrayed in a very short doublet trimmed with a row of square tabs round the waist.

The records we find of the Spanish rule in Florida, which lasted until 1763, when that province was ceded to Great Britain in exchange for Havana, captured by the English the preceding year, bear witness to the charms of the women, their lovely expressive black eyes, clear brunette complexion, and carefully arranged hair. "At mass they are always well dressed in black silk basquinas with little mantillas (or black lace veils) over their heads. The men are in military costume." Dancing, as in all the Spanish provinces, was a favourite amusement, and the Posey Dance, now obsolete, was very popular many years ago. It is thus described: †

"The ladies of a household arrange in a room of their dwelling an arbour decked with garlands of flowers and lighted with many candles. This is understood by the gentlemen as an invitation to drop in and admire the decorations. Meanwhile the lady who has prepared it selects a partner from among her visitors and hands him a bouquet of flowers. The gentleman who receives this posey becomes for the nonce the king of the ball, and leads out the fair donor as queen of the dance. The others take partners and the ball thus inaugurated may continue several successive evenings. Should the lady's choice fall upon an unwilling swain, which seldom happened, he could be excused by paying the expenses of the entertainment."

* By John Esquemeling.
† History and Antiquities of St. Augustine, by George R. Fairbanks.

FIGURE 5.—Portrait of Fernando De Soto, showing Spanish armour of the six-
teenth century.
FIGURE 6.—Portrait of Sieur de La Salle, showing French costume of his day.
FIGURE 7.—Portrait of Pedro Menendez de Aviles, showing Spanish dress.
FIGURE 8.—Portrait of Sir Francis Drake in the dress of an English sea-cap-
tain.

Figure 5.

Figure 6.

Figure 7.

Figure 8.

These assemblies were always informal and frequented by all classes, all meeting on a level, but were conducted with the utmost politeness and decorum, for which the Spanish character is so distinguished.

The customs, as well as the costumes, of their native land were followed by these Spanish colonists, and as both California and Florida closely resemble Spain in climate and vegetation, the old modes of life were found particularly appropriate.

With the Spanish colonies, Texas may be included, for although this territory was the subject of numerous political intrigues between the Spanish authorities and the French in Louisiana, in 1692 it became a part of the Spanish province of Mexico.

The French Settlements

in

Louisiana and the Mississippi Valley

1680–1764

———

"A gay and gallant company
Those voyagers of old."

Undeterred by the failures and reverses of previous explorers, the French King Louis XIV sent out an expedition under Robert Cavalier de La Salle (Figure 6) in 1680, to discover if possible a waterway across the continent through which ships might pass to the South Sea, as the Pacific Ocean was called in those days.

La Salle experienced many hardships on the way, but finally reached the Mississippi River and sailed southward to its mouth in the Gulf of Mexico. At this point a wooden column was raised, hymns were sung, and La Salle proclaimed, "In the name of Louis the great King of France and Navarre, fourteenth of that name, I do take possession of this country of Louisiana—from the mouth of the river St. Louis and along the river Colbert, or Mississippi, from its source beyond the country of the Sioux as far as its mouth." A cross was raised by the side of the column and in the ground at its foot was buried a leaden plate bearing the arms of France and the inscription, "Ludovicus Magnus Regnat."

By this discovery La Salle had proved that ships from Europe might sail to the vast interior of the continent. He now hoped to colonize the valley of the Mississippi, and add a new lustre to the crown of France.

Father Hennepin, writing in 1683, says: "Le Sieur de la Salle appeared at Mass very well dress'd in his scarlet cloak trimmed with gold lace."* A picture of the fashionable cloak of that period is given in Figure 3.

Discouraged by many hardships, on their way up the Mississippi River some of La Salle's men mutinied and killed the great explorer, but, despite his failure to found a colony at the outlet of the Mississippi, he stands out in history as the foremost pioneer in North America.

Trading posts and mission stations grew up in many places, and were gradually augmented by bands of emigrants from other parts of the country.

Louis XIV still cherished the ambition to found a Colonial Dominion on the shores of the Gulf of Mexico, so dramatically claimed for him by La Salle,—a colony which in time might rival the flourishing English settlements on the Atlantic coast. Accordingly, in 1698, he sent out to Louisiana a squadron of two frigates and two smaller ships bearing a company of mariners and about two hundred colonists. Among the latter were many ex-soldiers of the French army accompanied by their wives and children. Others were artisans, labourers, and needy adventurers. "They were all supplied with necessary clothing, provisions, and implements for beginning a settlement in the remote solitudes of Louisiana."

In 1704, twenty unmarried women were sent out under the charge of two nuns, and shortly after their arrival in Louisiana were married to bachelor colonists. The same ship brought troops to reinforce the garrison, and four priests.

The costume of these early French settlers was somewhat motley in its composition. The women were dressed in coloured bodices and short gowns of handmade woolen stuffs, or of French goods of finer texture. In summer most of them went without shoes, but in

* Description of Louisiana 1683, translated by J. G. Shee.

winter and on holidays they wore Indian moccasins gaily decorated with porcupine quills, shells, and coloured beads. Instead of hats they wore kerchiefs of bright colours interlaced with gay ribbons or wreathed with flowers.

The men wore long vests drawn over their shirts, leggings of buckskin or of coarse woolen cloth, and wooden clog shoes or moccasins of heavy leather. In winter they wrapped themselves in long capotes or overcoats with capes and hoods which could be drawn over their heads, thus serving for hats. In summer their heads were covered with blue handkerchiefs worn turbanlike as a protection from mosquitoes as well as from the sun.

FIGURE 9.
French Peasant Women (from a Contemporary French Print).

The French settlements were usually small villages on the edge of the prairie or in the heart of the woods. They were always near the bank of a river, for the watercourses were the only roads, and the light canoes, such as the Indians used, the only means of travel. In these villages the French settlers lived like one family, ruled by the village priests and the elders of the community. Their houses were built along a single narrow street, and close enough together for the villagers to carry on a neighbourly gossip, each from his own doorstep.

Adjoining the village was a large enclosure, or common field, for the free use of all the villagers. It was divided into allotments, one for each household, the size proportioned to the number of persons in the family.

The village traders always kept a small stock of French goods, laces, ribbons and other useful and ornamental articles, which they exchanged with the settlers for the products of the forest. Some of the young men became voyageurs or boatmen in the service of the traders. When the wood-rangers returned once a year to their village homes, great was the rejoicing, and old and young gathered around them to hear the story of their adventures. These French settlers took characteristic delight in amusement and "had almost as many holidays as working days." *

Indian converts lived in amicable intercourse with the settlers, learning from them to cultivate the ground, and to manufacture various useful articles from the hair of the buffalo.

Many of the original settlers married Indian women; their descendants were called half-breeds or Gumbos, the latter being a nick-name given to them by the French. The language of the Louisiana colonists was a patois, a corrupted provincial French.

FIGURE 10.
Jesuit Missionaries.

Among them were a few carpenters, tailors, stone-masons, boat-builders, and blacksmiths, the latter capable of repairing a firelock or a rifle.

The city of New Orleans was founded in 1717 and rapidly grew in size and importance. For many years a "rude semblance of a Court" was maintained and social amusements of various sorts could be engaged in, even duelling and brawling, for some of the Louisiana colonists were of noble birth and many were military officers. "All the people shared alike the harmless merriment and

* Discovery of the Old Northwest and Its Settlement by the French, by James Baldwin.

3

frolic of the carnival. All, too, observed the self-denying ordinances of the Lenten season which terminated in the festival of Easter."

The treaty of Paris, in 1764, gave to the English Government the Illinois and Louisiana colonies as well as the province of Acadia, in Nova Scotia,* originally peopled by Normandy peasants whose pathetic story Longfellow has made so familiar to us. More than six hundred of the Acadian exiles were sent to Louisiana, where they had at least the comfort of hearing their native language, and where the customs and pursuits were more congenial than in the northern colonies. The quaint costumes and the peculiar head-dresses worn by Normandy peasants at the end of the seventeenth century are minutely described in Mrs. Stothard's "Letters written during a tour through Normandy, Brittany and other parts of France," illustrated in colour by her husband. This book was published in London in 1818, and is the earliest authority on the subject I have found. The descriptions are not quoted here, as there is not any evidence that very elaborate peasant dress was ever worn in the American colonies.†

* Thus named by a company of Scots who planted a settlement there in 1622.

† For Spanish and French costumes, see Racinet's Le Costume Historique and Kretchmer's Trachten der Völker.

PART I

THE SEVENTEENTH CENTURY

THE ENGLISH COLONIES

IN

VIRGINIA, MARYLAND, THE BARBADOES, AND THE CAROLINAS

1607–1700

During the Reigns of
James I, Charles I and II, James II, and
William and Mary

TOBACCO

Tobacco is but an Indian weed,
Grows green in the morn, cut down at eve.
    It shows our decay,
    We are but clay.
Think of this when you smoke tobacco!

The pipe that is so lily white,
Wherein so many take delight,
    It breaks with a touch,
    Man's life is such;
Think of this when you take tobacco!

The pipe that is so foul within,
It shows man's soul is stained with sin;
    It doth require
    To be purged with fire;
Think of this when you smoke tobacco!

The dust that from that pipe doth fall,
It shows we are nothing but dust at all,
    For we came from dust,
    And return we must;
Think of this when you smoke tobacco!

The ashes that are left behind,
Do serve to put us all in mind
    That into dust
    Return we must;
Think of this when you take tobacco!

The smoke that doth so high ascend,
Shows that man's life must have an end;
    The vapour's gone,
    Man's life is done;
Think of this when you take tobacco!

                —Thomas D'Urfey, **1719.**

The English in Virginia, Maryland, the Barbadoes, and the Carolinas

1607–1700

FIGURE 11.

AMESTOWN in Virginia was the first actual settlement of the English people in America. The Virginia Company, of which Sir Edwin Sandys was President, was formed under the patent of King James I. The first ships sent over arrived in 1607, at the mouth of the James River, where a fortified village was built, and trade established with the surrounding Indians. One hundred colonists came in the first expedition, a great number of them being men of quality. As Captain John Smith, in his delightful "History of the Virginia Settlement," puts it:

"We had far too many gentlemen adventurers amongst us, and of a necessity some of these must needs be not quite all we could wish as reliable companions. Out of one hundred colonists there are fifty-two gentlemen adventurers besides Master Robert Hunt, the Preacher, and Masters Thomas Wotton and William Wilkinson, the Chirurgeons. We had four carpenters, twelve labourers, a blacksmith, a sailor, a bricklayer, a mason, a tailor and a drummer, four boys and some others."

The Company in London advised each emigrant to provide him-self with the following articles of dress:

A Monmouth cap,	Three falling bands,
Three shirts,	One waistcoat,
One suit of canvas,	One suit of frieze,
One pair of garters,	One suit of broadcloth,
Four pairs of shoes,	Three pairs of silk stockings,

One dozen pairs of points.

From original prints in this book of Captain John Smith's, we get the costume of the gentleman adventurer, similar in style, of course, to the garments worn by men of rank in England during the reign of James I. A portrait of Sir Edwin Sandys, or Sandes as it is sometimes written, is given in Figure 13, show-ing the prevailing dress of an English gentleman, a brocade doublet, a lace-trimmed ruff, and a pointed beard. The strange fashion which was conspicuous at

FIGURE 12.

King James's Court, of padding and stuffing the breeches, called farthingale breeches on account of the resemblance to that most disfiguring but popular article of fashion worn by women in the reigns of Elizabeth and James I, was probably followed in a modified form by these gentlemen adventurers, as the padding was supposed to be a protection against rapiers and arrows.

Stays were also worn by men in those days beneath long-waisted doublets; and ruffs too were used, although they gradually dimin-ished in size and stiffness (Figures 11, 15, and 21).

FIGURE 13.—Portrait of Sir Edwyn Sandys, showing a turned-down ruff, the predecessor of the Vandyke collar. Reign of James I.

FIGURE 14.—Portrait of George Sandys, Secretary of the Virginia Colony, showing slashed doublet and Vandyke collar. Reign of Charles I.

FIGURE 15.—Portrait of Sir Isaac Pennington, showing the style of hat worn in the Virginia House of Burgesses. Reign of Charles I.

FIGURE 16.—Portrait of Sir John Pennington, showing English armour and Vandyke collar. Reign of Charles I.

FIGURE 13.

FIGURE 14.

FIGURE 15.

FIGURE 16.

In the portraits of the Earl and Countess of Somerset,* so often reproduced, may be seen the costumes worn by the nobility of this time, but there were no radical changes in English costume from 1550, the middle of Elizabeth's reign, until the accession of Charles I in 1625. If any change of fashion appeared in the early days of life at Jamestown, the tailor of the Company was probably responsible for it, and the old adage, "Cut your coat according to your cloth," was very likely his inspiration.

FIGURE 17.
The Farthingale.

The present of a cloak of raccoon skins from King Powhattan to Captain John Smith must have been very acceptable as, according to Stith, the first winter was very damp and cold.

FIGURE 18.
Ordinary Dress of a Boy at this Period, 1602–1676 (from a Contemporary Print).

The first women to come to Virginia were Mrs. Forrest and her maid Anne Burroughs, who, soon after her arrival, married John Laydon. This was the first English wedding on American soil.† Figure 21 represents the style of dress worn by Mrs. Forrest. Her maid's costume was of similar cut, but of linsey-woolsey, with cuffs and falling band of plain linen.

As early as 1621 the Company resolved to establish a free school for children. The costumes of children given in Figures 18 and 23 are taken from a picture of a Dame's School in England by A. de Bosse, 1602–1676.

In 1622 the College, afterward known as "William and Mary," was first talked of, but it was in this year that occurred the horrible

* Fairholt's History of English Costume.
† History of the First Discovery and Settlement of Virginia, by William Stith.

massacre of the English by the Indians which sadly reduced their numbers. However, the survivors struggled valiantly on, and gradually comfortable houses were built, even for the labouring men, while the houses of the people of quality could boast of many conveniences.

In 1624 an attempt was made to produce silk from the mulberry trees which flourished in Virginia, and skilled workmen were sent over by Nicholas Farrar from France to raise silkworms, but the effort was not successful.

King James died in 1625 and the accession of Charles I proved a blessing to the Virginia Colony, for the new king left the affairs of government to Sir Edwin Sandys and the Virginia House of Burgesses which held its meetings in the church at Jamestown. The Representatives coming in barges from their plantations along the river were usually accompanied by their wives and daughters, who embraced these opportunities to show off their fine apparel (Figures 20, 21, 32, 33, 35, 36). Very gay and elaborate the finery of that period seems, even from our twentieth century standpoint.

In the body of the church, facing the choir, sat the Burgesses in their best attire, with starched ruffs or stiff neckbands (Figure 22) and doublets of silk or velvet in bright colours. All sat with their hats on in imitation of the time-honoured custom of the House of Commons (Figures 15, 19, and 22).* These same Burgesses, however, did not approve of too general a display of fine clothing, it seems, for among many astute laws passed by them was the following, to prevent extravagance in dress: "Be it enacted that for all public contributions every unmarried man must be assessed in church according to his own apparel, and every married man must be assessed according to his own and his wife's apparel."

The years from 1625 to 1642 were marked with great prosperity and progress, and when Berkeley was sent over with the title of English

* Old Virginia and her Neighbours.

REIGNS OF JAMES I—CHARLES I
1607–1640

FIGURES 19 and 20 represent a colonial governor and his wife of the time of Charles I dressed in the fashion of the English Court.

The man has a short-waisted doublet with trimmings of gold braid, and the breeches are finished with loops of ribbon. The slashed sleeves show the Holland shirt underneath. The boots are the style called " French falls" with large buckles on the instep. Hat and plumes are of the recognized Cavalier type, and the collar a Vandyke of rich lace.

His lady (Figure 20) has a low-cut, short-waisted bodice finished with square tabs. The sleeves are full and reach a little below the elbow. Ruffles and falling band are of rich lace. No farthingale is worn with this gown which falls in soft folds on the ground both back and front. The hair is arranged in short ringlets across the forehead, hangs to the shoulders in curls, and is coiled in the back.

FIGURE 21 shows a planter's wife in the usual costume of the time of James I. This lady wears a gown of prunella opening over a brocaded petticoat. The ruff is of stiffened lace. The coif of white linen is shaped over it in the back. A modified farthingale supports the dress which hangs in heavy plaits to the ground. The trimming on the bodice is of silk galloon with a design in gold thread.

FIGURE 22 represents a gentleman planter in the ordinary costume of James I's day. The doublet and padded breeches of coloured velvet or cloth are fastened together with points; long oversleeves hang from the shoulders. The stiff band is of starched linen. The stockings are of silk fastened with garters tied in a bow at one side. The hat of felt is ornamented with an embroidered band and a short plume of feathers.

FIGURE 19.

FIGURE 20.

FIGURE 21.

FIGURE 22.

Governor, the inhabitants of Virginia numbered eighteen thousand English and three hundred negroes.

At that time London fashions were strictly followed by the quality, and seem to have been not only the chief amusement of the women, but matter of great moment to both sexes (Figures 13, 14, 19, 20, 32, 33, 35, 36).

The fashionable costume in England during the reign of Charles I, made familiar to us by the magic brush of Vandyke, was picturesque in the extreme.

A gentleman of those days wore a doublet of satin or velvet with large loose sleeves slashed up the front (Figures 45, 46); the collar covered by a falling band of richest point-lace with the peculiar edging now called Vandyke (Figures 14 and 16), and a short cloak worn carelessly over one shoulder. Bands were called "peccadilles" when trimmed with this pointed lace, so fashionable in the middle of the seventeenth century, and it is interesting to read that the fashionable London thoroughfare, Piccadilly, gets its name from a shop where "peccadilles" were made and sold in the reign of Charles I. Under slashed doublets, loose shirts of Holland linen were worn. (See portrait of George Percy [Figure 29], second Governor of the Virginia Colony.) The breeches, fringed or pointed, met the tops of the wide boots (Figures 51, 55), which were ruffled with lace, lawn, or soft leather. A broad-leafed Flemish beaver hat, with a rich hatband and plume of feathers (Figure 19), was set on one side of the head, and a Spanish rapier hung from a most magnificent baldrick or sword-belt worn sash-wise over the right shoulder. In troublous times the doublet of silk or velvet was frequently exchanged for a buff coat (Figures 83, 84, 85, 86, 87) which was richly laced, sometimes embroidered with gold or silver, and enriched by a broad silk or satin scarf tied in a large bow either behind or over the hip, in which case, the short cloak was perhaps dispensed with; in some instances the buff jerkin without sleeves was worn over the doublet

(Figure 87). The beard was worn "very peaked with small up-turned mustaches; the hair long on the neck."

George Sandys, the celebrated traveller, a younger brother of the President of the Company in London, was sent over to Jamestown in the capacity of treasurer. During his stay in the colony, he trans-lated ten books of Ovid. This was the first poetical achievement in America. The portrait of him (Figure 14) shows the slashed doublet and the Vandyke collar of this reign.

FIGURE 23.

Ordinary Dress of a Little Girl of the Period 1602–1676 (from a Contemporary Print).

A gentlewoman of the same time wore a long soft skirt, with a low-cut bodice finished with square tabs about the waist (Figures 20, 32, 49), full sleeves a little below the elbow, with soft ruffles of rich lace, a wide collar of the same lace being worn over the shoulders but allowing the throat and neck to show. Soft breast-knots of ribbon were also much worn. The hair was usually curled over the brow, falling to the shoulders in rather tight ringlets, and arranged in a knot at the back (Figures 20, 73).

Earrings were very popular in England in Vandyke's time, not only for women but for men, as we may see by the numerous specimens in his portraits. In his famous painting of Charles I in the National Gallery in London, the King is represented with a pear-shaped pearl-drop in one ear. This was the most advantageous way of displaying a pearl of more than usual beauty, but the origin of the fashion of piercing the lobe of the ear has been ascribed by many authorities to the common belief that it was a cure for weak eyes. Tradition also associates the fashion with navigators and seamen. Probably it was thought to be a safe way of carrying precious stones found in perilous adventures by land and sea, but there is not any evidence that earrings were at any time a fashion favoured by men in the Colonies of America.

Mr. Bruce, in his "Economic History of Virginia," remarks: "The incongruity of shining apparel with the rude surroundings of new settlements in the wilderness does not seem to have jarred upon the perceptions of the population except so far as it implied an unnecessary expenditure, and this view was only taken when the resources of the Colony were seriously impaired.

"About the middle of the century a law was passed prohibiting the introduction of silk in pieces except for hoods or scarfs, or of silver, gold or bone lace, or of ribbons wrought in gold or silver. All goods of this character brought into the colonies were confiscated and then exported."

FIGURE 24.

An English Mariner (from a Contemporary Print).

The typical workingman's costume of this period consisted of loose breeches and jerkin of canvas or frieze; hose of coarse wool, shoes of tanned leather tied in front; hat of thrums or felt. "The carpenters, the labourers, the blacksmith, the mason, and the bricklayer" of the Virginia Company were in all probability dressed in this way. The tailor and the drummer may have worn their breeches fastened at the knee with points, and all these useful members of the Company wore aprons of dressed leather when at work. Mariners, according to contemporary authorities, wore a similar costume (Figure 24).

Randle Holmes, another contemporary authority, gives the following picture of a countryman in 1660, showing that the hat, doublet, and short breeches of the reign of James I were worn in country districts of England as late as the Restoration; the short breeches probably being of leather and the hose of stout woolen cloth.

Bishop Coleman tells us that in the Jamestown Settlement "church services, according to the English ritual, were held daily by

1660.

FIGURE 25.
Countryman in Doublet (from a print by Randle Holmes, 1660).

the Reverend Robert Hunt, formerly rector of a living in Kent. Soon after the arrival of the Colonists sent over by the Virginia Company, in 1607, an altar was erected under the shade of the forest trees, and the emigrants gladly attended the celebration of the Holy Communion. English churchmen came to Massachusetts in 1623; to Maryland in 1629; Lord Baltimore wrote that four clergymen of the Church of England were in his province with decent maintenance in 1676." Surplices were very expensive in the Colonies; 5000 pounds of tobacco was the price paid for three of them in Virginia, and probably they were not available in every parish. Regular services were held in New England in 1638, in South Carolina in 1660, in New York in 1674, in New Jersey in 1678, and in Pennsylvania in 1694.*

These dates are quoted to show that in the English Colonies, under English rule, the clergy wore, as in England, the customary dress of the period: a black coat (ancestor of the cassock), full breeches to the knee, silk hose fastened with points, a soft brimmed hat, and plain stock or falling band for outdoor wear; the white surplice with bands and a close cap of black silk or velvet in church. Bishops

* History of the American Church.

ordinarily wore the usual full-sleeved white robes with black stoles. Out-of-doors long full cloaks were worn universally for protection from the weather.

FIGURE 26.
Soldier in Cuirass and Morion (from an Old English Print, Seventeenth Century).

Hard, indeed, must have been the lives of the pioneer clergy of every denomination in America before 1700, and in remote parts

4

they were probably constrained to wear whatever they could have made at home.   The general outlines of the accepted dress of the times, given here, are based upon careful historical research.   Further details will be found in the authorities quoted.

Close-fitting black caps were worn habitually by the clergymen of all denominations.   Instead of the white surplice, the black Geneva or preaching gown was adopted by Non-conformists, Presbyterian ministers and Puritan divines in all the Colonies.

The Roman Catholic Church was represented chiefly by the Jesuits, a missionary priesthood, who habitually adopted the dress of the people with whom they sojourned.   Maryland was the active centre of Catholicism in the Colonies.   When Father Greaton of the Jesuit Order was sent from there to Philadelphia and founded the Parish of St. Joseph in that city, we are told that he entered the Province of Penn in the dress of a Quaker.*   But this did not happen until 1731.

Maryland was settled in 1633 by Lord Baltimore, whose ambition was to found a commonwealth in the Colonies where Roman Catholics might escape the oppressive legislation to which they were subjected in England.   He brought with him his wife, children, and many servants, and following the English customs of living, naturally brought over the prevailing costumes of his day.

That armour was sometimes worn by the Colonists, ample proof is given in the early records.   In the archives of the first colony of Jamestown it is stated, among the proceedings of the Virginia Company, that

Brigandines, alias plate coats	100
Jacks of mail	40
Jerkins or shirts of mail	400
Skulls	2000
Calivers and other pieces, belts, halberts, swords,	

* History of Old St. Joseph's, Philadelphia, by Martin I. J. Griffin.

FIGURE 27.—Silver frontlet, bearing the English coat-of-arms, given to the Queen of the Pamunkeys by Charles II.

FIGURE 28.—Silver mace used in the Virginia House of Burgesses.

FIGURE 29.—Portrait of George Percy, second Governor of Virginia, showing the full shirt of Holland linen customarily worn under slashed doublets, and the Vandyke collar and cuffs of Charles I's reign.

FIGURE 30.—Steel vambrace dug up near Jamestown, and preserved by the Historical Society at Richmond, Virginia.

FIGURE 27.   FIGURE 28.   FIGURE 29.

FIGURE 30.

were sent out from London upon request of the Burgesses, July 17, 1622.   In the Historical Society at Richmond, portions of a steel vambrace are preserved which were dug up at Jamestown in 1861 (Figure 30).

At the time of the first Colony in America, heavy plate armour had gone out of use, and back and breast plates with overlapping

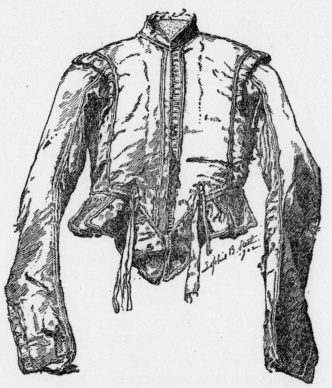

FIGURE 31.

A Doublet of Satin Trimmed with a Narrow Galloon and Points of the Same Colour with Padded Lining, 1600–25 (Reign of James I).

tuilles or tassetts to protect the thighs, and helmets for the head, were generally worn.   Whole suits of armour may have been worn on occasions, but so great had been the improvement in firearms that armour was no longer a safeguard, according to Fairholt, and in the time of Charles I, stout buff coats thick enough to resist a sword thrust, under a cuirass and a gorget (Figures 88, 89, and 90) affording special protection for the throat and chest, a helmet of metal, and breeches and boots of tough leather, formed the customary uniform of the soldier. The armour of a mounted officer, judging from effigies on old English tombs and from prints of the day, was more formidable, the arms and legs being encased in steel, at least all that part of the body not hidden by the saddle. Pictures of buff coats (Figures 83, 84, 85, 86, and 87), and drawings of a pikeman and a musketeer are given (Figures 26 and 78).

There is an anonymous pamphlet called "A Perfect Description of Virginia," printed in Force's Tracts, which shows the inducements set forth in England to bring people to the Colony. The great advantages of the country, its resources, agricultural and even educational, are announced in glowing terms, and one citation at least bears directly upon the history of costume. In describing the fine house of one, Sir John Harvey, the author says: "He sows yearly stores of hemp and flax, and causes it to be spun, he keeps weavers, and hath a tan house, causes leather to be dressed, hath eight shoemakers employed in their trade."

After the execution of King Charles I, a great many of the Cavaliers of England sought a haven of refuge in Virginia and Maryland. They were followed by many other representatives of distinguished families who could not brook the rule of Cromwell.

We realize how luxurious life in Virginia had already become for the prosperous, when we read that Governor Berkeley (against whom Bacon rebelled in 1675) retired to his rural estate of "Green Spring" near Jamestown from 1652 to 1660, where he had an orchard of more than two thousand fruit trees—apples, pears, peaches, and apricots—and a stable of seventy fine horses. Here he lived in ease, entertaining Cavalier guests and drinking healths to King Charles, until recalled to Jamestown as Governor. In 1661 he went to London and remained a year. While there he saw the performance of his play,

"The Lost Lady," described by Pepys in his diary. This play contained the following mention of the costumes of the day:

> "Observe with me how in that deep band,
> Short cloak, and his great boots, he looks
> Three stories high, and his head is the
> Garret where he keeps nothing but lists of
> Horse matches and some designs for his next clothes."

In the first part of the reign of Charles II, doublets were worn much shorter and opened over a Holland shirt, which hung over the waistband of the loose breeches, the latter as well as the large full sleeves were ornamented with points and "ribbands" (Figures 29 and 68). The falling collar was also of lace. With this costume a high-crowned hat with plume of feathers was sometimes worn (Figure 19).

A year or so later the fashion of petticoat breeches, trimmed with "many rows of loops of ribbon overlapping like shingles," came into vogue for a short time (Figure 68). A certain Captain Creedon appeared in the street of Boston with this fantastic garb, much to the astonishment of the pedestrians, we are told. Probably this particular style was more popular with the gayer Colonists in Virginia and the Carolinas, who kept in touch with the Court fashions.

Later in the same reign (Charles II) "the doublet was worn much longer with sleeves to the elbows, finished with hanging ribbands from under which the ruffled sleeves of the shirt hung out." Thus the doublet became transformed into a coat, and in an inventory of apparel provided for the King in 1679, a complete suit of one material is mentioned as "coat and breeches." Neck-cloths were worn toward the close of this reign.

For a few years extending into the reign of James II, a long coat reaching to the knees and closely buttoned down the front came into fashion. Full breeches hanging in full folds over the garters were worn with this style of coat (Figures 137 and 138).

"The gowns of the ladies of the English Court at this period were cut very low, with slashed sleeves, and were trimmed with lace and jewels"* (Figures 20, 32 and 49). Long gloves reaching to the elbow were worn with low cut dresses (Figures 33 and 35).

The fashion of wearing patches came in towards the end of the reign of Charles I, and continued in vogue until George III's day. They are mentioned in 1650. "Our ladies have lately entertained a vain custom of spotting their faces out of affectation of a mole, to set off their beauty such as Venus had; and it is well if one black patch will serve to make their faces remarkable, for some fill their faces full of them, varied into all manner of shapes." Patches are associated with the fashion of powdering the hair (1720–1778), but when Mrs. Pepys was permitted by her husband to wear a patch we have his word for it that she looked "very pretty." It is not likely that the extreme of this fashion, as described in Bulwer's satirical lines, was seen in the Colonies:

> "Her patches are of every cut,
>   For pimples or for scars.
>   Here's all the wandering planets' signs
>   And some of the fixed stars;
>   Already gummed to make them stick
>   They need no other sky."

A seventeenth century author gives the following concise definition of the muff, which figures so frequently in English portraits of the day: "A fur worn in winter in which to put the hands to keep them warm. Muffs were formerly only for women: at the present day they are carried by men. The finest muffs are made of martin, the common of miniver. The country muffs of the cavaliers are made of otter and of tiger. A woman puts her nose in her muff to hide herself. A muff-dog is a little dog which ladies can carry in their muffs." It is not easy to imagine the pioneer men of the Colonies carrying muffs; in fact even a Patroon would have found one sadly

* Book of Costume by a Lady of Rank. (London, 1846.)

inconvenient in the days when "a musket with six shoots of powder" was his constant companion. Towards the end of the century, however, when the peaceful days of William and Mary's reign afforded a life of comparative luxury, the fashion at its height in England was followed in the Colonies by men as well as by women, with whom muffs have ever been deservedly popular (Figure 36).

Mr. Fiske, speaking of Virginia hospitality at that early date, suggests that "in the time of Bacon's Rebellion (1675) your host would have appeared, perhaps, in a coat and breeches of olive plush or dark red broadcloth, richly embroidered waistcoat, shirt of holland, long silk stockings, silver buttons and shoe buckles, lace ruffles about neck and wrists, and his head encumbered with a flowing wig; while the lady of the house might have worn a crimson satin bodice trimmed with point-lace, a black tabby petticoat, and silk hose with shoes of fine leather, gallooned. Her lace head-dress would be secured with a gold bodkin, and she would be likely to wear earrings, a pearl necklace, finger rings set with rubies or diamonds, and to carry a fan."

This description may be very nearly correct of the man's dress in regard to colour and material, but the style of the coat described is of a later period. To the feminine mind a few items are needed to complete the costume of the lady. For instance, all the pictures of the time show the bodice and skirt of the same material, up to the reign of James II; after that a long skirt still matching the bodice was looped over a gay petticoat sometimes richly trimmed with lace or gimp (Figures 1, 19, 20, 21, 22, 24, 32, 33, 35, and 36).

The Barbadoes and Carolina settlements date from 1650. The Colonists of these Southern ports, being mostly Cavaliers who had seen something of Court life in London, very soon surrounded themselves with comforts and luxuries unknown to the first-comers in Virginia. We read that the Barbadoes Colony resembled a little Court in itself, the planters maintaining large households and many slaves.

* Old Virginia and Her Neighbours.

There was frequent intercourse with the settlements in Virginia and Maryland. The brocade gown in the frontispiece was the property of an English lady who came to Barbadoes when James II was on the throne of England. Figure 104 depicts a gentleman of the same date.

The following description of the articles of dress is quoted from Mr. Bruce's "Economic History of Virginia," but may be reasonably considered typical of all English Colonies in America from 1660 to 1700:

"The shirt was made of holland, blue linen, lockram, dowlas and canvas, according to the quality desired; holland representing the most costly and canvas the least expensive. The buttons used on the shirt were either of silver or pewter, and in many cases were carefully gilded.

"The stockings were either of silk, woolen or cotton thread, worsted or yarn. The shoes worn by men were made of ordinary leather, or they were of the sort known as French Falls (Figures 19, 51, 53, and 55). The shoe buckles were manufactured of brass, steel or silver. There are many references to boots, the popular footwear of the planters, who were accustomed to pass much of their time on horseback (Figures 50, 54, and 57).

"The periwig was worn in the latter part of the century (Figures 134, 135, 140, and 141). In 1689 William Byrd forwarded one to his merchant in London with instructions to have it altered.

"The covering for the heads of men consisted of the Monmouth cap, the felt, the beaver or castor, and the straw hat, occasionally with a steeple crown.

"The neck-cloth, or cravat, was of blue linen, calico, dowlas, muslin or the finest holland. The band or falling collar was made either of linen or lace, in keeping with the character of the suit (Figures 16 and 82).

"The material of the coat ranged from broadcloth, camlet, fustian, drugget, and serge, which became less expensive with the progress of the century, to cotton, kersey, frieze, canvas, and buckskin.

FIGURE 32 represents the fashionable indoor dress of an English gentlewoman, reign of Charles I.

FIGURE 33 shows the usual outdoor summer costume of an English lady, reign of Charles I.

—*From Hollar's Sketches of "The Seasons," Spring and Summer.*

FIGURE 33.
SUMMER.

FIGURE 32.
SPRING.

When of broadcloth, it was lined with calico or coarse linen.   There are numerous references to the stuff coat, and the smock, and to the serge or linen jacket (Figure 48).

"The outer garment used in riding was usually a cloak of camlet. The buttons of the coat and waistcoat were made of various materials, from silk thread to brass and pewter, silver, gimp and mohair.

"Over the ordinary coat, a great-coat of frieze was worn in cold weather, or, on special occasions, a substitute was found in a cloak of blue or scarlet silk.

"Waistcoats in 1679 were made of dimity, cotton or drugget, flannel or penistone, of a great variety of colours, white, black, and blue being the most popular.

"The breeches for dress occasions were of plush or broadcloth; for ordinary wear, of linen, common ticking, canvas or leather. There are references in inventories of the period to serge breeches, lined with linen or worsted, with thread buttons, and also to cal-limanco breeches with hair buttons.   Occasionally the whole suit was of plush, broadcloth, kersey or canvas, or the coat was made of drugget, and the waistcoat and breeches of stuff cloth.   Olive col-oured suits were very popular.

"Handkerchiefs were of silk, lace, or blue linen.   Gloves were made of yarn, or of tanned ox-, lamb-, buck-, dog-, or sheepskin, and were of local manufacture.   The hands of children were kept warm by mittens."

It was the habit of the wealthy planters to have even their plainest and simplest articles of clothing made in England.   Mr. Fitzhugh, of Stafford County, Virginia, instructed his merchant in London, in 1697, to send him two suits of an ordinary character, one for use in winter and the other in summer.   The exact measurements for the shoes and stockings needed were to be guessed at, and the only direction given as to the two hats ordered was that they should be of the largest size.

The lists sent out to England show that costly garments were imported for the planters' wives. Many of the gowns worn in Virginia must have been as handsome as those worn by the women of the same class in England. There are numerous allusions to silk and flowered gowns, to bodices of velvet brocade and satin, trimmed with lace (Figures 32 and 49).

Petticoats were of serge, flannel, or tabby, a kind of coloured silk cloth. They were also made of printed linen or dimity and trimmed with silk or silver lace. An outfit of gown, petticoat, and green stockings, composed of woolen materials, is frequently mentioned in the inventories.

After
Romain de Hooghe. 1675.
S.B.S.

FIGURE 34.

Back View of Outdoor Dress (from a Contemporary Print).

For outdoor wear, women of all ranks wore hoods and mantles. The hoods were made of camlet, sarsenet, or velvet, often trimmed with fur (Figures 34, 35, 36, 40, 67, 69, 128, 129, and 144). The mantles of silk (Figure 128) or tippets of fur (Figures 47, 69, and 129) were worn over the shoulders.

Hose varied very much in colour, being white, scarlet, or black. They were held in place by silk garters.

Shoes of the finest quality were either laced or gallooned (Figure 36). Wooden shoes with wooden heels were also worn.

Aprons were of muslin, silk, serge, and blue duffel (Figures 35 and 144). Small fans, many of which were richly ornamented, were favourite items of dress in the toilets of planters' wives (Figure 20), and silver and gilt stomachers were not unknown. Perfumed powders were imported and used in the English Colonies.

FIGURE 35 shows an English woman in hood and apron, reign of Charles I.

FIGURE 36.—An outdoor winter costume of an English woman, reign of Charles I.

—From Hollar's Sketches of "The Seasons," Autumn and Winter.

FIGURE 36.
WINTER.

FIGURE 35.
AUTUMN.

About 1661, we are told, a young English lady set out for Virginia, furnished with the following articles of clothing:

"A scarf, white sarsenet and a ducape hood, a white flannel petticoat, two green aprons, three pairs of gloves, a long riding scarf, a mask and a pair of shoes."

"The wardrobe of a rich planter's wife in Virginia, Mrs. Sarah Willoughby, consisted of a red, a blue, and a black silk petticoat, a petticoat of India silk and a worsted prunella, a striped linen and a calico petticoat, a black silk gown, a scarlet waistcoat with silver lace, a white knit waistcoat, a striped stuff jacket, a worsted prunella mantle, a sky-coloured satin bodice, a pair of red paragon bodices, three fine and three coarse holland aprons, seven handkerchiefs, and two hoods. The whole was valued at fourteen pounds and nineteen shillings.

"The wardrobe of another Virginia lady, Mrs. Frances Pritchard, was quite as extensive. It included an olive-coloured silk petticoat, petticoats of silver and flowered tabby, of velvet, and of white striped dimity, a printed calico gown lined with blue silk, a white striped dimity, a black silk waistcoat, a pair of scarlet sleeves, a pair of holland sleeves with ruffles, a Flanders lace band, one cambric and three holland aprons, five cambric handkerchiefs, and several pairs of green stockings."*

Aprons were at least on one occasion conspicuous articles of dress. Although some historians discredit the episode, in a history of costume we can hardly omit the story of Bacon's very ungallant behaviour to the ladies of Jamestown, whom he compelled to stand in a white-aproned row to screen his men while they worked on the entrenchments, as a protection from the Burgesses, who could not shoot without injury to the women. We may at least safely conclude that every woman of consequence was expected to have a white apron in her wardrobe.

* Bruce's Economic History of Virginia.

The favourite ornaments of women at this time were pearl necklaces, gold pendants and earrings, and rings of various kinds. It was customary to leave mourning rings to a large number of relatives and friends. One lady, Mrs. Elizabeth Digges, in her will desired that eight should be distributed among the members of her intimate circle. A gentleman of Middlesex bequeathed twenty-five pounds sterling for the purchase of rings of the same character; sixteen pounds of this sum were to be expended in such as would cost one guinea apiece.

A rich planter of Lower Norfolk County, at his death, was in possession of "a sapphire set in gold, one ring with a blue stone, another with a green stone, and another still with a yellow stone, two hollow wrought rings, a diamond ring with several sparks, a mourning ring, a beryl set in silver, and an amber necklace."

As real pearls were very costly, a Frenchman, named Jacques, invented a substitute for them in this century (seventeenth). He had observed that the water in which small fish, called "ablettes," had been washed, contained a quantity of silvery particles, and by filling hollow blown glass beads with this sediment, he succeeded in producing an admirable imitation; but about twenty thousand white-bait were required to supply one pound of this essence of pearls.*

Small gold and silver bodkins were used by the wives of the planters for the purpose of keeping the head-dress in place.

Plantation life, even toward the end of the century, gave but few opportunities for display. There were no towns where, as at Williamsburg in the following century, the leading families might gather at certain seasons and show off their fashionable costumes. The church of the parish was the social centre of each community. It was there that fine clothes could be exhibited on Sundays, while at weddings and other festal meetings, the most costly suits and dresses were worn.

* History of Fashion in France.

The store, which every planter of importance maintained on his place, was a notable feature of colonial life. A list of the articles for sale in one of those rural establishments is almost as varied as the advertisement of one of our city department stores to-day. For instance, the Hubbard store in York County in 1667 contained:

Lockram, canvas, dowlas, Scotch cloth, blue linen, oznaburg, cotton, holland serge, kersey and flannel in bales, full suits for adults and youths; bodices, hoods and laces for women; shoes, gloves, hose, cravats, handkerchiefs, hats and other articles of dress. Hammers, hatchets, chisels, augers, locks, staples, nails, sickles, bellows, saws, knives, flesh forks, porringers, saucepans, frying-pans, gridirons, tongs, shovels, hoes, iron-pots, tables, physic, wool-cards, gimlets, compasses, needles, stirrups, looking-glasses, candlesticks, candles, funnels, 25 pounds of raisins, 100 gallons of brandy, 20 gallons of wine, 10 gallons of *aqua vitæ*.

FIGURE 37.
A Peddler (from an Old Print).

The contents of this store was valued at £614 sterling, a sum which represented about $15,000 in our present currency.

Mr. Fiske says: "One can imagine how dazzling to the youthful eyes must have been the miscellaneous variety of desirable things. Not only were the manufactured articles pretty sure to have come from England, but everything else, to be saleable, must be labelled English, insomuch that fanciers used to sell the songsters unknown to England, if they sang particularly well, as English mocking birds."

It was the habit of the early Virginia planters from time to time to purchase silver plate in England. This they looked upon as a sort of wealth which could never lose its value, and pieces of such plate engraved with the crest of the original owner, have in many cases been handed down as family heirlooms, even to the present day. Candlesticks and snuffers, castors for sugar, pepper, and mustard, saltcellars and beakers are frequently mentioned in the wills of the latter part of the seventeenth century.

In one instance dishes weighing eighty and ninety ounces apiece and a case containing a dozen silver-hafted knives and a dozen silver-hafted forks are specified. Mrs. Elizabeth Digges bequeathed two hundred and sixty ounces of silver plate to her friends and relatives. Specimens of old silver, etc., are shown in Figure 159.

FIGURE 37½.
Drawn from an Original Monmouth Cap at the Rolls Hall, Monmouth, Wales.

We read also of the following musical instruments among the household goods of the richer planters: Virginals, hand-lyres, cornets, violins, recorders, flutes, and hautboys.

In the kitchen, various utensils were in use, being made of brass, tin, pewter, wood, clay, and copper.

Another feature of colonial life was the itinerant peddler, who travelled from plantation to plantation carrying the latest fashions and, oftentimes, the latest piece of gossip. He was always sure of a welcome from the people of every class, from the mistress and master at the hall fireside to the maids and men in the servants' quarters, for his pack contained, like that of Autolycus, wares to suit all needs and tastes.

"Lawn as white as driven snow;
  Cypress black as e'er was crow;
  Gloves as sweet as damask roses;
  Masks for faces and for noses;
Bugle-bracelet, necklace-amber,
Perfume for a lady's chamber;
Golden quoifs and stomachers,
For my lads to give their dears;
    Pins and poking-sticks of steel;
    What maids lack from head to heel;
    Come buy of me, come; come buy, come buy;
    Buy lads, or else your lasses cry: come, buy."

REIGNS OF JAMES II—WILLIAM AND MARY

1685-1700

FIGURE 38 represents a lady of quality in the fashionable dress of William and Mary's reign. Her gown is of rich silk trimmed with pretintailles, or patterns cut out and laid on in rows across the petticoat. The flounce is edged with gold lace, also the gown which is looped back to show the underskirt. The stomacher is stiff and high; the sleeves loose, ending below the elbow with full ruffles of lace to match the commode head-dress, which has long streamers down the back. The hair is worn low and in soft loose curls on the forehead.

FIGURE 39 is a typical dress of a child of the period. In this case it is of blue Holland, but silk and brocade were much used. Apron with bib is of white linen. Under the loose silken hood is a close-fitting cap of linen which was always worn by little children and sometimes beautifully embroidered.

FIGURE 40 shows the outdoor costume of a tradeswoman late in the seventeenth century. Her gown is of woolen fabric, paragon or linsey-woolsey, made with sleeves short enough to show the undersleeves of white kenting which reach a little below the elbow. Her mantle is of durant trimmed with bands of gimp. The hood is of black ducape and is the popular style of head covering of that period. It is lined and turned back round the face with sarsinet of a contrasting colour.

FIGURE 41.—A man on his way to work about the end of the seventeenth century in leggings of tanned leather and coat of frieze under which is a woolen jerkin. His wide-brimmed hat is of coarse felt.

FIGURE 42 represents a gentleman of William and Mary's day, costumed in dark red broadcloth trimmed with gold braid and gold buttons. He wears a cravat of fine linen with lace ends, and carries his three-cornered hat edged with feathers, rather than crush his voluminous periwig. His shoes have small buckles rather high on the instep.

FIGURE 38.　　　FIGURE 39.　　　FIGURE 40.　　　FIGURE 41.　　　FIGURE 42.

There is not much to be said about dress among the American Indians. However, the costume of the Queen of the Pamunkeys, who accompanied her husband, Totto Potto Moi, to a conference with the English in Virginia, and who was a lady of some distinction, is worthy of description. She wore a turban made of a wide plait of black and white wampum and her robe was of deerskin, with the hair on the outside, ornamented (from the shoulders to the feet) with a twisted fringe six inches deep. An effective but rather an uncomfortable dress for the season, as this conference took place in May (1677).

The King of the Pamunkeys was afterward killed in fighting with the English under Colonel Edward Hill. His wife, the Queen, made an appeal to the House of Burgesses, whereupon Charles II sent to her, in recognition of her husband's services, a crown consisting of a red velvet cap with a silver plate as a frontlet, to which were attached many chains. During the latter part of the year 1800, the Pamunkeys determined to move westward, and, being under stress of weather, and, also, it is supposed, lacking food, came to Mr. Arthur Morson, who gave them shelter and protection for a time on his plantation. Upon leaving, they expressed their gratitude by presenting their benefactor with this crown, their greatest treasure, which still existed in the original shape. The cap becoming in time moth-eaten, the chains lost and scattered, the Administrator of the Morson Estate sold the frontlet to the Association for the Preservation of Virginia Antiquities, and it was placed in the Historical Society's rooms for safe-keeping (Figure 27).

For descriptions and pictures of the native Indians, the reader is referred to Schoolcraft's exhaustive history, which illustrates the life and customs of the various tribes in North America from the landing of Columbus to the middle of the nineteenth century.*

* History of the Indian Tribes of the United States, by Henry Rowe Schoolcraft, LL.D.

THE ENGLISH COLONIES

IN

MASSACHUSETTS, CONNECTICUT, NEW HAMPSHIRE, MAINE, AND RHODE ISLAND

1620–1700

During the Reigns of
James I, Charles I, Charles II, James II, and
William and Mary

"A Dosen of Points, Sent by a Gentlewoman to Her Lover as a Newe Yeare's Gifte."

As I on a New Yeare's day
　　Did walcke amidst the streate,
My restless eyes for you my hart,
　　Did seke a fayring mete.
I sercht throughout the faire
　　But nothing could I fynde:
No, no, of all ther was not one
　　That would content my mynde.
But all the boothes were filled
　　With fancyes fond attyre,
And trifling toyes were set to sale,
　　For them that would requyre.
Then to myself quoth I,
　　What meanes theise childish knacks;
Is all the faire for children made,
　　Or fooles that bables lackes?
Are theise the goodly gifts,
　　The new yeare to beginne;
Which friends present unto their friends,
　　Their fayth and love to winne?
I se I came in vayne,
　　My labour ali is lost,
I will departe and kepe my purse,
　　From making any cost.
But se my happy chaunce,
　　Whilest I did hast away;
Dame Vertue doth display her booth,
　　My hasty feete to stay.
I joyfull of the sight,
　　Did preace unto the place,
To se the tricke and trimmed tent,
　　For such a ladye's grace.
And after I had viewed
　　Eache thing within her seate,

I found a knotte of peerlesse points
  Beset with posyes neate.
Theise points in number twelve,
  Did shew themselves to be:
The sence whereof by poet's skil,
  I will declare to the.

1. With meate before the set,
    Suffice but nature's scant;
2. Be sure thy tongue at table tyme,
    Noe sober talke doe want.
3. Let word, let thought, and dede,
    In honest wise agree:
4. And loke the pore in tyme of nede,
    Thy helping hand may see.
5. When foes invade the realme,
    Then shew thy might and strength:
6. Tell truth in place wher thou dost come
    For falshed failes at length.
7. Be fast and firm to friende,
    As thou wouldst him to be:
8. Be shamefast there wher shamefull dedes
    Be offred unto the.
9. Weare not suche costly clothes,
    As are not for thy state:
10. Heare eache man's cause as thoh he wer
    In wealth thine equall mate.
11. In place thy maners shewe,
    In right and comly wyse:
12. From the let peace and quietnesse,
    And wars from others ryse.

With these twelve vertuous points,
  Se thou do tye thee round,
And lyke and love this simple gifte,
  Till better may be found.
Yet one point thou dost lacke,
  To tye thy hose before:
Love me as I love the, and shall
  From hence for evermore.—Farwell.

The English in Massachusetts, Connecticut, New Hampshire, Maine, and Rhode Island

1620–1700

FIGURE 43.
A Puritan Dame.

IN 1620 came the first English settlers to Massachusetts—the Pilgrims, or Separatists, as they are sometimes called, in their sombre coloured garments, of the same shapes and fashions, however, as those in vogue at the gay court of Charles I, the superfluous trimmings, knots of bright ribbon, rich laces and feathers, being conspicuously absent.

In this company of one hundred and four Pilgrims, which arrived at Plymouth, December 20, 1620, were the following:

Two carpenters
One fustian worker and silk dyer
One lady's maid
Two printers and publishers
One tailor

One wool-carder
One cooper
One merchant
Four seamen
One soldier
Two tradesmen

Ten adult servants
One lay reader
One hatter
One physician
One smith

The Pilgrims, like the Roundheads in England, were minded to discourage extravagance, and made strict laws to control fashions of dress. Three years later they were followed by the Puritans of the Massachusetts Bay Company, who, according to Weedon, settled first at Cape Ann and afterward removed to Salem. This Company was a large and rich organization and provided each man with a suitable outfit:

Four pairs of shoes
Four pairs of stockings
A pair of Norwich gaiters
Four shirts
Two suits of doublet and hose of
    leather lined with oil skin
A woolen suit lined with leather
Four bands
Two handkerchiefs

A green cotton waistcoat
A leather belt
A woolen cap
A black hat
Two red knit caps
Two pairs of gloves
A mandillion or cloak lined with cotton
    and an extra pair of breeches were
    allotted each man (Figure 44).

There were many women in this band of settlers, but no mention is made of their garments.

This outfit was much more liberal than that provided by the Virginia Company, but the climate of Massachusetts was bleak and cold compared with that of Virginia, although the air apparently agreed with Francis Higginson, who wrote the following letter from Boston in 1629:

"But since I came hither on this voyage I thank God I have had perfect health and I, that have not gone without a cap for many years together neither durst leave off the same, have now cast away my cap, and do wear none at all in the day time; and whereas beforetime I clothed myself with double clothes and thick waistcoats to keep me warm even in summer time, I do now go as thin clad as any, only wearing a light stuff cassock upon my shirt and stuff breeches of one thickness without lining."

This company of Puritans, which numbered about two hundred, eventually founded Boston and other places in the neighbourhood: Charlestown, Watertown, Dorchester, Roxbury, Mystic, Lynn, etc. They kept in touch with the Mother Country and imported many comforts, which the Plymouth Bay Company eschewed.

About 1630 a body of this Massachusetts Bay Company, composed chiefly of yeomen of Dorsetshire, England, settled in Connecticut. They were mostly Church of England people of the representative Anglo-Saxon type, and in their laws we find few restrictions concerning dress, although at the dawn of the Revolution the people of Connecticut were among the first of the Colonists to renounce foreign luxuries and augment the use of homemade articles. We read that "master-tailors were paid 12 pence, inferior 8 pence per day, with dyett."

In 1634, the Massachusetts Court forbade the purchase of "Any apparell, either woolen, silke, or lynnen with any lace on it, silver, golde, silk, or thread." They shall not "make or buy slashed clothes, other than one slashe in each sleeve and another in the backe"; there shall be no "cutt works, imbroid'd or needle work'd capps, bands & Rayles; no gold or silver girdles, hatt bands, belts, ruffs, beaver hatts."

In 1636 lace was forbidden; only the binding of a small edging on linen was allowed.

FIGURE 44.

A Puritan Cloak or Mandillion of Black Silk with Small Embroidered Buttons. The original garment from which the drawing is taken is in the South Kensington Museum, London.

Points were the usual fastenings in use during the sixteenth and seventeenth centuries. Sometimes they had metal tags at the ends and were more or less ornamental. Frequent mention is made of them by Shakespeare:

"Their points being broken, down fell their hose;"
"With one that ties his points," etc.

Like their successors, the modern suspenders, they were often very dainty and were appropriately given as love tokens.

Margaret Winthrop, in a letter to England written from Massachusetts, gives a note of daily wear: "I must of a necessity make me a gown to wear every day and would have one bought me of good strong black stuff and Mr. Smith to make it of the civilest fashion now in use. If my sister Downing would please to give him some directions about it, he would make it the better."* Slight as is this note, it proves that Dame Winthrop was not indifferent to the prevailing fashions, and we know that English gentlewomen of that time were dressed as in Figures 21, 32, 33, 35, and 36. The familiar portrait of Governor Winthrop in a ruff and long hair indicates that he had not adopted the dress of the strict Puritans (Figure 93). Unfortunately, no portrait of his wife has been handed down to posterity, and we are left to conjecture that the dress of "good strong black stuff" to "wear every day" was made of durant, something after the fashion of Figure 21, or, perhaps, like that of the Puritan gentlewoman in the initial letter of this chapter, which represents a typical Puritan of the Massachusetts Bay Company.

Abundant evidence of the various styles of dress of English women in the reigns of Charles I and II is preserved in the clever sketches of Hollar. They are invaluable to the historian.

Wenceslaus Hollar (1607–1677) went from Cologne and Antwerp to London in the train of the Earl of Arundel, English Ambassador, in 1635, and was appointed teacher of drawing to the young Prince, afterwards Charles II. A volume of sketches by the royal pupil, to which Hollar had given the finishing touches, may be seen among the Harleian manuscripts at the British Museum. In 1640 appeared his "Ornatus Muliebris Anglicanus, or the Severall Habits of English Women from the Nobilitiee to the Country Women as they are in these times."

* Margaret Winthrop, by Mrs. Earle.

FIGURE 45.—Doublet of black cloth trimmed with silk braid and crochet **buttons.** The sleeves are slashed. The lace collar is not put on properly. It should turn down over the neck-band and fit close up to the throat, as in Figure 14. Worn in Reign of Charles I. (Photographed from the original garment.)

FIGURE 46.—Doublet of black silk trimmed with points of galloon with silver aiglets. The collar should be turned over the neck-band and fit close to the throat, as in Figure 14. Worn in the reign of James I. (Photographed from the original garment.)

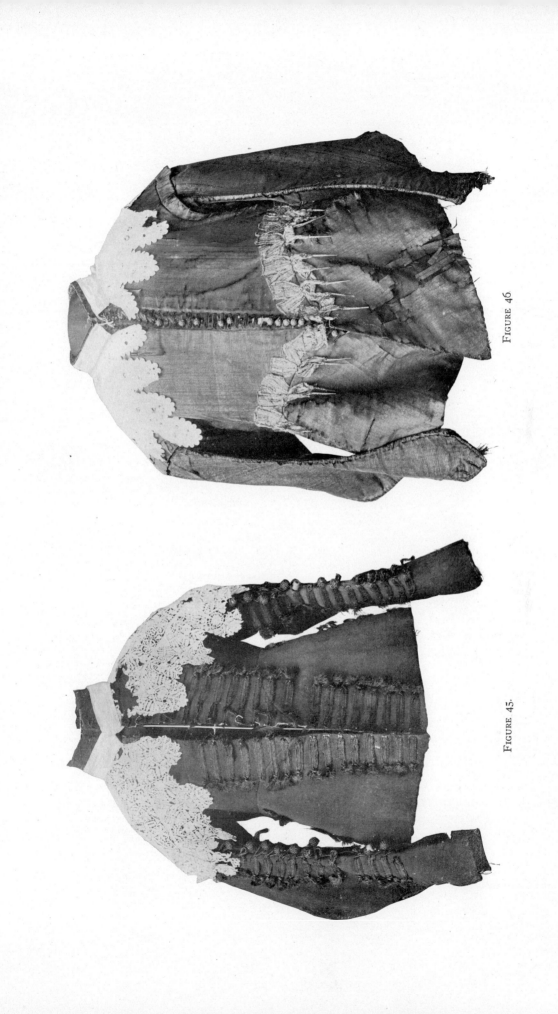

FIGURE 46

FIGURE 45.

In 1643 appeared a second book, "Theatrum Mulierum," in which are represented the various styles of dress in the leading nations of Europe. On the accession of Charles II, Hollar was appointed His Majesty's Designer.

His books are now very rare. Copies may be seen in the Library of the British Museum, but I do not know of any in a public library in this country. The "Theatrum Mulierum" shows the costumes of the women of Holland in the seventeenth century, specimens of which are given in Figures 106, 107, 110, 124, and 126.

In the Colony at Plymouth a manifesto against long hair was published, in which it was called an impious custom and a shameful practice for any man who had the least care of his soul to wear long hair. An old song about the Roundhead Puritans runs thus:

> "What creature's this? with his short hair,
> His little band, and huge long ears,
> That this new faith has founded?
> The Puritans were never such,
> The Saints themselves had ne'er so much—
> Oh such a knave's a Roundhead."

The majority of the Puritans, however, were very much in earnest on the subject of reform in dress, and it has been said they expressed their piety not only in the choice of sombre hues and simplicity of cut, but even worked into the garments religious sayings and quotations from Holy Writ. As Fairholt puts it, "they literally moralized dress."

> "Nay Sir, she is a Puritan at her needle too,
>   Indeed,
> She works religious petticoats; for flowers
> She'll make church histories: besides
> My smock sleeves have such holy embroideries,
> And are so learned, that I fear in time
> All my apparel will be quoted by
> Some pure instructor."*

* The Citye Match. Jasper Mayne, L. 1639.

This fashionable custom in England is also mentioned by Ben Jonson. "The linen of men and women was either so worked as to resemble lace or was ornamented by the needle into representations of fruit and flowers, passages of history," etc.*

FIGURE 47.
Typical Winter Costume of a Lady of the Period, 1640.

The inventories of about 1641 show that

3 suits of clothes were valued at	£3		
3 coats	" " "	2 6s.	
1 hat and doublet	" " "	3	
4 pairs of shoes	" " "	9	
4 " " stockings	" " "	6	
1 stuff petticoat was	" "	6	
2 pairs of linen breeches	" "	1 6s.	

In 1652 is found the first mention of shoemaking, at Salem. It was about this time that the General Court of Massachusetts passed sumptuary laws to repress the spending of too large a proportion of income on apparel. Weedon says: "When the Court was not occupied with grave business of State, it devoted itself to correcting morals and regulating dress. The function of dress in the minds of the anxious Fathers was not only to cover and protect people, but to classify and arrange them. The same conserving prejudice which marked their treatment of labourers and apprentices controlled their notions of dress. Social prestige, rank, caste, and breeding were to be formulated in the garments of the wearer. It was not only that the precious capital of the community was wasted by expensive dressing, but the well ordered ranks of society were

* Every Man out of his Humour.

FIGURE 48.—A boy's doublet of white linen quilted, and embroidered with gold-coloured silk. The sleeves are slashed and the whole garment is edged with needle-point lace. Worn in reign of Charles I, 1639. (Photographed from the original garment.)

FIGURE 49.—Bodice of white satin slashed and pinked. A chemisette of silk or embroidery would show in the openings. Worn in reign of Charles I. (Photographed from the original garment.)

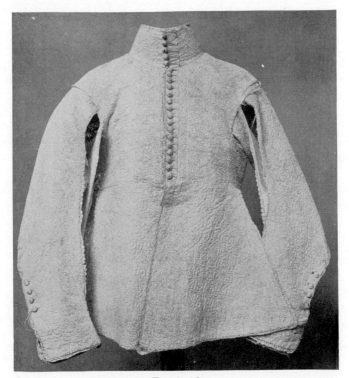

FIGURE 48.

FIGURE 49.

jostled and disturbed by the glitter of lace and the show of silken hoods, the tramp of strong boots."

Mrs. Lake, who came over with the Dorsetshire Company in 1635, sent out to England for the following articles for the furnishing of the new household of her daughter, who married John Gallup of the same settlement in 1645. We give the list in full as thoroughly typical of the time:

"A peare of brasse Andirons
A brasse Kittell,
2 grate Chestes, well made,
2 armed Cheares with rushe bottums,
2 carven Caisse for Bottels wch my Cuzzen Cooke has of mine
A Warming Pann,
A Big Iron Pott,
6 Pewter Plates
2 Pewter Platters,
3 Pewter Porringeres
A small Stew Pann of Copper
A peare of Brasse and a peare of Silver Candle-sticks (of goode plate)
A Drippe Panne
A Bedsteede of carven Oake (ye one in wch I sleept in my father's house, with ye Vallances and Curtayns and Tapestry Coverlid belongynge & ye wch my sister Breadcale hath in charge of Mee)
Duzzen Napekins of fine linen damasque & 2 table cloathes of ye same. Also 8 fine
Holland Pillowe Beeres and 4 ditto sheetes.
A skellet,
A pestel & mortar
A few Needels of different sizes
A carpet (that is, a table cover; the name was universally applied thus) of goodly stuff and colour, aboute 2 Ell longe.
6 Table knifes of ye beste Steal with such handles as may bee.
Also 3 large & 3 smal Silvern Spoones, and 6 of horne."

We are told that Mrs. Lake left a wardrobe of considerable extent and richness, besides a goodly list of linens and other household treasures, with several carved chests to contain them, all of which she bequeathed to friends and relatives: "To my daughter Martha Harris," she says, "I give my tapestry coverlid and all my other apparell which are not disposed of to others particularly, and I give unto her my mantel and after her decease, to all her children as their need is."* This "mantel" was supposed to have been Russian sable, even then as costly as it was rare, and presumably brought from the far East, perhaps China.

We read also in "Colonial Days and Ways" that "all the better class among the Colonists seem to have disproportionately liberal supplies of 'mantels and pettycotes' of velvet or brocade, with other 'garments to consort therewith,' but this was not due so much to vanity as to thrift, the best being literally the cheapest in the days when the fine fabrics were so honestly made as to wear for decades and

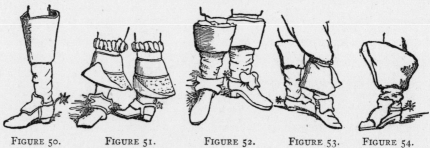

FIGURE 50.   FIGURE 51.   FIGURE 52.   FIGURE 53.   FIGURE 54.
Reign of Elizabeth,   Reign of Charles I, 1625+   During the Commonwealth,
1595–1603+.   1649–1660.

the cost of carriage was the same for a coat of frieze as for one of velvet." Mrs. Smith throws a new light on the subject, which also helps us to understand the wills and inventories in which these beautiful old stuffs were handed down as family heirlooms. Fortunately for this book of costume, some Colonial garments have been preserved in their original fashion, while, of course, others bear the marks of many alterations to suit the times.

In 1638 an order was passed by the General Court of Massachusetts:

"No garment shall be made with short sleeves, and such as have garments already made with short sleeves shall not wear the same

* Colonial Days and Ways, by Helen Evertson Smith.

unless they cover the arm to the wrist; and hereafter no person whatever shall make any garment for women with sleeves more than half an ell wide."

The town records were full of prosecutions, acquittals, and convictions for offences against these laws. In Salem in 1652 "a man was presented for excess of bootes, ribands, gould and silver laces, and Ester Jynks for wearing silver lace"; while in Newbury in 1653 "two women were called upon to pay taxes for wearing silken hoods and scarves, but were discharged on proof that their husbands were worth two hundred pounds each."

"John Hutchins' wife was also discharged upon testimony of her being brought up above the ordinary ranke." "The latter," observes Weedon, "is an interesting instance showing that rank as well as property condoned these offences."

FIGURE 55.   FIGURE 56.   FIGURE 57.
Reign of   Reign of   Reign of
Charles II,   James II,   William III,
1660+.   1685+.   1690+.

Any one of less estate than two hundred pounds was held to strict account in dress. The women offended especially by wearing silk and tiffany hoods; but they also wore broad-brimmed hats (Figure 43). Under the stiff bodice of a gown a lady wore a petticoat either of woolen stuff or of rich silk or brocade. The ruff had given place to a broad collar, plain or embroidered, falling over the shoulders (Figures 20 and 33).

As leather was much used, a tannery was almost the first industry started in every settlement. In 1676 the price of shoes was regulated by law. "Five pence half penny a size for all pleyne and wooden heel'd shoes, and above seven pence half penny a size for well wrought 'French falls.'" Wooden heels were worn all through the seventeenth century. Even at this early date, Lynn, Massachusetts, was the centre for the manufacture of shoes, which were usually made with broad straps and buckles; women's shoes being of neat leather or woolen cloth and occasionally of silk.

During the seventeenth century leather clothing was much worn, especially by labourers and servants. The excellent brain-tanned deerskin, which the Indians taught the Colonists to prepare, served well for garments. Hampshire kerseys were used for common wear. Monmouth caps and red knit caps are mentioned among the articles used by the lower classes, and the mandillion, or over-garment, fastened with hooks and eyes, is frequently spoken of. Irish stockings, so often mentioned in this century, have been compared to modern socks, but they were of cloth and were very warm. While rich apparel is noted here and there, in spite of statute law, it is evident that the great majority of the people dressed plainly. Their

1610.—   1610.—   1640.   1643.   1647.   1663.—   1682.—   1695.—

FIG. 58.   FIG. 59.   FIG. 60.   FIG. 61.   FIG. 62.   FIG. 63.   FIG. 64.   FIG. 65.

frugality and abstinence made a foundation on which sumptuary statutes could be based.

Doublets were worn by both sexes; they were always lined or padded for extra warmth (Figure 31). The sleeves were often slashed and embroidered extravagantly, as indicated in the "restraining acts" of the Pilgrim Fathers. Falling bands at the neck were very common, and often they were embroidered. A deep linen collar was sometimes preferred in place of the bands.

> "This pretty new fashion indulge him to wear
> There's no law in bands, I may venture to swear,
> But they set off an old fashion face I declare.
> Which nobody can deny, deny, which nobody can deny."

Shoes were ornamented with rosettes (Figures 59 and 61). A beaver or felt hat covered the head. Embroidered gloves were

FIGURE 66.—A Puritan Colonist of the Massachusetts Bay Company. Suit of black cloth of the same cut and general make as the Cavalier's costume in Figure 19. Stockings or hose of dark grey or green wool fastened to the breeches by points of black galloon or ribbon. Falling band and cuffs of white Holland. Hat of black felt finished with a narrow band of ribbon and a small silver buckle. The mandillion or cloak is of black cloth lined with drugget or fustian.

FIGURE 67.—A woman of the same Company. Her gown is of cloth, either purple or grey, or perhaps brown; for outdoor wear it is turned under and looped back showing petticoats of homespun or linsey-woolsey. The apron is of white Holland linen. A falling collar or band turns down round the neck of the gown and white linen cuffs are turned back over the sleeves. The kerchief is put on for outdoor wear as well as the hood, which is made of dark coloured silk or camlet and lined with soft silk or fur to match the muff. This was the ordinary dress of a Puritan gentlewoman from 1620 to 1640. In cold weather a cloak and hood of heavy cloth or fur was worn with a velvet mask as a protection from the wind. See Figure 36. Stout shoes with wooden heels and woolen stockings completed the costume. The hair is drawn back under a white linen cap.

FIGURE 68.—The dress of an English gentleman about 1666. Petticoat breeches trimmed with wide ribbon arranged in overlapping loops. Short doublet to match with slashed sleeves opening both back and front and held together by loops of braid and buttons. A collar of linen trimmed with rich lace turns down over the coat, but is much deeper and fuller in front, where it is laid in box-plaits under the chin. The shirt of Holland hangs out from under the doublet. The cloak is of a fine woolen stuff made full and long and gathered into a rolling collar at the neck. The hat is of Flemish beaver with long full plumes of a contrasting colour. The boots are French falls with very wide tops, known as bucket tops. The peruke is long and full without powder.

FIGURE 69.—A lady of the same date (1666) in a walking hood and fur tippet. The gown is of rich silk trimmed with fancy gimp. The bodice is pointed in front and back over a full-gathered skirt and is cut low in the neck and finished by a falling collar of lace under the tippet. Under the short full sleeves of the gown are white puffed sleeves to the wrist. Silken shoes tied with ribbon on the instep match the gown in colour and texture. The hair is worn in curls to the shoulders and held back by a ribbon which is tied in a bow either on top or above the left ear.

FIGURE 69.

FIGURE 68.

FIGURE 67.

FIGURE 66.

always worn with full dress, the flaps of the gauntlets being richly figured or fringed (Figures 72, 74, 75, 76, and 77). Swords were suspended from embroidered shoulder-belts. Gold and silver lace was often used for trimming.

In the Massachusetts Colony, armour was provided for the emigrants. Bandoliers, horn flasks, corselets, and pikes are mentioned frequently.

In an old book called an "Abridgement of the laws in force and use in Her Majesty's (Queen Anne) Plantations of Virginia (viz.) of Jamaica, New England, Barbadoes, New York, Maryland, Carolina, etc., London 1709," will be found under the heading "Ammunition, Or Laws Concerning the Colonial Militia": "I. an. 1662. Every man able to bear arms shall have in his house a fixed gun, 2 l. of powder and 8 l. of shot, at least, to be provided by the Master of the Family, under the Penalty of being fined 80 l. of tobacco. II. an. 1666. Every County shall

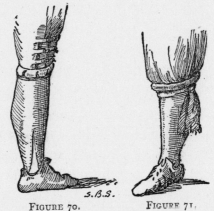

FIGURE 70.   FIGURE 71.

Cannons or Breeches Fastenings (from an
Old Print, 1650).

be empowered by their By-Laws to make such provision of ammunition at the county charges as their several occasions require. III. Captains of foot and horse shall take a strict account of what arms are wanting and represent the same to the Colonel," etc. This affords valuable proof of the familiarity with firearms expected of the Colonists in everyday life, also of the early origin of the American militia. With regard to the latter organization, we read under the date of 1660 as follows:

"Every person neglecting to appear at the Days of Exercising the Militia shall be fined 100 l. of Tobacco."

"Ten long guns or muskets with one Barrel of gun powder and Bullets proportionable shall be kept in each garrison as a Reserve and Defence for the same."

"For the better taking alarms upon the approach of Indians the frequent shooting of guns at Drinkings is prohibited."

"Six shoots of powder each man is required to bring with him on Training Days or pay a fine. The latter to be put aside for the purchase of Drums and Colours."

A portrait of Sir John Leverett, Governor of the Massachusetts Colony in 1673, in the Essex Institute at Salem, depicts a buff coat of dressed leather with metal fastenings, like ornamental hooks and eyes, down the front; a falling collar of linen tied with little tassels, and a very magnificent pair of embroidered gloves, which Sir John is holding in one hand, while on a table beside him is a hat ornamented with a long feather (Figure 82). Probably the portrait was taken when he was a Colonial soldier, for history records that he went to England in 1644 and took the side of the Parliament against the King, but after his return to Boston he filled several important offices, and in 1676 was magnanimously knighted by Charles II in acknowledgment of his services to the New England Colonies.

The women of New England in the last quarter of the seventeenth century were well, if not handsomely, dressed. Undoubtedly the gentlewomen of that time had brocades and silks for festive occasions and fur-trimmed cloaks and hoods for the cold season, but the ordinary dress was a short gown of camlet over a homespun petticoat with a long white apron of linen. The sleeves of the gown were supplemented by mittens reaching to the elbows and leaving a part of the fingers and thumbs bare. The cloak worn at that time was short, with a hood to cover the head, which was thrown back in meeting; and those who wore hats took them off. The matrons wore caps habitually and the young women had their hair curled

FIGURES 72, 74, 75, and 77 show different specimens of embroidered gloves, made of doeskin, embroidered in coloured silks and gold thread, worn in the seventeenth century.

FIGURE 76.—Gloves worn by Sir John Leverett, Governor of Massachusetts Colony. (From the original gloves in the Essex Museum, Salem, Massachusetts.)

FIGURE 73.—Fashionable style of hair-dressing, reigns of Charles I and II. (By Hollar.)

FIGURE 72.

FIGURE 74.

FIGURE 73.

FIGURE 76.

FIGURE 77.

FIGURE 75.

and tied back with a ribbon or arranged in a soft coil at the back, with short curls on the forehead.

Scarlet robes are said to have been worn by the judges in the

FIGURE 78.
A Man in Buff-coat and Bandolier, 1620–1660.

Massachusetts Colony. Mrs. Earle gives a picture of one stated to have been worn by Judge Curwen, of Salem, during the gruesome witch

6

trials, but the garment in question is so exactly like the cloaks worn by the women of the Puritan days that one is tempted to think it was borrowed from his wife for these solemn occasions. However, scarlet was a favourite colour for men in those days, and a very romantic story has recently been written by Mrs. Austin about the red riding cloak worn by Governor Bradford, 2d, about the middle of the seventeenth century.

Mourning for the dead was attended by various solemn ceremonies in the Colonies. Judge Sewall, of Massachusetts (Figure 81), describes minutely the funeral of Lady Andros, the wife of the Governor (Figure 97), on the 10th of February, 1688, to which he had been invited by the "Clark of the South Company." "It took place between 7 and 8 P. M. probably. The hearse, surrounded by torch bearers, was drawn by six horses, and escorted by a guard of

FIGURE 79.
Points with Aiglets Drawing Together a Slashed Sleeve.

FIGURE 80.
Points with Aiglets or Tags Fastening a Buff-coat and Sleeve Together (from an Old Print, 1650–1660).

soldiers from the Governour's house to the South Meeting House where the body was placed before the pulpit, with six mourning women by it. There was a great noise and clamour to keep the people out of the house, which was made light with candles and torches." He tells of himself that he went home, and about nine o'clock heard the bell tolled again for the funeral. He missed the sermon, whether purposely or not is not told, but knows that the text was "Cry, all flesh

FIGURE 81.—Portrait of Samuel Sewall, Governor and Judge of Massachusetts Colony, showing the periwig and long coat of the reign of James II.

FIGURE 82.—Portrait of Sir John Leverett, Governor of Massachusetts Colony, showing buff coat and plain band of a soldier in reign of Charles I.

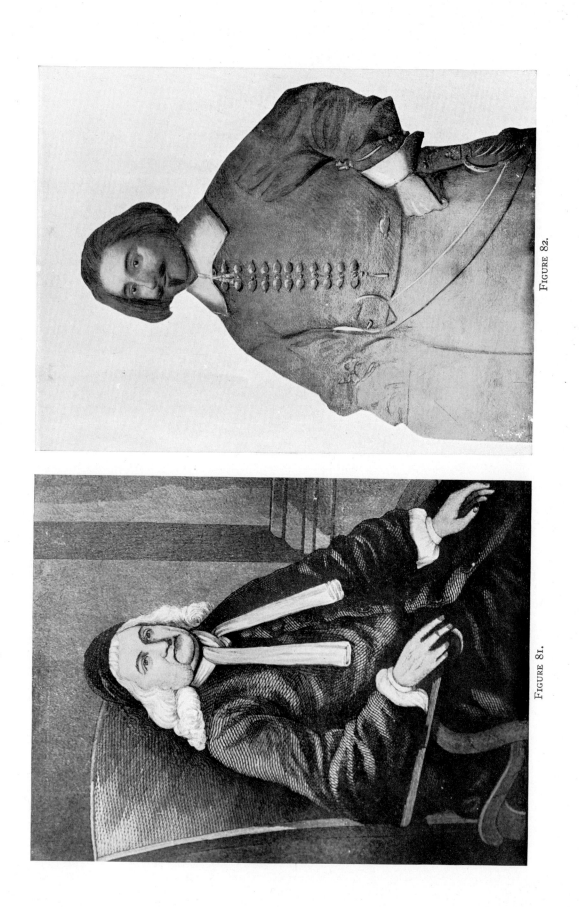

FIGURE 82.

FIGURE 81.

is grass." After naming a number of the people who were present, he remarks, "Twas warm thawing weather and the wayes extreame dirty. No volley at placing the body in the tomb." On Saturday, February 11th, another entry in this instructive diary reads: "The next day the mourning cloths of the pulpit is taken off and given to Mr. Willard." Frequent mention is made throughout this diary, and others of the time, of the gloves, scarves, and mourning rings given friends and relatives at funerals, and there is evidence that the general custom of wearing black as a token of sorrow was followed throughout the Colonies, the women wearing gowns and hoods of

FIGURE 83.   FIGURE 84.   FIGURE 85.   FIGURE 86.   FIGURE 87.

Various Forms of the Buff Coat.

black stuff with trimmings, cuffs, and veils of crêpe, at least such was the "customary woe," but it was observed with less formality by the Non-Conformists than by the Orthodox Church people. Little children were dressed in black and wore black ribbons for a time, and it was not unusual for the servants of a household to be dressed in black when the head of the family died: as in nearly every other respect, English ways and English customs were very closely followed throughout the Colonies in America. In the Philadelphia Library there is preserved, among many other interesting relics of the past, an old hatchment formerly used in the Dickinson family,

—probably brought from England,—which was placed over the doorway when a death occurred in the family. Another specimen is also to be seen at Christ Church, Philadelphia.

The portrait of a widow given in Figure 150 represents Lady Mary Fenwick, in high widow's cap and tippets, black dress and veil, in one hand holding a portrait of her husband, Sir John Fenwick, who by an act of attainder was beheaded 27th of January, 1696, without a trial, for conspiracy in favour of James II. Lady Fenwick made the greatest exertions to save her husband's life and became an object of much interest to the Jacobite Party. The cap is of the shape known as the "commode" in William and Mary's reign (Figure 38).

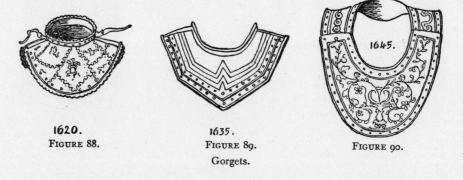

1620.
FIGURE 88.

1635.
FIGURE 89.
Gorgets.

1645.
FIGURE 90.

Though the Massachusetts General Court admonished men against long hair and inveighed against excess in apparel in 1675, the laws in this direction were dropping into disuse in many districts. In the same year the grand jury threatened the selectmen of Dedham with prosecution for their neglect in enforcing the sumptuary statutes. These worthy burghers did not relish the work "of stripping silken hoods and ribbands from irate dames and of arraigning the great boots of dandies. There is no record to show that they heeded the mandate of the grand jury."

The inventories in Boston prove that sumptuous dress was in fashion notwithstanding the written laws against it. Robert Richbell, in 1682, leaves two silver hilted rapiers and a belt worth £12. His wardrobe contained a satin coat with gold flowers, and blue breeches, £4; a stuff suit with lace, several other suits, all accompanied by seven cravats and seven pairs of ruffles and ribbons, valued at £7.

Periwigs came into fashion at the Restoration, 1660. Richbell must have vexed poor Judge Sewall sorely, for he was the possessor of three.

We know that silver buttons were very common in the Colonies in the seventeenth century, and gold ones were also used. Captain Hudson, whose dress was modest in comparison with Richbell's, had two suits equipped with them. In a trading stock, mention is made of 4 gross of silver and gold buttons valued at £3 12s. A curiosity of the time was "Beggars' velvet," 14 yards worth 21s.

The long periwigs introduced into England from France in the latter part of Charles II's reign were promptly assumed by the women of fashion, together with the plumed hats of the same period. Pepys records the fact thus:

"Walking in the gallery of Whitehall, I find the Ladies of Honour dressed in their riding garbs, with coats and doublets with deep skirts, just for all the world like men's, and their doublets buttoned up the breast, with periwigs and hats on, that only for a long petticoat dragging under their men's coats, no body would take them for women on any point whatever, which was an odd sight and a sight that did not please me."

About 1680, the long straight coats, which took the fickle fancy of Charles II for a time, were introduced into New England. They were made without a collar and were worn with a neck-cloth which fastened with a silver buckle under the hair in the back. Specimens of this fashion are given in Figures 137, 138, photographed from the original garments in the South Kensington Museum. They belonged to Sir Thomas Isham (1657–1681), third baronet, who was born at Lamport in Nottinghamshire. When still a boy he wrote a diary in Latin, by the command of his father, which gives a vivid picture of the everyday doings of a family of the period. This diary was translated and privately printed (1875) by the Rev. Robert Isham, rector of Lamport, where the original is still preserved. Isham succeeded to the Baronetcy in 1679. He is described as a young gentleman of great expectations. Figure 137 represents the suit of light brocade prepared for his wedding, which he never wore, as he died after a brief illness on the day fixed for the ceremony.

Weedon again records: "In the inventories of women, house-linen generally formed an important part. Mistress Anne Hibbins in 1656 had relatively more of the luxuries her sex cherishes in all periods. A gold wedding ring at 16s., a ring with a diamond at 8s., a 'taffaty' cloak at £2 10s., a black satin doublet at 10s., a green wrought cup-board cloth with silk fringe at 15s., 5 painted callico curtains and valiants at £1 10s., show that Anne loved the things hated by the Puritans.

"In William Paine's stock in 1660 were silk wares in two boxes at £31 14s. These occasional luxuries stand out conspicuously. Usually the assorted merchandise of the traders is in solid wares and goods for the everyday use of everyday people. The women selected them carefully and conscientiously. In 1647 one writes: 'She have three peeces of stuf, but I think there is but one of them yt you would like yrself. It is pretty sad stuf, but it have a thred of white in it; it is 3 quarters broad and ye priz is 5s. 6d ye yard.'"*

Towards the close of the seventeenth century we note a tendency to display in all inventories and descriptions left by the wealthy colonists of New England, as well as those in the same period in Virginia, Maryland, and the Carolinas. It was the reign of William and Mary in England, and the Colonies were not subject to any form of oppression. Intercourse between the two countries was frequent,

* Weedon's Economic History of New England.

FIGURE 91.—Portrait of John Winthrop the second, showing the typical garb of the Puritan in the Massachusetts Colony.   1640 +

FIGURE 92.—Picture of Sir John Leverett as Governor of Massachusetts Colony, about 1680.

FIGURE 93.—Picture of John Winthrop, Governor of Massachusetts Colony in 1629.

FIGURE 94.—Picture of Edward Winslow, Governor of Plymouth Colony, in Puritan dress, in 1644.

FIGURE 91.

FIGURE 92

FIGURE 93.

FIGURE 94.

and every ship brought over comforts and luxuries, also fine clothes made by fashionable London tailors, wigs from the popular wig-makers, etc. It is quite safe to conclude that fashions in the Colonies were never more than a year behind those of old England.

Children in the New England Colonies, as elsewhere at that time, were dressed as much like their parents as possible. The baby clothes of the seventeenth century were marvellous specimens of needlework. The earliest garments I have seen are the christening blanket, shirts, and mitts said to have been worn by Governor Bradford, of Plymouth, and now exhibited at Salem in the Essex Institute.

A portrait of Robert Gibbs, aged four and a half, painted in Boston in 1670, also one of John Quincy, at a little more than one year of age, painted in 1690, show the long hanging sleeves usually worn by children under ten years of age (Figure 39). There is also a portrait of Jane Bonner at the age of eight, painted in 1700, which looks almost like a diminutive court lady, with stiff stomacher, ruffles of point-lace, and a necklace of pearls; in one hand a fan, a rose in the other.*

New England by this time included New Hampshire and Maine, settled in 1623 by an English Company in search of gold, and Rhode Island, founded by Roger Williams in 1636.

The attitude of the New England Colonists towards the Mother Church is not clearly outlined in all the authorities of the time; and, in order to prevent anachronisms in costuming a story of that period, it may be well to explain here that the emigrants who came over in 1630 under Governor John Winthrop, and who the day before they embarked sent an address to the "rest of the brethren of the Church of England" calling the Church their "dear mother," had, notwithstanding their dutiful address, when they arrived in America, allowed a sense of freedom to overcome their allegiance, and, following the

* Child Life in Colonial Days, by Mrs. Earle.

example of the Pilgrims of Plymouth and the Puritans of Salem, established separate churches, choosing their own officers. The Plymouth settlers had not openly renounced the authority of the Church of England, but they had laid aside the established ritual. Endicott followed this example and organized the first New England Church at Salem. A few members of that Colony objected, but he had them arrested and sent to England. From that time (1630) Non-Conformist Churches were established in every New England settlement. A simple method of choosing their leaders was adopted. Each member wrote his vote on a piece of paper, stating the Lord moved him to think this man is fit to be pastor, and this one to be teacher. The first pastor thus chosen was Skelton, with Francis Higginson, whose journal is quoted on page 84, for teacher. The choice was confirmed by a number of the leading members of this Company laying their hands on them in prayer.

With the disuse of the English ritual came the abandonment of the white surplice during the service, but the Geneva gown (Figures 148, 149), or preaching gown as it was often called, was worn in the pulpit, not only by the Puritan Non-Conformists, but also by the Presbyterians, who adopted it even before they came to the Colonies. A close-fitting black cap or coif is seen in many of the pictures of New England divines.

From "The Judicial History of Massachusetts" I have gleaned the following account of lawyers in the New England Colonies:

"It was many years after the settlement of the Colony, before anything like a distinct class of Attorneys at Law was known. And it is doubtful if there were any regularly educated Attorneys who practiced in the Courts of the Colony at any time during its existence. Several of the Magistrates, it is true, had been educated as Lawyers at home, but they were almost constantly in the magistracy, nor do we hear of their being ever engaged in the management of cases. If they made use of their legal acquirements, it was in aid of the great object which they had so much at heart—the establishment of a religious Commonwealth, in which the laws of Moses were much more regarded as precedents than the decisions of Westminster Hall, or the pages of the few elementary writers upon the Common-law which were then cited in the English Courts. It was thus, therefore, that the clergy were admitted to such a direct participation in the affairs of the Government, and that to two of their number was committed the duty of codifying the laws by which the Commonwealth was to be governed thereafter.

"There were Attorneys, it is true, and there were lawyers, and all the concomitant evils growing out of the bad passions involved in litigation, and there was a law against barratry, passed in 1641, because even then there was barratry practiced in the Courts. The profession seems to have now but little favor in the public mind, although for the first ten years of the Government there were no fees allowed to the 'patrons,' as they were called, who defended or aided parties in their suits."

This statement explains the similarity in the dress of judges, governors, and clergymen of this period of colonial history, as will be noticed in the portraits of the day, given in Figures 91, 92, 94, and 149.

THE DUTCH AND ENGLISH

IN

NEW YORK, LONG ISLAND, THE JERSEYS, DELAWARE, AND PENNSYLVANIA

1621–1700

with brief mention of
the Walloons, Huguenots, and Swedes, as well as of the
Quakers and German Settlers
to which is added an account of the dress of English
Lawyers in the Seventeenth Century

TIME'S ALTERATION;

or

THE OLD MAN'S REHEARSALL, WHAT BRAVE DAYS HE KNEW,
A GREAT WHILE AGONE, WHEN HIS OLD CAP WAS NEW.

When this old cap was new,
    'Tis since two hundred yeere;
No malice then we knew,
    But all things plentie were:
All friendship now decayes
    (Beleeve me, this is true),
Which was not in those dayes
    When this old cap was new.

Good hospitalitie
    Was cherisht then of many;
Now poor men starve and die
    And are not helpt by any:
For charitie waxeth cold,
    And love is found in few:
This was not in time of old
    When this old cap was new.

Where-ever you travel'd then,
    You might meet on the way
Brave knights and gentlemen
    Clad in their countrey gray,
That courteous would appeare,
    And kindly welcome you:
No puritans then were
    When this old cap was new.

Our ladies in those dayes
    In civil habit went,
Broad-cloth was then worth prayse,
    And gave the best content;
French fashions then were scorn'd,
    Fond fangles then none knew,
Then modistie women adorn'd
    When this old cap was new.

A man might then behold
　　At Christmas, in each hall
Good fires to curbe the cold,
　　And meat for great and small;
The neighbours were friendly bidden,
　　And all had welcome true;
The poore from the gates were not chidden
　　When this old cap was new.

Blacke-jackes to every man
　　Were fill'd with wine and beere;
No pewter pot nor kanne
　　In those days did appeare:
Good cheare in a noble-man's house
　　Was counted a seemely shew;
We wanted no brawne nor sowse
　　When this old cap was new.

We took not such delight
　　In cups of silver fine;
None under the degree of a knight
　　In plate drunke beere or wine:
Now each mechanicall man
　　Hath a cup-boord of plate, for a shew,
Which was a true thing then
　　When this old cap was new.

The Dutch and English in New York, Long Island, the Jerseys, Delaware, and Pennsylvania

1621–1700

FIGURE 95.
A Dutch Colonist in New Amsterdam.

VEN in a study of costume it is difficult to draw a distinct line between the Dutch and English elements in the Colony of Manhattan.

To an English seaman belongs the honour of discovery in 1609. When Henry Hudson, sometimes called Hendrick (Figure 98), brought the first ship to the mouth of the river which bears his name, he was a navigator of experience, well known to the merchants of Holland, who on this occasion had engaged him to make the voyage, and it is likely that he had under him as many Dutch as English sailors in his ship, "The Half-Moon." After a few weeks spent in exploring the adjacent country, he returned with an enticing report of a great many fur-clad animals near the shore. The trading proclivities of the Dutch merchants were at once aroused and they hastened to send over men to establish trading posts. But the first Colonial settlement was in 1621, when the great West India Company was chartered by the States General of Holland and given the monopoly of the American trade.

Peter Minuit, who was appointed Governor in 1626, arrived with a large number of colonists, men, women, and children, with cattle and household goods. Many of this company were Walloons of French extraction whose forefathers had been driven from their homes in Flanders and Belgium during the Inquisition, and had afterward formed an industrious community in Holland. They were skilled in various trades and were a valuable acquisition to the new colony, but they do not appear to have worn a distinctive dress.

In 1628 an act was passed in Holland giving to every man who raised a company of fifty colonists and brought them to America a large tract of land and the title of Patroon. In fact, many privileges were granted as an inducement to form a settlement in the Colony, and the Patroons became very rich and very powerful. A thousand square miles were included in the estate of Patroon Van Rensselaer (Figure 141). Fine cattle were imported, fruits, wheat, rye, buckwheat, flax, and beans were cultivated. The religious toleration prevailing in this Colony induced men from New England to remove there, and the Huguenots from France also sought shelter from persecution in New Amsterdam, as the town was called under the Dutch supremacy (Figures 145, 146).

In spite of the hardships they had endured before they reached the safe shelter of America, these people were distinguished for a happy, thrifty temperament and gentle manners, and knew many graceful accomplishments in the way of lace-making and embroidery, which they cheerfully taught to their neighbours. They are said to have been the first to weave carpets and hangings of odds and ends of material. They were also versed in the concoction of delicate coloured dyes, which they used for their garments and house decorations.

The Huguenots settled also in Pennsylvania, Massachusetts, the Carolinas, and in Virginia, and their descendants have taken a conspicuous part in the development of our country.

Almost from the outset, Manhattan was a cosmopolitan community, and costumes were as varied as the wonderful tulips in the

FIGURE 96.—Portrait of Peter Stuyvesant, Governor of New York Colony, showing armour and a black skull-cap, 1647.

FIGURE 97.—Portrait of Sir Edmund Andros, Colonial Governor of New York, 1674–1681, and Governor of the Dominion of New England, which included all the English settlements between Maryland and Canada except Pennsylvania, 1686–1690, showing periwig of reign of James II.

FIGURE 98.—Portrait of Henry Hudson, the English navigator, 1609, showing the ruff, reign of James I.

FIGURE 99.—Portrait of Sir William Keith, Governor of the Province of Pennsylvania, showing armour and campaign wig, 1717.

FIGURE 96.

FIGURE 97.

FIGURE 98.

FIGURE 99.

Dutch gardens. As there were neither sumptuary laws nor religious restrictions to control the manner or material of dress, we find the prevailing fashions among the citizens, both Dutch and English, very elaborate. The mercantile spirit ever pervading New York probably stimulated the wearing of fine clothes.

We read of the stalwart Peter Stuyvesant, Governor of New Amsterdam for many years, that "he was never otherwise than faultlessly dressed and always after the most approved European standard. A wide drooping shirt collar fell over a velvet jacket with slashed sleeves displaying full white linen shirt sleeves. His breeches were also slashed, very full and fastened at the knee by a handsome scarf tied in a knot, and his shoes were ornamented with large rosettes."* The leg which he lost in battle was replaced by a wooden one with silver bands, which accounts for the tradition that he wore a silver leg. Mrs. Lamb, in her "History of New York," says of Governor Stuyvesant that "he had sterling excellence of character, but more knowledge than culture," also that "his whole heart and soul became interested in the country of his adoption. In bearing he seems to have been somewhat haughty and exacting. One of his contemporaries recorded that, during his inauguration speech as Governor of New Amsterdam in 1647, he kept the people standing with their heads uncovered for more than an hour while he wore his chapeau, as if he were the Czar of Muscovy. Habitually he wore a close cap of black velvet on his dark hair, which imparted a still deeper shade to his dark complexion, and his stern mouth was not hidden by the slight mustache which he wore" (Figure 96).

From the same authority we learn that Governor Stuyvesant's wife, Judith Bayard, "was a beautiful blonde and followed the French fashions in dress, displaying considerable artistic skill in the perfection and style of her attire." Also that "the purity of morals and decorum of manners for which the Dutch were distinguished

* History of New York, by Mrs. Lamb.

7

had been ascribed to the happy influence of their women, who mingled in all the active affairs of life and were consulted with deferential respect." As early as 1640 we read of many richly furnished houses with well-kept gardens and choice conservatories in Colonial New York. Governor Schuyler called his town house "White Hall," and he owned a beautiful country-seat in the neighbourhood, for which, it is said, he paid 6400 guilders in 1659.

FIGURE 100.
A Dutch Woman in Working Dress (from a Contemporary Print, Middle of Seventeenth Century).

Markets were held every Saturday in 1656 and after, where laces, flax, linen, linsey-woolsey, duffels, etc., were sold by the farmers' wives.

The annual Fair, or Kermiss, was an occasion of festivity which attracted the people in their holiday garments from the neighbouring villages. It was inaugurated on the 20th of October, 1659, and usually lasted six weeks. The working garb of the Dutch peasant women consisted of a short woolen petticoat with a loose jacket of red cotton or blue Holland; a white kerchief folded around the shoulders, and a close white cap. In Figure 100 a sketch is given in which the long white apron of coarse homespun linen is caught up with the petticoat for convenience.

The Dutch women of the Manhattan Colony were marvellous housewives. They concocted medicines and distilled perfumes from the plants in their flourishing gardens. They instructed the maids in carding and weaving, for the woolen garments worn by the family, as well as the household linen and underwear, were usually made under the home roof. Moreover, they had a shrewd knowledge

REIGNS OF CHARLES I AND II, AND JAMES II
1640–1686

FIGURE 101.—A Dutch lady of New Amsterdam, wife of a patroon, about 1640. Her gown is of crimson silk with a pointed bodice, low neck and full slashed sleeves showing white undersleeves beneath. The ruff and cuffs are of lace starched and wired. A fold of soft lawn edged with lace finishes the bodice in front, held in place by a rosette of ribbon, or a jewelled brooch. An over-garment, the predecessor of the samare, of a woolen fabric, fitting in at the back and confined by a ribbon at the waist, opens down the front. It has full open sleeves tied with ribbons at the elbow. The hair is worn in a knot at the back and in short wavy locks in front with a fringe of short curls across the forehead.

FIGURE 102.—A patroon, about 1640. The baggy breeches and slashed doublet are of cloth or velvet. Woolen hose with a scarf of silk below the points which fasten them to the breeches. The falling ruff (collars were also worn at this time) is of white Holland laid in fine knife-plaits. The hat with a soft flapping brim is of felt trimmed with plumes of two colours. Leather shoes with wooden heels are tied at the instep with large bows of ribbon.

FIGURE 103.—A Dutch lady, about 1660, in a furred samare or jacket of velvet over a gown of amber satin. The arrangement of hair is copied from a portrait of the period; the ends of the side locks are turned under and tied with a ribbon, the rest is taken back and fastened in a coil in which narrow ribbon is twisted.

FIGURE 104.—An English gentleman at the end of Charles II's reign and the first half of James II's. His long coat is of flowered silk, cuffs of rich brocade. The breeches are full and hang over the garters or points which fasten the silk stockings. The shoes are cut rather high and are fastened with a strap of leather through a buckle on the instep. The hat is cocked a little to one side of the front in the fashion called the "Monmouth cock." The periwig is very long and full. An embroidered baldric is worn with the sword and a walking-stick ornamented with a large bow of ribbon is carried in the right hand. The neck-cloth tied in a bow under the chin is the new fashion of this date.

FIGURE 101.　　　FIGURE 102.　　　FIGURE 103.　　　FIGURE 104.

of mercantile pursuits and often carried on business for themselves and invested their savings in trading ventures. Their houses were scrupulously neat; white curtains usually hung in the leaden sashed windows, and pots of flowers stood on the ledges, while a great loom was placed under the sloping roof of the back stoop. Every family in the Colony made a coarse cloth called linsey-woolsey, the warp being of linen and the woof of wool, which they kept ready to be finished off by one of the itinerant weavers. About the middle of the seventeenth century we read of a rattle-watch dressed in a costume of blue cloth with facings of orange, and armed with lanterns, rattles, and long staffs. The duty of this company of watch-men was to patrol the town by day as well as by night. In the early days of the Colony a licensed herdsman was put in charge of all the cattle of the community. The distinctive badge of his office was a twisted cow's horn fitted with a mouth-piece suspended by a green cord across his shoulders. The ordinary working dress of a man was probably of homespun linsey-woolsey with hose of hand-knitted yarn. Monmouth hats of thrums were commonly worn in all the Colonies (Figure 37½).

FIGURE 105.
A Dutchman in Working Dress (from a Contemporary Painting, Middle of Seventeenth Century).

Mrs. Van Rensselaer, in her "Goode Vrow of Mana-ha-ta," aptly describes the quaint costumes of the Dutch people in New York. We will borrow her description of Dutch babies. "Upon the birth of a child, the infant was wrapped in swaddling clothes and put into an elaborately embroidered pocket, which was trimmed with

frills of ribbon, the colour indicating the sex of the child. A tiny
ruffled cap confined its ears closely to its head, and the baby was
wrapped so firmly in its bands that it could move neither hand nor
foot, and was laid in its cradle, or hung suspended on a nail in the
wall without fear of its stirring from any position in which it might
be placed. The birth of an infant was announced to the neighbours
by hanging an elaborately trimmed pincushion on the knocker of
the front door, the colour of which denoted the sex, blue indicating
a boy and white a girl. This cushion was usually provided by the
grandmother and was handed down as an heirloom from one genera-
tion to another to serve for similar occasions."

All authorities tell us of the many petticoats worn by a bride one
over another, and of the bridal crown which in Holland was a token
of the wealth of the family. It was made often of silver and adorned
with jewels, but when the family was not rich, it was of pasteboard
covered with embroidered silk. Only matrons wore coifs, and they
varied with the rank and affluence of the wearer (Figures 121, 131).

The inventory of the wife of a respectable and well-to-do Dutch
settler in New Netherlands, Vrouentje Ides Stoffelsen, in 1641 contained a gold hoop ring, a silver medal and chain, and a silver undergirdle to hang keys on; a damask furred jacket, two black camlet
jackets, two doublets, one iron-gray, the other black; a blue
petticoat, a steel-gray lined petticoat, a black coarse camlet-lined
petticoat, one of Harlem stuff, a little black vest with two sleeves,
a pair of Damask sleeves, a reddish morning gown, not lined, four
pairs of pattens, one of Spanish leather; a purple apron and four
blue aprons, nineteen cambric caps and four linen ones, a fur cap
trimmed with beaver, nine linen handkerchiefs trimmed with lace,
two pairs of old stockings and three shifts. Pictures of fur-trimmed
jackets and of fur caps are given in Figures 103, 106, 110, 111.

Officials could easily be distinguished by their dress. The leather
aprons worn by labourers and craftsmen were often dyed red, and

FIGURE 106.—Dutch girl in fur cap and fur-trimmed jacket, 1641. (By Hollar.)
FIGURE 107.—Dutch lady, hair arranged in puffs at the side, 1645. (By Hollar.)
FIGURE 108.—A little Dutch girl, seventeenth century. (By DeVos.)
FIGURE 109.—A little Dutch boy (from a portrait by Cuyp).
FIGURE 110.—A Dutch lady in fur cap and mantle, 1644. (By Hollar.)
FIGURE 111.—A Swedish lady in pointed fur cap and ruff, 1640. (By Hollar.)

FIGURE 106.

FIGURE 107.

FIGURE 108.

FIGURE 109.

FIGURE 110.

FIGURE 111.

when the wearer was not at work, one corner was usually tucked under his belt.

Different concoctions of bark taught them by the Indian squaws were used by the women to dye their homespun petticoats and short gowns (Figure 100).

The caps, chatelaines, and gowns of the well-to-do matrons were of costly materials and invariably of bright colours. The garments of the men, too, were of satin, velvet, and silk, trimmed with lace and fur. Buttons and buckles were often of gold set with precious stones.

The samare or loose jacket with "side laps" or skirts reaching to the knee, sometimes with elbow sleeves turned back and faced, was worn by the Dutch ladies over a waistcoat and petticoat. A picture of one trimmed with fur is given in Figure 103. The prevailing shapes of coats and hats were not unlike the English. Late in the seventeenth century coats had long wide tails with wide cuffs. Hats were large and low of crown (Figures 42, 104).

Dr. Jacob de Lange and his wife (New York, 1682) left lists of their wardrobes which are documents of great value to a history of costume.

> One under petticoat with a body of red bay,
> One under petticoat, scarlet
> One Petticoat, red cloth with black lace
> One striped stuff petticoat with black lace
> Two coloured drugget petticoats with white linings,
> One coloured drugget petticoat with pointed lace.
> two coloured drugget petticoats with gray linings
> One black silk petticoat with ash gray silk lining,
> One potto-foo silk petticoat with black silk lining,
> One silk potoso-a-samare with lace,
> One tartanel samare with tucker
> One black silk crape samare with tucker
> Three flowered calico samares,
> Three calico nightgowns, one flowered, two red,
> One silk waistcoat, one calico waistcoat
> One pair of bodice,
> Five pairs white cotton stockings,

Three black love hoods,
One white love-hood
Two pair sleeves with great lace
Four cornet caps with lace
One plain black silk rain cloth cap
One black plush mask,
Four yellow lace drowlas
One embroidered purse with silver bugle and chain to the girdle, and silver hook and eye.
One pair black pendants, gold nocks
One gold boat, wherein thirteen diamonds & one white coral chain,
One pair gold stucks or pendants each with ten diamonds.
Two diamond rings.
One gold ring with clasp beck
One gold ring or hoop bound round with diamonds

Dr. de Lange's wardrobe was abundant, but not so rich:

One grosgrained cloak lined with silk,
One black broadcloth coat,
One black broadcloth suit,
One coat lined with red serge
One black grosgrained suit
One coloured cloth waistcoat with silver buttons
One coloured serge suit with silver buttons
Three silk breeches
Three calico breeches
Three white breeches
One pair yellow hand gloves with black silk fringe
Five pairs white calico stockings
One pair black worsted stockings
One pair gray worsted stockings
One fine black hat, one old gray hat, one black hat.

When in 1664 the English sailed into the harbour and made bloodless conquest of the Colony, they introduced but few changes in the mode of living. In 1675 Manhattan was re-taken by the Dutch, and affairs of government and life went on as before for another year.

"The colours in the Dutch gowns were almost uniformly gay— in keen contrast to the sad coloured garments of New England. We hear of Madam Cornelia de Vos in a green cloth petticoat, a red and blue 'Haarlamer' waistcoat, a pair of red and yellow sleeves, and a purple 'Pooyse' apron."

Figure 121 shows a coif or cap worn in New Amsterdam. It is made of gray and white brocade and trimmed with silver lace of an elaborate pattern, put on flat across the top.   Around the

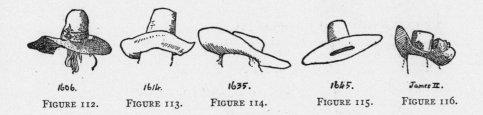

1606.   1614.   1635.   1645.   James II.
FIGURE 112.   FIGURE 113.   FIGURE 114.   FIGURE 115.   FIGURE 116.

face is a plaited ruffle of lace held in place by three rows of silver wire run through the plaits.

The children, too, were gaily dressed, as we can see in the Dutch contemporary portraits (Figures 108, 109, 132, and 133).

A leading man of New Amsterdam, a burgomaster, had at the time of his death, near the end of the Dutch rule, this plentiful num-

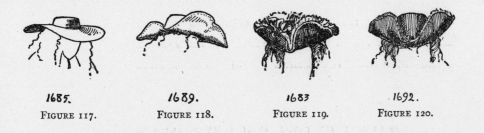

1685.   1689.   1683   1692.
FIGURE 117.   FIGURE 118.   FIGURE 119.   FIGURE 120.

ber of substantial garments: A cloth coat with silver buttons, a stuff coat, cloth breeches, a cloth coat with gimp buttons, a black cloth coat, a silk coat, breeches and doublet, a silver cloth breeches and doublet, a velvet waistcoat with silver lace, a buff coat, with silk sleeves, three grass-green cloaks, several perukes, "tets and fox-tails after the genteelest fashion."

One romantic element in the history of New Amsterdam not found in the other colonies is that of the pirates who carried on a vigorous business at sea and brought into the shops and markets many rich stuffs captured from the ships returning to England and France from the East Indies. The government made no effort to interfere with them, and sometimes, as in the case of Captain Kidd, these maritime marauders finally settled down and became respectable citizens. We are not surprised to read that Captain Kidd started housekeeping in New York with three hundred dollars' worth of plate.

FIGURE 121.

Coif of a Dutch Matron (from the Original Garment, late Seventeenth Century).

The English again conquered New Amsterdam and, under Sir Edward Andros, as Governor (Figure 97), it became an English colony, and was called New York in honour of the Duke of York, brother of Charles II.

There were Dutch and English settlements likewise in Long Island, the Jerseys, and Delaware, more or less under the jurisdiction of the Governor of New York, where doubtless the costumes, like the customs, reflected both nationalities.

THE SWEDES ON THE DELAWARE

In 1638 a colony of Swedes was sent out to America with instructions to settle the land not belonging to the Dutch and English. Selecting a spot on the west shore of the Delaware, they built a fort and called the settlement New Sweden. In 1656 the Dutch sent a company from New Amsterdam to establish a trading post on the Delaware, and they founded the town which is now known as New Castle.

FIGURE 122.—Shows the dress of an English gentlewoman of 1640.　(By Hollar.)
FIGURE 123.—Swedish woman in clogs, 1640.　(By Hollar.)
FIGURE 124.—A Dutch lady in outdoor dress, 1640.　(By Hollar.)
FIGURE 125.—An English lady in house dress, 1640.　(By Hollar.)

FIGURE 122.

FIGURE 123.

FIGURE 124.

FIGURE 125.

Frequent skirmishes followed between the Swedish and the Dutch settlers (Figures 95, 106, 111, 123, 124, also 100, 105), and finally the English claimed, by virtue of a patent from Charles II in 1664, all the land from the west side of Connecticut River to the east side of Delaware Bay, which was named for Thomas West, Lord Delaware, one of the early Governors of Virginia; and thus all the colonies of America came under English rule. This was in the latter part of the reign of Charles II.

In Figures 1, 68, and 69 we have the characteristic dress of the English gentleman and gentlewoman of this date, and in Figures 101 and 102 the typical costume of a Dutch Patroon and his wife.

THE QUAKERS IN PENNSYLVANIA

When the Quakers came to Pennsylvania with William Penn, they had not adopted any distinctive style of dress. From choice only were the colours rather grave than gay, for no strict rules had been formulated at this time (1682) prohibiting the use of bright colours or trimmings by the Quakers. The sash of sky-blue silk worn by Penn, either as a badge of office or mark of his rank, is an agreeable note of colour. This sash is described as made of silk network and as being of the size and style of that of a military officer. In an old English publication we read: "This sash is now in the possession of Thomas Kett, Esq., of Seething Hall, near Norwich."*

Shoe and stock buckles were usually of silver, and the ruffles at neck and wrist were of linen, either plainly hemmed or trimmed with rich lace. Heels were rather high, the toes of the shoes square. A gentleman of our day would seem to modern eyes very gaily dressed in such a costume as the first followers of the benign Founder of Philadelphia habitually wore (Figures 143, 144).

However, a certain neatness and staidness distinguished both the men and the women from the earliest days of this Quaker colony,

* Hone's Every Day Book.

although family portraits still in possession of their descendants prove that gowns of blue and red satin were not infrequently worn by members of the Society of Friends previous to 1700. There was nothing of the so-called Quaker simplicity about Penn's household. Pennsbury, his beautiful manor on the banks of the Delaware, was furnished and maintained on a substantial and most liberal scale. Costly silver, fine china, rich curtains and rugs made it a fitting abode for a royal governor. The twelve-oared barge in which Penn usually made his journeys to town was also stately and imposing.

Although the hats of the Quakers (Figures 117, 118, and 143) were of a shape similar to those worn by King Charles and his courtiers, they were put on the head with a certain rigidity, and the fact that they were never doffed in deference to rank or the fair sex may have added a touch of grimness and austerity to the expression of the broad brims in striking contrast to the graceful plumed hats worn by cavaliers and used by them to express every degree of courtesy.

> "The Quaker loves an ample brim,
> A hat that bows to no salaam."

In 1693 Penn, with the welfare of the province always in mind, put into his book, "Some fruits of Solitude," a message of counsel in matters of dress. "Choose thy cloaths by thine own eye, not anothers. The more simple and plain they are, the better. Neither unshapely nor fantastical, and for use and decency, not for Pride."

Mrs. Gummere, who has made an exhaustive study of Quaker dress, says that green aprons were so much worn by Friends at this period as to be regarded "almost as badges of Quakerism"; also that Friends not only called their cloaks by the popish title "Cardinal," but wore them in red and all bright colours.

"Wigs were as generally worn by genteel Friends as by other people" (Figures 134 and 135). This was the more surprising because they religiously professed to exclude all superfluities, and

FIGURE 126.—A portrait of a Dutch lady, middle of seventeenth century, showing wide-brimmed hat and ruff. (By Hollar.)

FIGURE 127.—An English lawyer of the seventeenth century. (By Hollar.)

FIGURE 128.—An English woman in silk hood and tippet. (By Hollar.)

FIGURE 129.—A Dutch lady in fur tippet and hood, middle of seventeenth century. (By Hollar.)

FIGURE 130.—Portrait of a boy in periwig in the Massachusetts Colony, end of the reign of Charles II.

FIGURE 131.—An English woman in a coif and kerchief trimmed with Vandyke lace, 1640. (By Hollar.)

Figure 128.

Figure 131.

Figure 127.

Figure 130.

Figure 126.

Figure 129.

yet nothing could have been offered to the mind as so essentially useless."* In the year 1685, William Penn wrote to his steward, James Harrison, requesting him to allow Governor Lloyd, his deputy, the use of his wigs in his absence.

In England there were but few striking changes in the fashionable dress of the upper classes from the end of the reign of Charles II to the end of the reign of William and Mary.

The straight square-cut coats were worn opening over waistcoats of equal length reaching to the knees; the breeches were held in place beneath the knee by long stockings, which were drawn up over them; long neck-cloths of Flanders or Spanish point-lace were used; the shoes, the upper leather of which rose considerably above the instep, were fastened by a small strap over it, passing through a buckle placed rather on one side; the hat was bent up or cocked all round and trimmed with feathers (Figures 118, 119, 120); fringed gloves and monstrous periwigs, which it was the fashion to comb publicly, completed the habit of the beaux of London in the reign of William and Mary.

"The ladies seem to have adopted some of the Dutch fashions," says a contemporary writer. "The stomacher appeared more formally laced. The sleeves of the gown became straight and tight, and terminated with a cuff at the elbow in imitation of those of the male sex. Rows of flounces and furbelows, or falbalas, bordered the petticoat, which was disclosed by the gown being looped completely back. The head-dress was exceeding high in front, being composed of a cap, the lace of which rose in three or more tiers almost to a point above the forehead, the hair being combed up and disposed in rows of wavy curls one above the other (Figure 38). Hair powder was used occasionally, but not generally. Muffs were carried by both sexes. They were very small and ornamented often with large bows of ribands.

* The Quaker: A Study in Costume, by Amelia Mott Gummere.

"The dress of the commonalty underwent no change" (Figures 40, 41).*

We find the same costumes in the colonies. In Tod's "History of New York" is the following description of the fashions about 1695 (reign of William and Mary):

"Broadway on a Sabbath morning, as the bells were ringing for Church, must have presented an animated and even brilliant spectacle far exceeding that which modern beaux and belles present. In these days, however, both ladies and gentlemen shone rich as Emperor moths. These worshippers, whom we imagine ourselves watching, come in groups moving down the wide shaded street, some entering Trinity, others turning into Garden Street and passing into the new Dutch Church on that thoroughfare. Both places of worship are equally fashionable. The Dutch Church is the wealthier, but then Trinity has the Governor's pew, and the prestige that comes of State patronage and emolument. Let us describe, as showing the fashions of the day, the dress of this group bearing down abreast of the church yard. They are Nicholas Bayard and Madam Bayard, William Merritt, Alderman and Madam Merritt, and Isaac de Riemer. Bayard, who has been Secretary of the Province, Mayor, and Colonel of the City Militia, wears a cinnamon coloured cloth coat with skirt reaching quite to the knee, embroidered four or five inches deep with silver lace, and lined with sky-blue silk. His waistcoat is of red satin woven in with gold. His breeches, of the same colour and material as his coat, are trimmed with silver at the pockets and knees. Dove coloured silk stockings and low shoes adorned with large silver buckles cover his nether extremities. His hat, of black felt, has a wide flapping brim and is adorned with a band of gold lace. His full-bottomed wig is plentifully powdered with starch finely ground and sifted, to which burnt alabaster or whiting has been added to give it body, and is scented

* Knight's Pictorial History of England.

FIGURE 132.—A portrait of Elisabeth and Philadelphia Wharton, showing the prevailing styles of dress for little girls in reign of Charles I. (By Vandyke.)

FIGURE 133.—A portrait of two Dutch boys, showing the fashionable dress in the middle of the seventeenth century. (By Rubens.)

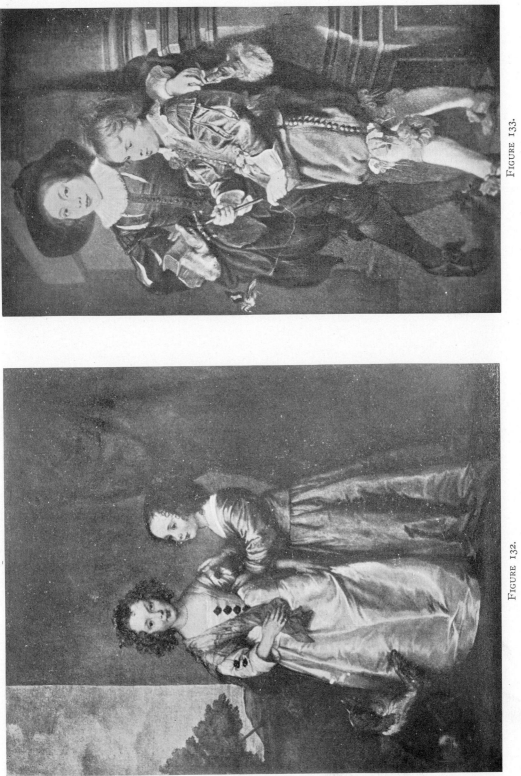

FIGURE 133.

FIGURE 132.

with ambergris. A steinkirk of fine muslin encircles his neck, the
ends of which are laced and tucked into his expansive shirt bosom.
The latter is of fine holland adorned with colebatteen ruffles, the
waistcoat being left open to better display them. He carries a cane,
too, with a gold head elegantly engraved in cypher and crown, but
the sword, with its gay sword knot, then an almost indispensable
adjunct to a gentleman's dress, in deference to the day has been
left behind. The two other gentlemen are dressed much in the
same style except that there is a pleasing variety in style and colour.
Merritt, for instance, wears a salmon coloured silk drugget coat,
with silver brocade waistcoat and small clothes, while De Riemer
has a sagathie cloth coat with waistcoat and breeches of drap du
Barre.

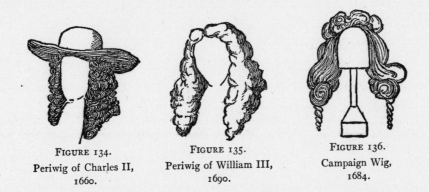

FIGURE 134.   FIGURE 135.   FIGURE 136.
Periwig of Charles II,   Periwig of William III,   Campaign Wig,
1660.   1690.   1684.

"But if the gentlemen are thus brilliant, what is to be said of the
ladies, who are apt to lead the sterner sex in matters of personal
adornment? Instead of a bonnet, Madam Bayard wears a 'front-
age' (commode), a sort of head-dress formed of rows of plaited muslin stiffened with wire one above the other, and diminishing in size
as they rise. She, too, wears the steinkirk, or neck-cloth. The
bodice of her purple and gold atlas gown is laced over very tight
stays, and the gown itself is open in front to display the black
velvet petticoat edged with two silver orrices and high enough to

show the green silk stockings and beautiful embroidered shoes of
fine morocco."

> "My high commode, my damask gown,
>   My lac'd shoes of Spanish leather.
>   A silver bodkin in my head,
>   And a dainty plume of feather."
>   —"*Young Maid's Portion.*"

THE DRESS OF ENGLISH LAWYERS IN THE SEVENTEENTH CENTURY

Very little is said by the early authorities on the costumes of
lawyers and judges in the Colonies, but there are numerous indica-
tions of the fact that scarlet, the judicial colour in England, was
worn on the Colonial bench, and Martin, in his "History of the
Bench and Bar in Pennsylvania," states that undoubtedly the courts
were conducted with much of the state and formality of the Mother
Country. It will be interesting in a study of the dress of the day to
recall the complicated costumes of the English law courts, although
the pomp and display therein detailed were not even possible in the
enforced simplicity of the early Colonies. In New England, Virginia, Maryland, the Barbadoes, and the Carolinas, as well as later
in New York and even in Pennsylvania, the forms and ceremonies
of government were as similar to the English code as circumstances
permitted.

In the Southern Colonies especially it is probable that much formality was observed in the dress of lawyers and judges; at all events
we do not read of any departure from the English methods of pro-
cedure in documents of the Colonies.

In a historical sketch of the English law courts by Inderwick,*
we find a description of the gradual changes in legal dress
and customs in England during the Colonial period. In the

* The King's Peace, by F. A. Inderwick.

FIGURE 137.—Coat and full breeches of buff brocade with flowers and leaves in bright colours scattered over it. Very large cuffs of a richly coloured brocade. A wedding suit of 1681. Reign of Charles II. (Photographed from the original garments.)

FIGURE 138.—Coat and full breeches of dark red flowered silk, 1681. Reign of Charles II. (Photographed from the original garments.)

FIGURE 139.—Coat and breeches of silk trimmed with fancy braid fringed out at the ends and caught with buttons. Worn in reign of James II. (Photographed from the original garments.)

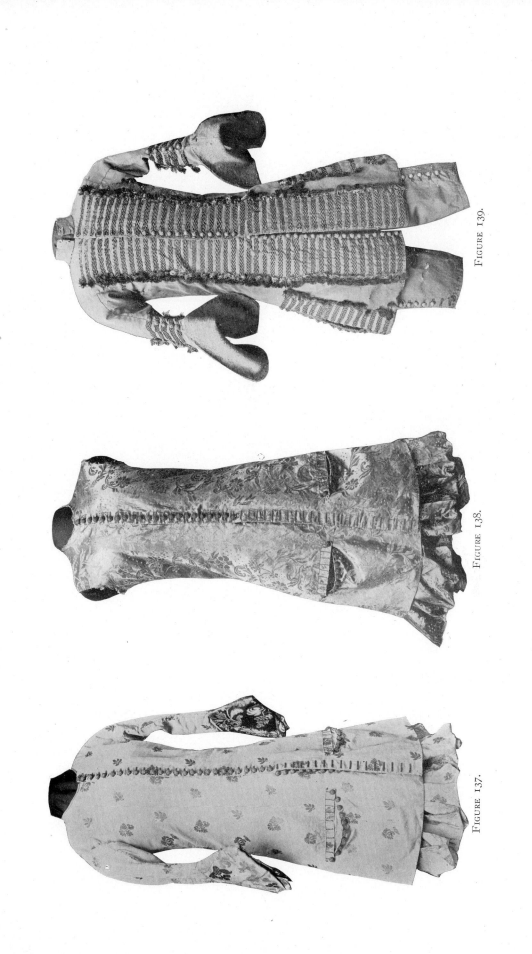

FIGURE 139.

FIGURE 138.

FIGURE 137.

time of Charles I questions relating to the attire of the common-law judges were involved in so much doubt and surrounded with so many contradictory precedents and traditions that the judges resolved to simplify matters by conference. The result of their deliberations was a decree dated June 6, 1635, which, although it could not have direct application to the Colonial courts in every particular, throws important light on the ceremonies and etiquette to which every English lawyer of that date was accustomed. We therefore quote the extract from State Papers given by Mr. Jeffreson: *

"The judges in Term time are to set at Westminster in the Courts, in their black or violet gowns, whether they will, and a hood of the same colour put over their heads, and their mantles above all; the end of the hood hanging over behind; wearing their velvet caps, and coyfes of lawn, and cornered cap. The facing of their gowns, hoods and mantles, is with changeable taffata; which they must begin to wear upon Ascension-day, being the last Thursday in Easter Term, and continue those robes until the feast of Simon and Jude. And Simon and Jude's day, the judges begin to wear their robes faced with white furs of minever; and so continue that facing until Ascension-day again.

"Upon all Holydays, which fall in the Term and are Hall dayes, the judges sit in scarlet faced with Taffata, when Taffata facing is to be worn, and with furs, or minever, when furs or minever are to be worn.

"Upon the day when the Lord Mayor of London comes to Westminster to take his oath, that day the judges come in scarlet, and upon the fifth of November, being Gunpowder Day, unless it be Sunday, the judges go to Westminster Abbey in scarlet to hear the sermon, and after go to sit in Court and the two Lords Chief Justices, and the Lord Chief Baron, have their collars of S.S. above their mantles for those two days.

* A Book about Lawyers, by John Cordy Jeffreson.

"When the Judges go to St. Paul's to the sermon, upon any Sunday in the Term time, or to any other public church, they ought to go in scarlet gownes; the two Lords Chief Justices and the Lord Chief Baron in their velvet and satin tippets; and the hood is to be pinned abroad towards the left shoulder. And if it be upon any grand dayes, as upon the Ascension-day, Mid-summer day, All Hallows-day, or Candlemas-day, then the two Lords Chief Justices and the Lord Chief Baron wear collars of S.S. with long scarlet casting-hoods and velvet and satin tippets.

"At all times when the judges go to the Council-table, or to any assembly of the Lords in the afternoons in Term time, they ought to go in their robes of violet or black, faced with taffata, according as the time of wearing them doth require; and with tippets and scarlet casting-hoods, pinned near the left shoulder, unless it be Sunday or Holyday, and then in scarlet.   In the circuit the judges go to church upon Sundays in the fore-noon in scarlet gownes, hoods, and mantles, and sit in their caps.   And in the afternoons to the church in scarlet gownes, tippet and scarlet hood, and sit in their cornered caps.

"And the first morning at the reading of the commissions, they sit in scarlet gownes, with hoods and mantles, and in their coyfs and cornered caps.   And he that gives the charge, and delivers the gaol, doth, or ought for the most part, to continue all that assizes in the same robes, scarlet gown, hood, and mantle.   But the other judge, who sits upon the Nisi Prius, doth commonly (if he will) sit only in his scarlet robe, with tippet and casting-hood; or if it be cold he may sit in gown and hood, and mantle.

"And when the judges in the Circuit go to dine with the shireeve, or to a publick feast, then in scarlet gowns, tippets, and scarlet hoods; or casting off their mantle, they keep on their hood.

"The scarlet casting-hood is to be put above the tippet, on the right side, for Justice Wolmsley and Justice Warburton, and all the judges before, did wear them in that manner, and did declare that

FIGURE 140.—Jeremias Van Rensselaer of the New York Colony, end of the seventeenth century. Reign of William and Mary. (From the original portrait.)

FIGURE 141.—Kiliaen Van Rensselaer, first patroon in New Amsterdam, born 1637. Showing the fashionable coat worn in 1695. Reign of William and Mary. (From the original portrait.)

FIGURE 141.

FIGURE 140.

by wearing the hood on the right side, and above the tippet, was signified more temporal dignity; and by the tippet on the left side only, the judges did resemble priests.

"Whenever the judges or any of them are appointed to attend the king's majesty, they go in scarlet gowns, tippets, and scarlet casting-hoods; either to his own presence, or at the council-table.

"The judges and sergeants when they ride circuit, are to wear a sergeant's coat of good broad-cloth, with sleeves, and faced with velvet. They have used of late to lace the sleeves of the sergeant's coat thick with lace and they are to have a sumpter, and ought to ride with six men at the least.

"Also the first Sunday of every term, and when the judges and sergeants dine at my Lord Mayor's, or the shireeves, they are to wear their scarlets, and to sit at Paul's with caps at the sermon.

"When the judges go to any reader's feast, they go upon the Sunday or Holyday in scarlet; upon other days in violet, and the sergeants go in violet, with scarlet hoods.

"When the judges sit upon Nisi Prius in Westminster, or in London they go in violet gowns, and scarlet casting-hoods, and tippets, upon Holydays in scarlet."

"This order," Jeffreson says, "deserves attentive perusal, for it throws light upon departed manners, exemplifies the obsolete pomp of the law, and recalls the days when the humblest judge of assize was required to ride circuit with an imposing body-guard."

The author of "The King's Peace" records that "in the matter of courts, of officers, and of costumes, the judges of the Commonwealth differed but little from their predecessors, except that the King's Bench was called the Upper Bench, a name by which it also seems to have been occasionally known in previous reigns. The Keepers of the Great Seal wore a robe described by Whitelock, the historian of the epoch, as a 'handsome velvet gown' closely resembling that worn by Lord Bacon in the portrait in Lord Verulam's collection."

8

The same authority gives the modification of legal dress which followed towards the close of the seventeenth century. "The Common Law judges wore their scarlet, as we know from certain petitions presented to the Protector, praying that the judges who went circuit in their scarlet, and were at times escorted by a troop of horse, should no longer be permitted to 'affright the country with their blood-red robes and their state and pomp.' Sergeants wore their coifs and striped gowns; but the Bar, under the rank of sergeant, wore their own hair trimmed in such device as was prescribed by fashion and not forbidden by the regulations of the Inn to which they belonged. The head-dress of the judges, the sergeants, and the Bar had from the very earliest periods been fixed and determined. The judges wore the coif and velvet cap over their own hair, and with their beards and moustaches as they thought fit. Sergeants wore the coif, while counsel wore a serious dress of the costume of the period. Ruffs were in fashion during the reigns of Elizabeth and James I, when judges and counsel wore them. These were supplanted by a broad lace collar, which was in fashion under Charles I, and by white linen bands under the Commonwealth. In the reign of Charles II the monarch and people of position assumed the periwig, a fashion imported from France, where it was patronized by Louis XIV, and gradually left off wearing beards and moustaches. Some of the judges, but not all, accordingly wore the judicial robes with the

FIGURE 142.
Sergeant-at-law, Reign of Charles II.

REIGNS OF CHARLES II, JAMES II, WILLIAM AND MARY
1682–1700

FIGURE 143.—A Quaker gentleman in a suit of dark brown or plum-coloured cloth cut according to the English fashion at the end of Charles II's reign. The full shirt-sleeves hang in ruffles over the hand and the neck-cloth, though of the fashionable style and of the finest linen, is untrimmed. The hat is of the shape seen in the portraits of the time. The absence of feathers and lace was the only distinction of Quaker dress before 1700. The hair was occasionally powdered and periwigs were not uncommon, but the hair was usually worn in natural locks parted in the middle and hanging to the shoulders.

FIGURE 144 shows the typical dress of a Quaker lady of the same date—a gown of some soft coloured silk with fine white kerchief and undersleeves. The long full apron is also of silk, probably a dull green. Under the black silk hood for outdoor wear a ruffled cap of sheer lawn is worn. The hair is arranged in a coil at the back and parted in front. With various modifications of material and colour Figures 143 and 144 show the general style of Quaker dress for many years, coats, gowns and hats following very closely the fashions of the time.

FIGURE 145.—A Huguenot lady in the French dress of the period (1686). Mantle of black trimmed with embroidery. Her over-dress is looped up for walking, showing an embroidered underskirt. Under the black hood is worn a high cap of lace over a wire frame called a "commode." The sleeves are finished with plaited ruffles of the material of the gown and she wears long gloves of kid and a muff decorated with a bow and ends of brocaded ribbon. The hair is arranged in curls on the forehead and in a soft knot at the back. Long ear-rings adorn her ears.

FIGURE 146.—A Huguenot gentleman of the same date in a suit of dark blue cloth trimmed with gold braid. His neck-cloth and handkerchief are trimmed with ruffles of lace. The shirt-sleeves end in a ruffle at the wrist and show beneath the wide cuffs of the coat. The hose of dark red or blue are pulled up over the knee and fastened under the breeches. The shoes are cut high on the instep and fastened with a flap of leather through a buckle. The hat is cocked on both sides and worn over a periwig of moderate size without powder.

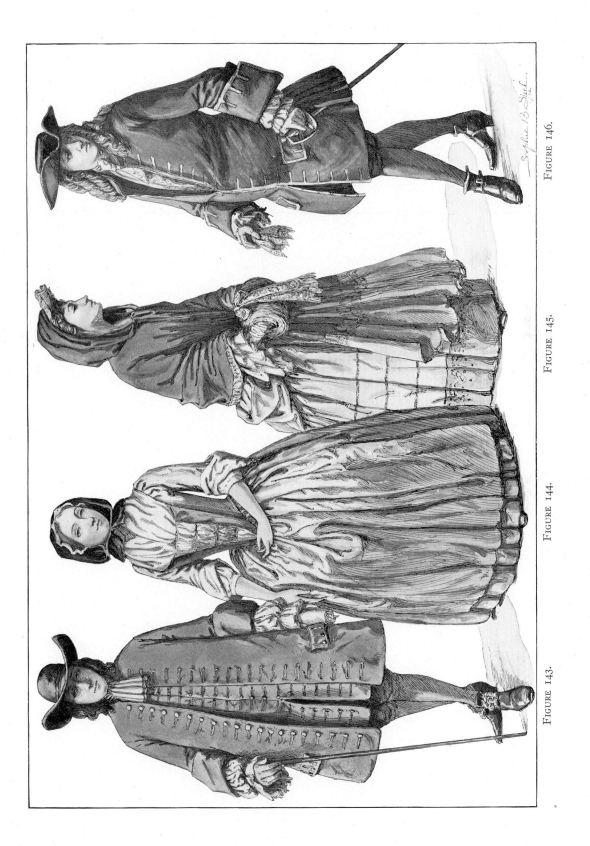

FIGURE 143.   FIGURE 144.   FIGURE 145.   FIGURE 146.

periwig in place of the coif; and this diversity of head-dress among the judges continued during the reign of James II, when Sir Thomas Street, one of the judges who was in office in 1688, still wore his own hair with the coif and the black velvet cap. The Bar, being younger than the judges, took more generally to the prevailing fashion, and wore first the long and then the short wig. In course of time, under William III, all classes of the community, including bishops and clergymen, wore the long or the short wig, judges and counsel being included in the number; and the sergeants, to indicate their status, wore a black patch on a white silk ground, fastened on to their wigs as a substitute for the black cap and the white coif. The lawyers, however, who followed the public taste in assuming periwigs, failed to follow it in leaving them off. The bishops, who continued to wear their wigs long after the public had ceased to do so, gave up the practice some fifty years ago; but the judges and counsel have continued till to-day the bands of the Commonwealth along with the head-dress of the Restoration, which is no more any portion of ancient or tradi-

FIGURE 147.
Sergeant-at-law, Reign of James II.

tionary legal costume than were the ruffs of Queen Elizabeth or the lace collars of Charles I. And thus it happens that, by a very perversity of conservatism, that head-dress, which in the seventeenth century was worn alike by kings and by courtiers, by clergymen and by soldiers, by Jeffreys on the Bench and by Titus Oates in the dock, has become in the nineteenth century the distinct characteristic of the advocate and the judge. King James I, interfering with the

Inns of Court, as with most other of his subjects' affairs, had ordered
that barristers were not to come to the hall of their Inn with their
cloaks, boots, swords, spurs, or daggers, showing their ordinary
habits were those of the gentlemen of the period, and further that
none were to be admitted into the Society who were not gentlemen
by descent. These directions were repeated by Charles I, and seem
to have been very generally followed, and it was not, I conceive, till
the middle of King Charles' reign, if not later, that counsel under
the rank of sergeants, when employed in court, took to wearing silk
or stuff gowns, and thus became 'gentlemen of the long robe.'"

I feel obliged to quote these items of legal costume and customs
in full, not being able to determine with exactness how nearly they
were followed in the Colonies in the seventeenth century. In Figure
127 a picture from a contemporary print is given of a lawyer in his
wig and parliament. The illustrations (Figures 142 and 147) are
also taken from authorities of the time. Much has been said in
print of the circuit and the county courts. It is well known that all
the pomp and dignity were observed that those occasions permitted
in the Colonies, but very grave offences and questions of State were
carried before the court in England.

THE GERMAN SETTLERS IN PENNSYLVANIA
1683–1790

The Mennonites, or German Quakers, who settled Germantown
in Pennsylvania under the hospitable encouragement of Penn (1683),
were speedily followed to America by other German sects from the
Palatinate or the low countries on the Rhine. They were the last
people to found colonies in the New World, for as a race they had
but little of the spirit of adventure in their composition.

Well equipped with implements for farming, the emigrants carefully selected the fertile country near the Blue Mountains, and, once
established as colonists, they were joined by large numbers of their

FIGURE 148.—Portrait of Count Zinzendorf in a preacher's robe.

FIGURE 149.—Portrait of Simon Bradstreet, Judge and Governor of the Massachusetts Colony, in gown and cap, 1630–1679.

FIGURE 150.—Portrait of Lady Fenwick, showing widow's mourning, 1695.

FIGURE 151.—Portrait of Mrs. Elisabeth Boehler in the Moravian settlement, Pennsylvania, 1787.

FIGURE 148.

FIGURE 149.

FIGURE 150.

FIGURE 151.

countrymen. In 1703, it is said there were nearly three hundred thousand Germans in Penn's province. At the time of the Revolution they warmly supported the struggle for independence.

Coming chiefly from the low countries along the Rhine, their costumes were not especially picturesque, but they were distinctive in character, and the fashion of them changed less frequently than in some other parts of Germany, so that for many years after their arrival in America they wore the quaint caps and head-dresses, clumsy boots, and odd looking cloaks of an earlier period.*

Not only in Pennsylvania, but in New York, Maryland, New Jersey, Virginia, the Carolinas and Georgia, the Germans also founded pastoral settlements.

The clothing of the new settlers consisted of "home-made cloth, woven from tow, made from flax grown on the virgin soil." Their costume did not admit of much change, and the men were dressed chiefly in shirt, trousers, and coat. In warm weather the shirt and trousers sufficed; in cold weather an additional top coat was worn for protection. The women wore short full skirts with dark bodices laced over coarse white shifts. Shoes were made to last a long time, and were worn only when absolutely necessary. Cobblers travelled through the country among the settlers and mended their shoes, in that way procuring a livelihood.

There were various sects among the German colonists: The Dunkers, whose doctrine was very much the same as the Mennonites, who still wear a peculiar costume; the Schoenkfelders from Silesia, who emigrated to Pennsylvania in 1734; the Moravians, who came to Georgia in 1735 and founded in 1790 a large and important settlement at Bethlehem, Pennsylvania, where they still practice the picturesque rites of their doctrine. The Moravians have many interesting customs, but their costume is decidely conservative, and resembles the accepted Quaker dress in sobriety of colour and simplicity of cut.

* See Trachten der Völker, by A. Kretschmer.

A Moravian community was divided into a number of choirs or bands. One object carefully kept in view was the avoidance of all unnecessary adornment in dress. Among other things, jewelry, lace, parasols, and fans were forbidden. The bonnets worn by the Sisters were usually of white straw with plain ribbon, the colour of which formed the distinction of the choir. White was worn by the widows, blue by the married women, rose colour by the unmar-

ried, and red by girls from fourteen to eighteen years of age. The male choirs were not distinguished by any badges, but they all wore very simple clothing, generally gray or brown. Mourning was never worn, as it was thought that death, or "returning to one's native land," as Zinzendorf called it, was not a proper subject for sorrow. Two curiously fashioned palls used for the funerals of children are still preserved

FIGURE 152.
Moravian Coif (from an Original Garment).

with the archives of the Moravians at Lititz. They are made of white damask linen and the inscription:

"Jesus er Mein Heiland lebt
Ich wird auch
Das Leben schauen,"

is embroidered thereon in ribbon gathered in a scallop pattern to form letters. They are bound around the edges with a broader ribbon—pink for the girls and blue for the boys. Similar palls were used for adults. A minute pillow used at infant baptisms is also to be seen. A wedding dress is still preserved of white satin trimmed with gauze roses and ribbon-work like the bag in Figure 153. It has a short waist and little puffed sleeves and was worn about 1790. The lady who wore it had also a white gauze shawl made to wear three-cornered-wise, with only one corner embroidered in an elaborate pattern, which she wore with a black velvet dress. She is

FIGURE 153.—A reticule of white silk embroidered in crêpe flowers.

FIGURE 154.—A waistcoat worn by Count Lemcke.

FIGURES 155 and 156.—Photographs of white silk pocket cases, embroidered in colours.

These relics are preserved in the Moravian archives of Lititz.

FIGURE 153.

FIGURE 154.

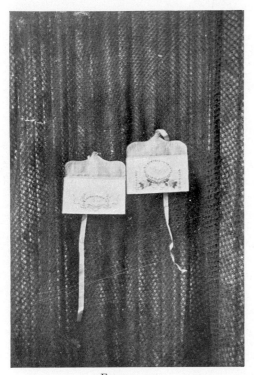

FIGURE 155.

FIGURE 156.

described as attending church in this garb, accompanied by a page carrying her train and a foot-stove.

A portrait of Count Zinzendorf and also one of the Countess are in possession of a direct descendant in Philadelphia. The wife wears a close-fitting cap with ribbons of blue (the distinctive trimming for a Moravian matron) (Figure 151) tied under her chin. The unmarried women were called Sisters. They dressed usually in white with a "nice handkerchief" pinned about the shoulders and a close-fitting cap with rose-pink ribbons, the hair all brushed back out of sight.

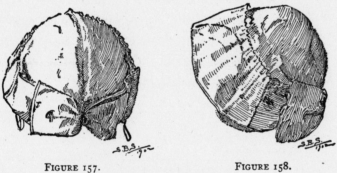

FIGURE 157.   FIGURE 158.
Moravian Cap of Lawn Worn over the Coif.

Before the Revolution, earthenware, paper, and linen were made at the cloister at Ephrata, Pennsylvania. In the Sister-House there may be seen at the present day the blocks of wood used instead of irons for smoothing linen. In Figures 155 and 156 are shown pictures of two white satin note cases, which were worked before 1790 for birthday gifts, each intended to hold a roll of bank-notes. The initials are done in hair and the flowers in silk.

Count Lemcke, the friend of Zinzendorf, brought over the first piano used in America. It was small enough to be carried under the arm, and he is said to have carried it with him when invited to evening parties. This piano may now be seen in the Smithsonian Institute at Washington.

Count Zinzendorf, the promoter and founder of the Pennsylvania settlement of Moravians, lived for a time in Philadelphia, and, according to his portraits, dressed simply in the fashion of his day in Germany. The long coat with many buttons and no collar or flaps, white shirt sleeves gathered into a band at the wrist, and a cravat or stock of plain white linen remind one of the portraits of William Penn about fifty years earlier. A portrait of him in a preaching gown is given in Figure 148.

The dress of the Seventh Day Baptists is peculiar and interesting. It consisted of a sort of cassock over which hung a stole, both back and front, and a close-fitting hood with large capes, or flaps. A picture of one of these hoods may be seen in a scholarly book, "The German Pietists in Provincial Pennsylvania," by Mr. Julius F. Sachse, where the curious customs of the German religious communities before 1700 are graphically described.

SEVENTEENTH CENTURY SILVER.

FIGURE 159.—Two pomanders
        One snuff-box
        One pair buckles
        Two patch boxes
        One watch fob of Dutch silver
        One porringer
        Travelling case with knife, fork, and spoon
        One sugar basin
        Hot milk jug
        One cream pitcher
        One pair salt cellars
        Two sugar tongs
        One cake basket
        One pap cup.

OTHER COLONIAL UTENSILS.

FIGURE 160.—Two Dutch knife-boards
        One flip glass
        Two tinder boxes
        One powder horn
        One pair snuffers
        One pewter pepper pot
        One pewter porringer
        One pewter tankard
        One pewter dish
        One folding pocket-knife and two forks
        One two-pronged table fork.

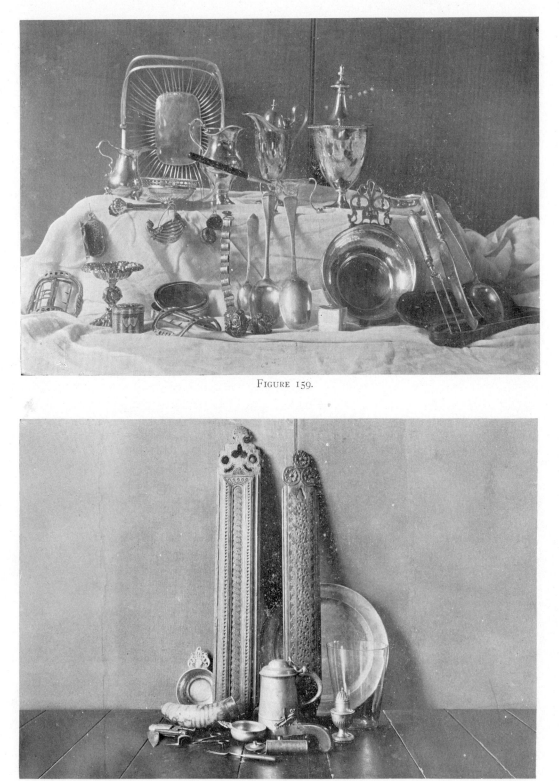

FIGURE 159.

FIGURE 160.

PART II

THE EIGHTEENTH CENTURY

WOMEN'S DRESS

1700–1800

During the Time of
Queen Anne, George I, II, and III of England,
Presidents Washington and Adams
of the United States

CAPRICES OF FASHION.

"The fickle head-dress sinks, and now aspires
A towery front of lace on branching wires;
The curling hair in tortur'd ringlets flows,
Or round the face in labour'd order grows.
How shall I soar, and on unwearying wing
Trace varying habits upward to their spring?
What force of thought, what numbers can express
The inconstant equipage of female dress?
How the strait stays the slender waist constrain,
How to adjust the mantua's sweeping train?
What fancy can the petticoat surround,
With the capacious hoop of whalebone bound?
But stay presumptuous Muse! nor boldly dare
The toilette's sacred mysteries declare;
Let a just distance be to beauty paid;
None here must enter but the trusty maid.
Should you the wardrobe's magazine rehearse,
And glossy manteaus rustle in thy verse;
Should you the rich brocaded suit unfold,
Where rising flowers grow stiff with frosted gold,
The dazzling Muse would from her subject stray,
And in a maze of fashions lose her way."

—"*The Fan.*"

Women's Dress

1700–1800

"Snuff or the fan supply each pause of chat."

FIGURE 161.
A Sacque, Early Eight-
eenth Century.

IN THE first half of the eighteenth century, which was the most prosperous and comfortable period of Colonial life in America, fashion was a conspicuous element.

Merchant ships from China and the Indies brought to all the seaport towns rich silks, tissues, and embroidered gauzes, as well as beautiful china and tapestry. These imported stuffs were known by odd sounding names, corruptions of the places of their manufacture. Thus, for instance, we have Nankeen, made in Nankin, China; and calico, originally a silken material first imported from Calicut in India.

Uninterrupted intercourse with England and France enabled the Colonists to keep up with the prevailing fashions in dress, which at that time became most whimsical and capricious. But as there were many people in England who, like Mrs. Hardcastle, "only enjoyed London at second-hand," and depended on the letters of their friends for descriptions of the fashions, so many of the leading families in the Colonies also living remote from seaport towns were content to follow at a distance the bewildering transitions prescribed by *la mode*.

177

Before the days of fashion plates, jointed dolls were dressed in the latest style and sent from Paris to London every month. Not quite so often, but at regular intervals, similar dolls were sent to the Colonies. The mantua-makers of the day copied them for their fashionable patrons. In "The Spectator," the anxiety caused by the delay in the arrival of one of these dolls in London is described: "I was almost in despair of ever seeing a model from the dear country, when last Sunday I overheard a lady in the next pew to me whisper to another that at the Seven Stars in King Street, Covent Garden, there was a Mademoiselle completely dressed just come from Paris. I was in the utmost impatience during the remaining part of the service, and as soon as ever it was over, having learnt the milliner's address, I went directly to her house in King Street, but was told that the French lady was at a person of quality's in Pall Mall and would not be back again until late that night. I was therefore obliged to renew my visit this morning and had then a full view of the dear puppet from head to foot. You cannot imagine how ridiculously I find we have all been trussed up during the war and how infinitely the French dress excels ours."

This puppet, we are told, was dressed "in a cherry coloured gown and petticoat with a short 'working' apron, her hair was cut and divided very prettily with several ribbons stuck up and down in it. The milliner assured me that her complexion was such as is worn by all the ladies of the best fashion in Paris. Her head was extremely high. Her necklace was of an immoderate length, being tied before in such a manner that the two ends hung down to her girdle." Though the fashion dolls were longer in their voyage to the Colonies, they were apparently expected with the same eagerness described by the London satirist. Could the representative of her tribe whose portrait may be seen in Figures 166 and 167 speak, she would surely tell us that she received a warm welcome and was entertained by the people of "the best fashion in Philadelphia." Her costume

REIGNS OF QUEEN ANNE AND GEORGE I

1702-1725

FIGURE 162.—A Colonial costume of 1711, gown of buff chiné silk with variegated flowers over a blue silk hooped petticoat. The open skirt is pinked at the edges. The elbow sleeves are rather loose with large armholes reaching on to the shoulder, the seams being covered by revers of silk which taper slightly at the waist. The picture is taken from a genuine old gown lent by a direct descendant of the original owner (for back see Figure 174). The hair is arranged in soft curls drawn back loosely from the forehead and fastened to the head with combs. Long loose curls fall on each shoulder.

FIGURE 163.—The typical costume of a gentleman from 1702 to 1720, differing but little from the fashion of William and Mary's reign (Figure 42). The periwig with big curls arranged high on top and hanging in long drop curls to the front is sometimes called the "campaign wig" and it was usually powdered. The square-toed shoes have red heels, according to the fashion introduced in Queen Anne's reign.

FIGURE 164.—A Colonial costume of George I's reign. The original gown is now in the National Museum, Independence Hall, Philadelphia. It is of yellow damask silk and looped back with narrow braid and buttons. The bodice is trimmed with ruchings of the material pinked, and the edges of the skirt are finished in the same way. The hooped petticoat in the picture is of white satin, and the slippers match the gown. The hair is arranged in a low pompadour without powder, which, though occasionally worn with court dress in England, was not in general wear for women until 1750.

FIGURE 165.—Two variations of fashion for men in George I's reign are shown in this figure. These are the fastening of the garters with small buckles below the knee and the wearing of a ramilie wig tied with a large black ribbon bow at the nape of the neck, and powdered white. The style of the coat is not changed, but the tails are stiffened with buckram or wadding and waistcoats were often elaborately trimmed with lace or embroidery. Square-toed shoes were gradually giving way to a more pointed shape, but red heels were still in high favour.

FIGURE 162.

FIGURE 163.

FIGURE 164.

FIGURE 165.

proclaims that she arrived during the reign of George I, probably about 1720. Mrs. Vanderbilt, in her "Social History of Flatbush," says: "We have a vivid remembrance of the old age of one of these fashion-dolls which had been sent from Paris to a fashionable mantua-maker in New York. When the dress was changed as to style, the dressmaker sold the doll to one of her customers, and 'Miss Nancy Dawson' passed into the obscurity of humbler dollies, who had never been sent as ministers plenipotentiary from the Court of Fashion."

REIGN OF QUEEN ANNE

"Tho' stiff with hoop
And armed with ribs of whale.

. . . .

" Invention we bestow,
To change a flounce, or add a furbelow." *

Queen Anne came to the throne of England in 1702, and for the first eight or nine years of her reign, dress differed but little from that introduced under William and Mary (Figures 38, 42), but in 1711 two striking changes are noted. The extravagantly high head-dress and cap, the "tower and commode," so scathingly satirized in "The Spectator," gave way to a simple arrangement of natural hair, noticeable in the portraits by Kneller† of Queen Anne and the ladies of her Court. This change is applauded by Addison, who says: "I remember several ladies who were once near seven feet high, that at present want some inches of five."

We read that these gigantic commodes held their place at Versailles in spite of the disapproval of the old monarch, who protested in vain against towering head-dresses. In 1714, two English ladies with their hair worn low having been presented at the French Court, Louis XIV said to the wives of the courtiers, "If Frenchwomen were reasonable beings they would at once give up their ridiculous

---

* Rape of the Lock.   † Born 1646; died 1723.

9

head-dresses and wear their hair in the English fashion." How could the court ladies bear to be called "ridiculous," especially by their king? They very soon made their appearance in the king's circle with their hair dressed low.* For once, at least, England set the fashion for France—a pleasing turn of the tables!

The next transformation was the hoop, invented by a mantua-maker named Selby, in 1711, and destined in one form or another to hold its sway over feminine taste for many years. Dresses which had been looped back over contrasting petticoats were hung out over these most awkward inventions. At first they were rather flat in front and in the back (Figure 162), projecting out on each side over the hips to such an extent that the wearer was often obliged to enter a door sideways. Mr. Wingfield, in his "Notes on Civil Costume in England," remarks that "in a sedan chair a lady would some-times pull up her hoop on both sides of her like wings." As sedan chairs were used in all the English colonies of America, fashionable colonial dames probably resorted to the same expedient.

The sacque, the name in use for many years to designate the loose over-dress, at this time hung in wide plaits from the shoulders to the ground over the large hooped petticoat. It was open in front and worn over a petticoat and stomacher of the same material, although a contrast of colour and of material was also popular. This garment was invariably worn by women of fashion in England and France, and in the Colonies for at least half of the century. It survived several generations of change. At first it was long and full as in Figure 161, then short to the knees and very full (Figure 170); later it became a graceful, stately garment, transformed by a few curved lines and worn over a laced stomacher and satin petticoat trimmed with flounces (Figure 204). This charming variety of sacque is usually called a "Watteau." Sacques were made in all materials and worn by all classes until 1777.

* History of Fashion in France, by Challomel.

FIGURES 166 and 167.—This fashion doll is dressed in a Watteau sacque of taffeta (a white ground with cross-bar lines of red) over a hooped petticoat of the same trimmed with a pinked flounce. The stomacher is plain without a point, but finished by robings of the silk from the shoulder to a little below the waist-line. An apron of soft green silk is worn under the stomacher. The sleeves end at the elbow and are finished with graduated ruffles of the silk pinked, very deep in the back and short in the front; a knot of red, the prevailing colour of the costume, is on each sleeve and also in the hair, which was powdered and worn close to the head, probably in French curls. Red slippers with high heels, a necklace, and bracelets complete this genuine "Fashion-baby's" attire. The original may be seen in the Colonial room of the National Museum at Independence Hall, Philadelphia.

FIGURE 166.

FIGURE 167.

"Let your gown be a sacque, blue, yellow or green,
And frizzle your elbows with ruffles sixteen;
Furl off your lawn apron with flounces in rows,
Puff and pucker up knots on your arms and your toes;
Make your petticoat short, that a hoop eight yards wide
May decently show how your garters are ty'd.
. . . .
But mount on French heels when you go to a ball,
'Tis the fashion to totter, and show you can fall."*

Figures 168 and 169 show the style of hood in general wear by
women of all ranks from 1690 to 1750. The original hood, lent

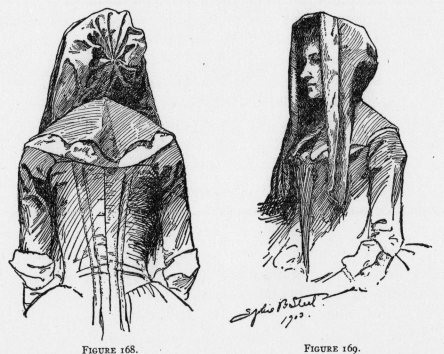

FIGURE 168.   FIGURE 169.
A Camlet Hood; taken from an Original Garment of about 1702. Reign of Queen Anne.

to us for this book, is made of drab camlet and lined with silk to
match, for it belonged to a Colonial Quakeress. The fashionable
dames of that time made them of gay silk, according to contemporary

* The Beau's Receipt for a Lady's Dress.

authority. The hood, which in the previous reign was commonly of black silk, velvet, or sarsenet, we now find of various colours; and cherry coloured hoods were all the rage in 1712. A group of ladies in coloured silk hoods at the theatre is thus described: "One of them was blue, another yellow and another philomot; the fourth was of a pink colour and the fifth was of a pale green. I looked upon this little parti-coloured assembly as upon a bed of tulips."*

From advertisements of this date (1712) in England, we can form some idea of the garments sent to the Colonies. In one of the papers we read of a black silk petticoat with a red and white calico border, a red and dove coloured damask gown flowered with large trees, a yellow satin apron trimmed with white Persian muslin, and headcloths with crow-foot edging.

An Isabella coloured kincob gown flowered with green and gold; a dark coloured cloth gown and petticoat with two silver orrices; a purple and gold atlas gown; a scarlet and gold atlas petticoat edged with silver; an underpetticoat edged with gold; a black velvet petticoat; an allejah petticoat striped with green, gold and white; and clogs laced with silver are also mentioned.

In the same year were advertised "a green silk knit waistcoat with gold and silver flowers all over it, and fourteen yards of gold and silver thick lace on it; and a petticoat of rich strong flowered satin, red and white all in great flowers or leaves, and scarlet flowers with black specks brocaded in, raised high like velvet or shag."†

A lady's riding suit of this period is described as consisting of "a coat and waistcoat of blue camlet trimmed and embroidered with silver, with a petticoat of the same stuff, by which alone her sex was recognized, as she wore a smartly cocked beaver hat, edged with silver and rendered more sprightly by a feather, while her hair, curled and powdered, hung to a considerable length down her shoulders, tied like that of a rakish young gentleman, with a long streaming

* The Spectator.   † Pictorial History of England.

FIGURE 170.—Picture of a short Watteau sacque worn over a petticoat to match and trimmed with ruchings of the same. It is taken from a garment in the South Kensington Museum, London, and is of biscuit-coloured taffeta with a damask pattern and scattered flowers and butterflies hand painted in water-colours—a specimen of the fancy-work of some lady of ease in the first half of the Georgian era. It is probable that this style of sacque was often made of Persian or dimity for home wear in the Colonies. The cap of muslin tied under the chin is often seen in contemporary pictures.

FIGURE 170.

scarlet riband."* But powder was not in general use by ladies at this time.

In Queen Anne's day patches meant more than one would suppose; they were not used simply to enhance the beauty of the complexion, but were worn as political badges. The ladies with Whig sympathies wore these patches on the left-hand side of the face, the Tories on the right. Mr. Andrew Lang has suggested that a revival of this fashion in England during the South African War would have greatly facilitated conversation. "If Pro-Boer ladies would only profess their opinion by way of patches, we should know where we are and could make no such mistakes as now occasionally occur in conversation."

Patch boxes (Figure 159) were carried, filled with patches of every shape; under the lid of the box was placed a small glass to assist the fair lady in adjusting them. These boxes were made of silver, ivory, and tortoise shell, and were often, like the snuff-boxes of the same period, very costly.

"That little modish machine," as Addison called the fan, was an indispensable article of fashionable dress. Flory, in his "History of the Fan," says: "We can scarcely imagine the rouged and powdered beauty of the eighteenth century without the fascinating trinket in her hand. Both in England and in France it had gradually become the mirror of the life and pleasure of the time. Political and social events, literature, music, and the fashions and follies of the day, were depicted upon them. Some were covered with words and bars from operas, or with scenes from popular plays, others bore the rules of various games, within decorative borders of playing cards." A picture of a fan painted by Gamble representing a scene from Ovid is given in Figure 241. "There were calendar fans, fortune-telling fans, fans with riddles and charades, political and social caricatures." One is noted representing the separation of America from England.

* The Spectator.

Addison declares there is an infinite variety of motions to be made use of in the flutter of a fan. "There is the angry flutter, the modest flutter, the timorous flutter, the merry flutter, and the amorous flutter. There is scarce any condition in the mind which does not produce a suitable agitation in the fan, insomuch that if I only see the fan of a disciplined lady, I know whether she laughs, frowns or blushes. I have seen a fan so angry that it would have been dangerous for the absent lover who provoked it, to have come within the wind of it; and at other times so languishing, that I have been glad for the lady's sake that the lover was at a certain distance from it."

> "What daring Bard shall e'er attempt to tell
> The powers that in this little engine dwell?
> What verse can e'er explain its various parts,
> Its numerous uses, motions, charms and arts?
> Its shake triumphant, its virtuous clap,
> Its angry flutter, and its wanton tap."

REIGN OF GEORGE I

Black and white beaver hats for ladies were advertised in 1719, faced with coloured silks and trimmed with gold or silver lace. The sacque was still in vogue. The paintings of Watteau, who died in 1721, and of Lancret, who died in 1724, are to a certain extent the authorities for the dress of the preceding reign (Queen Anne).

> "She takes her muff and goes
> To see some one she knows."

In 1720 women's muffs were narrow and long, the crossed hands filled one exactly; afterward they became wider. In various forms they continued in fashion throughout the century.

Stays, or "a paire of bodices," as they were called in the early part of the seventeenth century, were considered a necessary article of woman's dress throughout the eighteenth century, and very, very stiff and straight-laced were these colonial great-grandmothers of our modern corset! (Figure 188.)

FIGURE 171.—Shows a gown of yellow damask brocade worn over a blue quilted satin petticoat. Reign of George I.

FIGURE 172.—Shows a white satin wedding gown worn by Mrs. St. Clair in Philadelphia, 1760.

FIGURE 173.—Picture of a blue lutestring gown worn by the same lady.

FIGURE 174.—Is a very interesting dress of buff chiné silk, with coloured flowers, worn by Lady Stuart in the Barbadoes Colony in the reign of Queen Anne. (Photographed from original garments.)

FIGURE 171.

FIGURE 172.

FIGURE 173.

FIGURE 174.

About 1720 temple spectacles came into use; afterward "bridge spectacles," without any side supporters and held on solely by nipping the bridge of the nose. Perspective glasses, with long handles of tortoise shell or silver, were carried by gallants in London.

A mask of black velvet (Figure 194) was often worn in winter with a silver mouth-piece to keep it on; green silk masks were used in summer for riding in the sun on horseback, while for young girls in the Colonies they were made of linen and tied on under their hoods.

REIGN OF GEORGE II

At this time hooped petticoats were less exaggerated. Scarlet cloaks with hoods, called "cardinals," were worn out-of-doors (Figure 175). The hair was still worn low and was often covered by a much frilled cap or flat hat of moderate dimensions (Figure 195). During the next decade the caps became smaller, but the hats larger (Figure 216).

The use of powder, according to Mr. Wingfield, was never general in England, although it was worn on all occasions of ceremony in the reigns of George II and George III by both sexes, and was extremely fashionable from 1760 to 1776; but it was not habitually worn in home life with everyday costumes.

In 1735 we notice a change in the shape of the hoop, which was now made to project all around like the wheel farthingale, the petticoat being worn short and the gown without a train (Figure 196).

Lace tippets were now much worn, some having diamond solitaires to hook them together. Very broad laced tuckers, with diamond necklaces and earrings, were popular. Diamond and paste buckles were also very fashionable.

Mrs. Delany, who has been called not only the woman of fashion in her own age, but "the woman of fashion of all ages," records some charming costumes. The following is dated 1738 (when hoops were large):

"After much persuasion and many debates within myself I consented to go with Lady Dysart to the Prince's birthday, humbly dres't in my pink Damask, white and gold handkerchief, plain green ribbon and Lady Sunderland's buckles for my stays." The stays, evidently meaning the stomacher, were on this occasion straps of white silk covered with a lacing through which a handkerchief was passed. This costume is not unlike the yellow damask gown (Figures 164 and 183) worn in Philadelphia in 1740.

FIGURE 175.
Lady in a Cardinal (after Hogarth, Early Eighteenth Century).

Head-dresses at this time were made of three lace ruffles tucked to stand up in front. "Caskades of ribands" and artificial flowers were used as trimming. They were worn over powdered hair pinned up quite short in the back, and sometimes large curls were worn hanging down on the shoulder, as in Figure 198.

In another letter Mrs. Delany says: "I go to-morrow to pay my salutations to their Royal Highnesses at Carlton House in my Irish green Damask and my worked head; on the birthday, which is Tuesday next, in a flowered silk, I bought since I came to town, of a pale deer-coloured ground, the flowers mostly purple, and mixed with white feathers. I think it extremely pretty and very modest." The latter is not unlike the Colonial gown represented in Figures 218, 230. "Ruffles are much the same, large at the elbows and pretty narrow at the bottom. I think they pin their gowns rather closer than before; hoops are as flat as if made of pasteboard, and as stiff, the shape sloping from the hips and spreading at the bottom (Figures 164 and 183), enormous but not so ugly as the square hoops (Figure 162). There are hopes that they will soon be reduced to a very small size. Heads are variously dressed, pompons with some accompaniment of feathers, ribbons or flowers; lappets in all sorts of curli-murlis; long hoods are worn close under the chin, or tied with bows and ends behind."

FIGURE 176.   FIGURE 177.   FIGURE 178.   FIGURE 179.   FIGURE 180.   FIGURE 181.
            Caps, 1744.   Caps, 1745.

Long aprons were worn in 1740, then short ones, and before 1752 long ones again. In the same year (1740) we hear of a successor to the hood under the name of "capuchin."

The description which Mrs. Delany gives of a marvellous toilet worn by the Duchess of Queensbury, in 1741, is worth transcribing as a curious specimen of needle-work. "It was of white satin embroidered, the bottom of the petticoat brown hills covered with all sorts of weeds, and every breadth had an old stump of a tree that ran up almost to the top of the petticoat broken and ragged and worked with brown chenille, round which twined nasturtiums, honeysuckle, periwinkle and all sorts of twining flowers, which spread

and covered the petticoat; vines with the leaves variegated as you
have seen them by the sun, all rather smaller than nature, which
made them look very light.   The robings and facings were like green
banks covered with all sorts of weeds, and the sleeves and rest of
the gown loose twining branches of the same sort as those on the petticoat.   Many of the leaves were finished with gold, and part of the
stumps of the trees looked like gilding of the sun.   I never saw a
piece of work so prettily fancied and am quite angry with myself
for not having the same thought, for it is infinitely handsomer than
mine and could not have cost much more."

French curls (Figure 196), the mode in 1745, were described
as looking like eggs strung in order on a wire tied around the
head.   They were not always false, but could be made of the
natural hair.   The *crêpe toupée* was also a contemporary fashion.
Later came in the Italian curls (Figure 184), which had the effect
of scollop shells and were arranged back from the face in several
shapes.   In the *tête de mouton*, or *tête moutonée*, the hair was curled
close all over the back of the head.

In the summer of 1745 Gipsy straw hats appeared, being tied
under the chin (Figure 195).

We find that in 1745 the hoop had increased at the sides and di-
minished in front;   and a pamphlet was published in that year entitled "The Enormous Abomination of the Hoop Petticoat as the
Fashion now is" (Figure 184).   The hoop of this period was a great
bell-shaped petticoat or skirt of the dress stiffened by whalebone.
The material was placed directly upon it, so that, being a part of the
gown itself, it was customary to speak of "a damask hoop" or "a
brocade hoop."

Deportment was quite as important as dress in the fashionable
world of the eighteenth century.   Those were the days of back-
boards and of most unyielding stays.

The expression "she bridles well," which occurs in letters of this

REIGNS OF QUEEN ANNE AND GEORGE I

1702–1725

FIGURE 182 shows the cloak called a Roquelaure, after the Duke of that name who held the post of Gentleman of the Wardrobe under Louis XIV. It was made of velvet, silk or cloth and was usually lined with a bright coloured silk. Later in the eighteenth century the cloak was worn much longer and became a popular garment for both sexes. It is often mentioned in Colonial letters and papers as a "Roquelo." The cocked hat and campaign wig are typical of Queen Anne's reign, 1702–1714. The use of the muff is worthy of note.

FIGURE 183 represents the back of the yellow damask gown in Figure 164. The small cap, very fashionable in the reign of George I, is of sheer muslin trimmed with lace and has lappets in the back which could be worn hanging down the back or, as in this plate, turned up and fastened on top.

FIGURE 184 is a picture taken from a very handsome gown in the Art Museum of Boston. The ground of the brocade is of green with a pattern in bright colours. It is elaborately made and fitted in at the back like Figure 183. The stomacher is soft and full and held in place by bands of ribbon and rosettes. The hair of this figure is arranged in Italian curls which are fastened close to the head and finished with a small pompon of artificial flowers. It is copied from a contemporary portrait (1720).

FIGURE 185.—Back view of costume shown in Figure 165. The plaits in the coat-tail are very full.

FIGURE 182.

FIGURE 183.

FIGURE 184.

FIGURE 185.

time (1747), alludes to a manner of carriage which is now almost
unknown. "One of the first lessons in deportment at that period
was to hold up the head on entering a room, and to keep the chin
in, which is expressed by 'bridling,' and then, having curtseyed
at the door, to advance deliberately towards the person who had the
first claim to greeting—to sink low gradually—to rise slowly and
gracefully."*

The Boston "Evening Post" advertised in November, 1755,
"horse hair quilted coats to wear with negligees."

It is difficult to determine the exact limitations of a negligée.

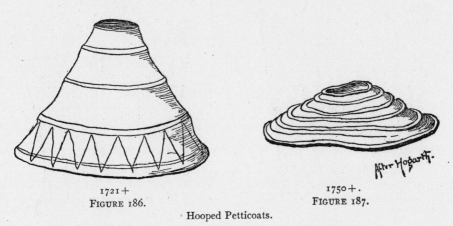

1721+
FIGURE 186.

1750+.
FIGURE 187.

Hooped Petticoats.

It was worn in full dress and was another variety of the sacque. The
advertisement quoted suggests an outdoor garment, a quilted coat
worn under it for warmth.

> "Put on her a sheperdee
> A short sack or negligee
> Ruffled high to keep her warm
> Eight or ten about an arm."†

A garment which became very popular about 1756 was a cloak
made of satin or velvet, black or any colour, lined or trimmed with
silk, satin, or fur, according to the fancy, with slits for the arms to

* Mrs. Woolsey's Notes to Autobiography of Mrs. Delany.
† Poem printed in New York, 1756.

pass through, and a hood like a capuchin. These cloaks were worn
by everybody and were called pompadours (Figure 216).

Night-gowns or night-rails correspond to our modern dressing-
gowns and were worn without hoops. One is represented in Figure
243 with a short cape over a skirt instead of a sacque.

An historian of Connecticut tells us that "the dress of the middle
period can hardly be praised for its simplicity or economy. In the
upper circles it was rich and extravagant, and among the females

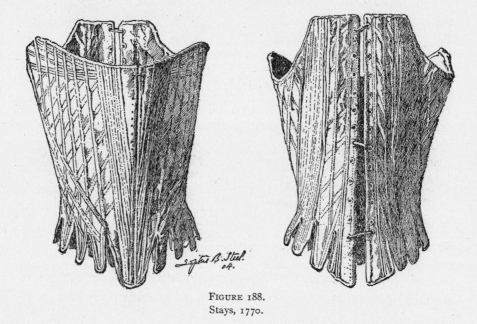

FIGURE 188.
Stays, 1770.

of all classes there was a passion for gathering and hoarding articles
of attire. It was an object of ambition to have a chest full of linen,
a pillow-beer of stockings, and other articles in proportion, laid by."

The inventory of the effects of Mrs. White of Norwich,* taken
August 16, 1757, contained "gowns of brown duroy, striped stuff,
plain stuff, black silk, crape, calico and blue camlet; a scarlet cloak,
blue cloak, satin flowered mantle, and furbelow scarf; a woolen

* History of Norwich, by F. M. Caulkins.

petticoat with calico border, a camlet riding-hood, long silk hood, velvet hood, white hood trimmed with lace, a silk bonnet, and nineteen caps; a cambrick laced handkerchief, silk do, linen do, sixteen handkerchiefs in all; a muslin laced apron, flowered laced apron, greer taffety apron, fourteen aprons in all; a silver riband, silver girdle and blue girdle, four pieces of flowered satin, a parcel of crewel, and a woman's fan; a gold necklace, death's head gold ring, plain gold ring, sett of gold sleeve buttons, gold

FIGURE 189.
Clog, Eighteenth Century (from an Old Print).

locket, silver hair peg, silver cloak clasps, and a stone button set in silver; a large silver tankard, a silver cup with two handles, a cup with one handle, and a large silver spoon."

FIGURE 190.
A Patten (from the Original in the Museum at Memorial Hall, Philadelphia).

We know that a salmon-coloured tabby made with a sacque and coat (probably, in this case, waistcoat or stomacher) was the correct thing in 1759, as an order for one for his wife is preserved in Washington's own writing. In the same order we read of "a cap, handkerchief and ruffles of Brussels or Point lace to be worn with the above negligée, to cost £20."

Also two fine flowered aprons
One pair women's white silk hose
Four pairs thread hose
Six pairs women's fine cotton hose
One pair black satin shoes
One pair white satin shoes of smallest 5's
Four pairs calamanco shoes
One fashionable hat or bonnet
Six pairs women's best kid gloves
Eight pairs women's best mits
One dozen round silk laces

One black mask
One dozen most fashionable pocket handkerchiefs
One piece of narrow white satin ribbon with pearl edge
Four pieces of binding tape
Six thousand miniken pins
Six thousand short whites
Six thousand corking pins
One thousand hair pins.

The following note from Washington's manuscripts shows the relationship between a sacque and a night-gown: "Mrs. Washington sends home a green sack to get cleaned, or fresh dyed of the same colour; made into a handsome sack again, would be her choice, but if the cloth wont afford that, then to be thrown into a genteel night-gown."* The latter being the old-fashioned name for a dressing-gown.

REIGN OF GEORGE III

In 1760 gowns began to be worn with a close-fitting bodice ending in a long point in the back (Figures 209, 210, 211, and 213), the skirt sewn on with a multiplicity of fine gathers, still opening over a petticoat, the latter often beautifully quilted. Aprons were worn, too, according to the dictates of fancy. Occasionally stomacher and apron matched, as in Figure 206. Sleeves were still trimmed with ruffles of lace, but often were edged with narrow cuffs turned back, the lace falling from underneath (Figures 205 and 230).

FIGURE 191.
Riding-hat of Fawn-coloured Felt. The original is in the Museum at Memorial Hall, Philadelphia. Reigns of George II and III.

Every lady of fashion wore an *étui*, or ornamental case, hanging from the waist, intended to hold thimble, scissors, and scent bottle. The snuff-box, the pomander, a box with perforated holes in the lid and used for perfumes, and the pouncet box, of a similar nature, were among the elegant accessories of the toilet of the eighteenth century

* Writings of George Washington, edited by Wm. C. Ford.

FIGURE 192.—Photograph of a kincob brocade, green figured with flowers in crimson, white, gold, and blue, with stomacher in white silk embroidered in colours to match. This dress was owned by a sister of Governor Hancock of Massachusetts, about 1735.

FIGURE 193.—Dress of a young Virginia lady, about 1775.

FIGURE 193.

FIGURE 192.

for both sexes. (See Figure 159.) Physicians made use of the pomanders to carry disinfectants; sometimes they had them inserted in
the handle of their canes, and a tap on the floor as they entered a
sick-room would scatter the powder through the atmosphere.

The recipe books of the time, written by each housewife for her
own use and pleasure, have in many cases been handed down to
posterity. Turning over the yellowed leaves of one written in the
careful penmanship of the eighteenth century by a notable New York
dame, an aroma of agreeable spices seems to
emanate from the pages as we read the following:

"Pot Pourri

"Dry your violets in a sunny window. Have
ready a quarter of a pound of finely powdered
bay salt. When the roses are out, gather all
kinds, and dry in the·same way. Then add
them to the violets, putting layers of salt between each layer.

FIGURE 194.
A Riding-mask, Eight-
eenth Century.

"Gather a good deal of lavendar, also the
leaves of the verbena, and, if possible, myrtle and orange blossoms.
After all the flowers and salt have filled the jar, its contents should
be constantly stirred for a month."

Here is another recipe from the same book:
"Take a Seville orange, and stick it as full as possible of cloves.
Put it in a jar. Pick the rose leaves when full blown. but before they
are ready to drop, and spread the petals to dry in the sun. When
dry mix them with a little bay salt, some cinnamon, ground cloves,
lemon peel, and powdered musk. Stir for some time until well mixed."

Old India jars filled with pot pourri stood in almost every house,
and lent a subtle fragrance to the draperies and carpets. This custom
was of the same origin as the use of pomanders.

Research on the subject of wedding veils at this period has pro-

duced nothing more satisfactory than the following passage from
Mr. J. Cordy Jeffreson's "Brides and Bridals":

"The origin of the English bride's veil is one of those disputed
questions which will never be settled. What of late years became
the most conspicuous feature of her costume may be nothing
more than a milliner's substitute for the flowing tresses, which in old
times concealed not a few of the bride's personal attractions and
covered her face when she knelt at the altar. This opinion is
supported by the fact that Elizabeth Stuart, daughter of James
I, was not thought to require an artificial veil, since nature had
given her such an abundance of circumfluent hair. Heyward says
of this wedding:

> 'At length the blushing bride comes with her
> hair disheveled aslant her shoulders.'

"It may be a mere amplification of the coif which medieval brides
used to wear between the garland and the hair, of such a coif, for
instance, as Margaret Tudor wore under the coronet at her wedding
with the King of Scotland."

In the early years of the reign of George III the veil and wreath fell
so completely out of vogue that they were for a time seldom seen on
brides of the "best ton." Horace Walpole, an earnest social reformer
in all trivial matters, was pleased by the neglect of old matrimonial
forms. He mentions that his niece Maria had never appeared more
lovely than when he watched the alternate blushes and paleness of
her unveiled face during her celebration of marriage with the Earl
of Waldegrave. The bride wore a hat and a white and silver gown,
and when the marriage service had been performed in the drawing-
room of a private mansion in Pall Mall by Dr. Keppel, the bridal
party sat down to dinner, which was over at eight o'clock in the evening. "It was," wrote Walpole to George Montague, "as sensible
a wedding as ever was." This wedding took place in the last year
of the reign of George II.

REIGNS OF GEORGE I AND II
1725-1745

FIGURE 195.—An everyday Colonial costume worn in Massachusetts about 1725. It is made of fawn coloured moiré camlet, and opens over a stiffened petticoat of durant. The ruffle of an under-garment of fine linen with knife-plaited sleeves turns down over the dress at the neck like a falling band. The original gown is exceedingly interesting as a specimen of the ordinary attire of the period. The hat worn over a ruffled cap was the popular style of that time, made familiar to us in the pictures of Hogarth and others.

FIGURE 196.—A Colonial gown of kincob, a very rich brocade imported from China. The original dress was owned by a sister of Governor Hancock of Massachusetts, Mrs. Whittington Allen. It was evidently made to wear over a large hoop (about 1735) and clears the ground. The stomacher is of white silk richly embroidered, the sleeves reach to the elbow and are finished with full pinked ruffles graduated so that they hang long in the back and are short in front. The back of this beautiful old gown is made with two large box plaits which hang out over the hooped skirt. It is of the style popularly termed a Watteau sacque and very fashionable in the Colonies from 1720 to 1776. The front of the skirt is made of two breadths of the kincob tied round the waist over the hooped skirt. The coiffure on this figure, known as French curls, was very fashionable at that time. Shoes match the gown, they have high heels and straps of the brocade pulled through handsome buckles. A strap of wide silver galloon runs up the front of the shoe and at the back from heel to counter; see first pair of slippers in Figure 262.

FIGURE 197.—A young gallant of George II's reign in a full-dress suit and a cocked hat. He wears the latest fashion in ties, 1740.

FIGURE 198.—A Colonial gown of green taffeta worn by Mrs. Wilimina Weemys Moore in Philadelphia about 1740 and lent for this book by a direct descendant. It is trimmed with ruchings and flounces of the material pinked. The bodice is laced in front over a white stomacher and is made without box plaits in the back (see Figure 174). The hair in the picture is copied from a contemporary portrait and is not powdered. As in Figure 196, the front of the skirt is separate and fastens round the waist over a hooped petticoat, evidently with a view to wearing a variety of combinations, for in the case of the kincob gown there was a white satin front to alternate with the kincob front.

FIGURE 195.

FIGURE 196.

FIGURE 197.

FIGURE 198.

In the Colonies the veil does not seem to have been a necessary article of a bride's costume.   Several beautiful wedding gowns which
have been handed down with care
from early in the eighteenth century are of coloured brocade or
damask (Figures 184, 213).

Orange-blossoms were not
used as wedding flowers until a
comparatively modern date,
although orange trees were growing in England at the time of
Henry VIII.

We read of an English bride *
in 1769 who wore "a sacque and
petticoat of the most expensive
brocaded white silk, resembling
network enriched with small
flowers, which displayed in the
variations of the folds a most delicate shade of pink; a deep and
pointed stomacher trimmed with
gimp; sleeves closely fitted the
elbow, from which hung three
point-lace ruffles of great depth;
a handkerchief of the same lace
covered the shoulders, fastened
in front with a large bow of white
satin ribbon and a bunch of delicate pink rosebuds.   A triple row
of pearls tied behind with a narrow white satin ribbon completed

FIGURE 199.

Maid in Sacque, Apron, and Clogs. Middle
Eighteenth Century.

* Mrs. Joseph Nollekens, wife of the noted sculptor.

10

the costume, although I believe a lace apron, previously worn by the bride's mother, was put on, but the fashion of wearing aprons in full dress had gone out at that date.

"The hair was arranged over a high cushion, with large curls on either side, and ornamented by a small cap of point lace with plaited flaps to match the ruffles in the sleeves. The shoes were like the gown and were ornamented with spangles and square buckles with heels three and one-half inches in height."

Lady Susan O'Brien, living in the Colonies, was kept informed by her cousin, Lady Sarah Lennox, of the latest changes in fashion in England. In 1766 she says:*

"I think that by degrees the French dress is coming into fashion, tho' 'tis almost impossible to make the ladies understand that heads bigger than one's body are ugly; it is growing the fashion to have the heads *moutonée*. I have cut off my hair and find it very convenient in the country without powder, because my hair curls naturally. . . . . I wear it very often with three rows of curls behind and the rest smooth with a fringe *toupé* and a cap; that is, *en paresseuse*. Almost every body powders now, and wears a little hoop.

"Hats are mostly left off; the hair down on the forehead belongs to the short waists [waists were apparently very long at the time this letter was written, 1766], and is equally vulgar with poppons [or pompons], trimmings, beads, garnets, flying caps and false hair.

"To be perfectly genteel, you must be dressed thus: *Your* hair must not be cut off, for 'tis much too pretty, but it must be powdered, curled in very small curls and neat, but it must be high before and give your head the look of a sugar loaf a little. The rest of the hair must be drawn up straight and not frizzled at all for half an inch above the rest. You must wear no cap and only little, little flowers dab'd in the left side; the only feather permitted is a black or white *sultane* perched up on the left side and your diamond feather against it (Figure 218).

* Lady Sarah Lennox to Lady Susan O'Brien in America, January 9th, 1766.

FIGURE 200.—Portrait of Mrs. Catharine Van Rensselaer, showing a popular style of cap worn by elderly ladies in the last half of the eighteenth century. (From the original portrait.)

FIGURE 201.—Portrait of Mrs. Nathaniel Appleton in an everyday costume.

FIGURE 202.—Portrait of Mrs. Nathaniel Appleton, Jr., showing a peculiar cap in 1784.

FIGURE 203.—Portrait of Mrs. Mary Faneuil of Boston, reign of George II.

FIGURE 200.

FIGURE 201.

FIGURE 202.

FIGURE 203.

"A broad puffed ribbon *collier* (Figure 206), with a tippet ruff, or only a little black handkerchief very narrow over the shoulders; your stays very high and pretty tight at bottom, your gown trimmed with the same straight down the robings, and a narrow flounce at bottom to button with a *compère* to be loose at the fore part of your robing. The sleeves long and loose, the waist very long, the flounces and ruffles of a decent length not too long, nor so hideously short as they now wear them. No trimming on the sleeve but a ribbon knot tied to hang on the ruffles."

Artificial flowers were worn in full dress. We learn from the newspapers of the day that "the biziness of making flowers" was a thriving one in Boston. Teachers in the art of flower making are often advertised in the Boston papers. We read, too, that Benjamin Franklin's sister and her daughter made a practical use of this accomplishment in the following extract from a letter from Mrs. Mecom, dated Boston, 1766:

"And I have a small request to ask. It is to procure me some fine old linen or cambric dyed into bright colours, such as red and green, a little blue but chiefly red, for with all my art and good old Benjamin's memorandums, I cannot make them good colours. My daughter Jenny, with a little of my assistance, has taken to making flowers for ladies' heads and bosoms with pretty good acceptance, and if I can procure these colours, I am in hope we shall get something by it worth our pains. It is no matter how old the linen is. I am afraid you never had any bad enough."

From a letter of Mrs. Mecom to Mrs. Franklin dated February 27th, 1766, we take the following: "We are now supplied not only with necessary but creditable clothing, for brother has sent each of us a printed cotton gown, a quilted coat, a bonnet, each of the girls a cap and some ribbons. Mine is very suitable for me to wear now, being black and purple cotton, but the girls' are light coloured."*

* Letters to Benjamin Franklin from his Family and Friends, 1751–1790.

The name bonnet, from the French *bonnet*, was often used throughout the eighteenth century in speaking of caps and hoods, but the first actual bonnet was the successor of the Gipsy hat in the latter part of the century, and in 1798 we read that "straw bonnets were in full fashion."

A New England authority tells us that "cushions stuffed with wool and covered with silk, used in dressing the hair, made a calash (Figures 222, 226, 227) necessary instead of a bonnet. This was large and wide, and an awkward article of attire, but often shrouding a health-beaming face in its depths, needing no other ornament than its own good humored smile."*

A gentleman of the courteous old school remarked of this fashion of the calash, "It was like looking down a green lane to see a rose blooming at the end."

From the "History of Norwich" quoted above we give the following description: "Women of mature age wore close linen caps (Figure 253). Parasols and umbrellas were unknown or of rare occurrence, but a fan nearly a foot and a half in length, and spreading like the train of a peacock, was often carried to keep off the sun as well as to catch the air. At one period feathers were much worn upon the head, surmounting a high turban of gauze or muslin raised on wire and adorned also with ribbon.

"A lady in full dress for great occasions displayed a rich brocade with open skirt and trained petticoat trimmed with lace; an embroidered stomacher and full ruffles at the elbows. Hood and scarf were of silk. No sumptuary laws restrained the feminine taste for rich attire at this period. When the ladies walked out, they threw the end of the train over the right arm. The foot was dressed in a silk stocking, a sharp-toed slipper, often made of embroidered satin, and with a high heel" (Figure 240). In winter beaver hats were worn over a lace cap, as in Figure 216, or with the brim curved downwards

* History of Norwich, by F. M. Caulkins.

REIGN OF GEORGE II

1735–1760

FIGURE 204 is a picture of a very dainty Colonial gown which in 1752 formed part of the wedding outfit of Mrs. West, *née* Mary Hodge, of Hope Lodge, White Marsh, Pa. The colouring is a soft fawn-coloured ground with nosegays of purple, red, yellow and white flowers scattered over it. The flounce and falbalas are of the silk pinked, the latter graduated as shown in the plate. The train has a graceful sweep in the back. The picture shows a stomacher of lace held in by ribbon tied in bows. The front of the gown and the elbow sleeves are finished with ruffles of lace. The head in this picture is copied from a contemporary portrait, the powdered pompadour being adorned with a string of pearls arranged with pins. Two soft curls hang on the neck in the back.

FIGURE 205 represents a costume worn in the Massachusetts Colony in 1750. It is of very rich crimson brocade over a petticoat of white satin. It belonged to Mrs. Faithful Hubbard, who, in spite of her Puritan name, possessed a very "modish gown." It is made without a Watteau back, like Figure 174, the skirt gathered into the bodice at the waist line. The hair is arranged in the height of fashion in 1759 and is powdered.

FIGURE 206 shows the green kincob gown of Figure 196, arranged over a white satin hooped petticoat with a full-dress apron of white silk embroidered like the stomacher in a bright coloured Chinese pattern. The fichu and sleeve ruffles are of lace and the "collier" of ribbon gathered into a ruche and edged with lace. This neck arrangement as well as the hair without powder are copied from a contemporary portrait.

FIGURE 207 represents the back of the kincob gown. The Watteau hangs out without the curved line shown in Figure 204, as the kincob gown was made some years earlier (about 1735) to wear over a large hoop. The hoop shown in Figure 207 is the fashion of about 1745. The cap is a very popular style of George II's reign, finished with a ribbon and bow at the back. The hair is powdered.

All the gowns in this plate have been lent for this book by direct descendants of the original owners.

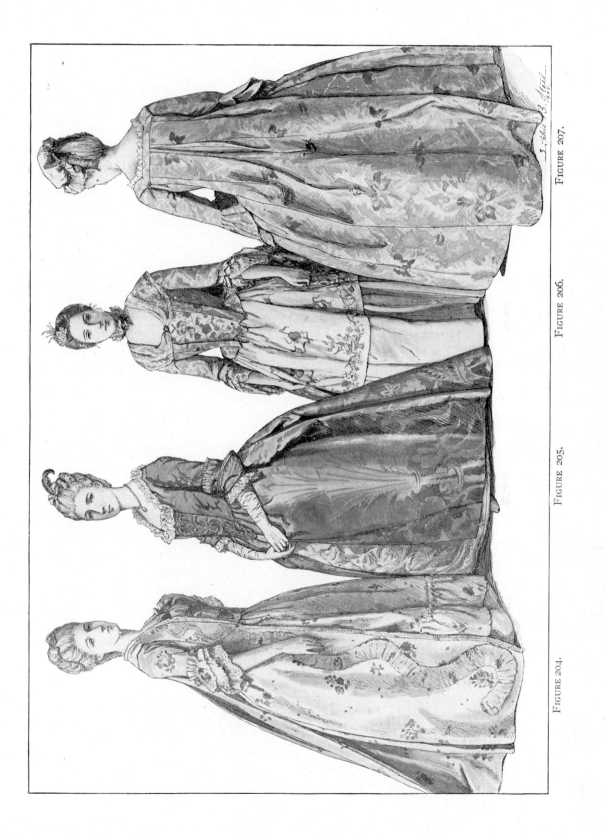

FIGURE 204.

FIGURE 205.

FIGURE 206.

FIGURE 207.

by broad ribbon strings tied under the chin (Figure 195). Loose cloaks trimmed with fur were the fashion in the middle of the eighteenth century, also long Roquelaures with short capes or a hood on the shoulders, like those worn by the men.

In Massachusetts, we are told, "ladies wore caps, long stiff stays, and high-heeled shoes. Their bonnets (hoods) were of silk or satin, and usually black. Gowns were extremely long-waisted with tight sleeves. Another fashion was a very short sleeve with an immense frill at the elbow. A large flexible hoop, three or four feet in diameter, was for some time quilted into the hem of the gown, making an immense display of the lower person. A large round cushion, stuffed with cotton or hair and covered with black crape, was laid across the head, over which the hair was combed back and fastened. It was almost the universal custom, also, for women to wear gold beads, thirty-nine little hollow globes, about the size of a pea, strung on a thread and tied round the neck.

FIGURE 208.
A Lady's Shoe, of a Cornflower-blue Serge Silk, Bound with White Ribbon.

"Working women wore petticoats and half gowns, drawn with a cord round the waist, and coarse leather shoes; though they generally had a pair of 'Lynn shoes' for Sunday."*

In Watson's famous "Annals" we read: "The women in Philadelphia wore caps (a bare head was never seen), stiff stays, hoops from six inches to two feet (Figure 184) on each side, so that a full-dressed lady entered a door like a crab. High-heeled shoes of black stuff with white silk or thread stockings, and in the miry times of winter they wore clogs, galoshes, or pattens (Figures 189 and 190).

"Ladies often had their hair tortured for four hours at a sitting, in getting the proper crisped curls of a hair curler. Some who

* History of Lynn, Mass., by Lewis and Newhall.

designed to be inimitably captivating, not knowing they could be sure of professional services, where so many hours were occupied upon one gay head, have actually had the operation performed the day before it was required, then have slept all night in a sitting posture to prevent the derangement of their frizzles and curls. This is a real fact, and we could, if questioned, name cases. They were of course

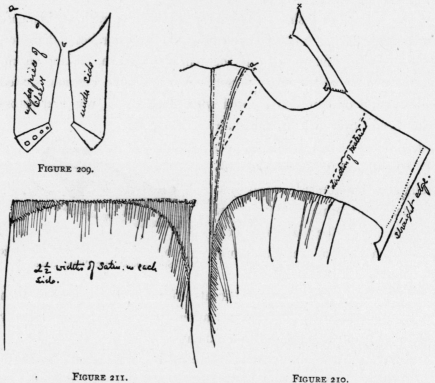

FIGURE 209.

FIGURE 211.   FIGURE 210.

Plan of White Satin Dress shown in Figures 218 and 230. Reign of George III.

rare occurrences, proceeding from some extra occasions, when there were several to serve, and but few such refined hair dressers in the place.

"This formidable head work was succeeded by rollers over which the hair was combed from the forehead. These again were superseded by cushions and artificial curled work, which could be sent out

FIGURE 212.—The wedding gown of Esther Marvel, a New England Quaker lady, married in Salem, Massachusetts, about the middle of the eighteenth century. It is white satin. The bodice fastens in the back with hooks and eyes, and the upper part of each sleeve is embroidered with a rosebud in white silk. The long sleeves are evidently of a later date and ruffles of sheer lawn like the fichu probably finished the shorter sleeves when the gown was first worn. The reticule carried in the hand is of white lutestring, embroidered like the sleeves in white silk. The cap is of the shape so much worn at that time by women of all classes. The hair is arranged very simply, drawn back softly over the ears and in a knot at the back. The absence of powder and of the fashionable hooped petticoat are the distinguishing marks of this Quaker costume.

FIGURE 213.—A gown of very rich brocade, blue on the surface and green underneath, with a narrow stripe of green at regular intervals and a running vine pattern of small bright flowers and leaves between. It is arranged over a quilted petticoat of blue satin. This gown is made without a Watteau plait, but has the long sweeping train so fashionable in the latter part of George II's reign, 1750–1760. The sleeves are longer than in the earlier part of the reign and reach below the elbows. The style of this gown is copied from one in the Art Museum in Boston, and the colouring from a piece of brocade which was part of a

gown worn by Mrs. Michael Gratz, *née* Miriam Simon, of Lancaster, Pennsylvania. The hair is copied from a contemporary portrait.

FIGURE 214.—A suit of uncut velvet worn by Robert Livingston, third Lord of Clermont Manor on the Hudson, New York. Coat and breeches are of the same material covered with a small design in soft shades of red and green, which does not show in the picture but gives a pinkish hue to the costume. The long waistcoat is of corded silk, a shade darker than the coat and embroidered by hand with a very graceful flowered pattern in which the soft red and green of the suit prevail. It is a very beautiful costume in material, colour, and design. The buttons are covered with velvet, and the coat and waistcoat are lined throughout with white corded silk and the knee breeches with heavy swanskin (Canton flannel), while the pockets of the latter are lined with white kid. Small straps of the velvet fasten with buckles below the knee.

FIGURE 215 shows the back of Figure 204, a charming specimen of the fashionable Watteau of George II's reign. Between the nosegays of lilac, yellow, and red flowers, a small brocaded bunch of daisies is seen in the original material, of the same colours as the silk (soft fawn), too small to be reproduced in the picture, but adding to the rich effect of the costume.

FIGURE 212.

FIGURE 213.

FIGURE 214.

FIGURE 215.

to the barber's block like a wig to be dressed, leaving the lady at home to pursue other objects, thus producing a grand reformation

FIGURE 216.
Beaver Hat and Short Cloak, Middle of Eighteenth Century.   Reigns of George II and III.

in the economy of time and an exemption from former durance vile.

"When the ladies first began to lay off their cumbrous hoops, they supplied their place with successive succedaneums, such as these, to wit: First came bishops—a thing stuffed or padded with horse hair; then succeeded a smaller affair under the name of *Cue de Paris*, also padded with horse hair. How it abates our admiration to contemplate the lovely sex as bearing a roll of horse hair or a cut of cork under their garments! Next they supplied their place with silk or calimanco, or russell thickly quilted and inlaid with wool, made into petticoats; then these were supplanted by a substitute of half a dozen petticoats. No wonder such ladies needed fans in a sultry summer, and at a time when parasols were unknown, to keep off the solar rays!"

Other articles of female wear are mentioned: "Once they wore a 'skimmer hat' made of a fabric which shone like silver tinsel; it was of a very small flat crown and big brim, not unlike the late Leghorn flats. Another hat, not unlike it in shape, was made of woven horse hair woven in flowers, and called 'horse hair bonnets,' an article which might again be usefully introduced for children's wear as an enduring hat for long service." Watson had himself seen what was called a "bath bonnet," date unknown, "made of black satin, and so constructed to lie in folds that it could be sat upon like a *chapeau bras*," and observes that "it would be a good article for travelling ladies!" This and the "musk melon bonnet," evidently a modification of the calash, used before the Revolution, had numerous whalebone stiffeners in the crown, set an inch apart in parallel lines and presenting ridges to the eye, between the bones. The "pumpkin hood" was made in the same manner with wadding between the ridges for cold weather.

"A 'calash bonnet,'" according to Watson, "was usually formed of green silk; it was worn abroad covering the head, but when in rooms it could fall back in folds like the springs of a calash or gigtop; to keep it over the head it was drawn up by a cord always held in the

REIGN OF GEORGE III
1760-1776

FIGURE 217.—Back view of the beautiful suit owned by Robert Livingston of Clermont, third Lord of the Manor, of which a front view is given in Figure 231. The powdered hair is tied in a black silk bag under the black ribbon bow—a fashion seen in many portraits of the time.

FIGURE 218.—Back view of the white satin gown in Figure 230. Like the blue lutestring (Figure 228), it is made with deep pointed bodice on to which the skirt is gathered with numerous small plaits. A diagram of this style of bodice is given on page 218. The elaborate powdered coiffure is copied from a contemporary picture. (1760.)

FIGURE 219.—A simple everyday costume of a young lady, 1770-1776, made of flowered chintz or dimity looped over a quilted petticoat. The frilled cap is of the fashion called "palisade," worn over a "fashionable head" too complicated to be arranged every morning.

FIGURE 220 represents an elderly man of business in a coat of strong fustian over nankeen breeches. This is a characteristic suit of the period from 1770 to 1790, and with the exception of the hat, which could be unlooped, was the costume of members of the Society of Friends to the end of the eighteenth century. The picture is taken from a suit worn by Mr. Joseph Johnson of German town.

FIGURE 217.

FIGURE 218.

FIGURE 219.

FIGURE 220.

sophie B. Steel. del.

hand of the wearer." When the calash was at the height of popularity, however, it appeared in many varieties of material and colour. I have seen mention of a pink dimity calash and of a flowered Persian worn over high heads, without disturbing the erection, and blue and brown calashes may be seen in the Museums in Philadelphia.

"The wagon bonnet, always of black silk, was an article exclusively in use among the Friends. When on the head it was thought to look not unlike the top of the Jersey wagons, having a pendent piece of the silk hanging from the bonnet and covering the shoulders. The only straw worn was that called the 'straw bee-hive bonnet,' worn generally by old people." Interesting specimens of bonnets may be seen in the Museum of Memorial Hall, Philadelphia, ranging from the calash and the pumpkin hood to the wagon bonnet mentioned by Mr. Watson, but the exact date of the latter is hard to determine.

Mrs. Gummere, in a very brilliant book on a very sombre subject, published recently,* says: "It has been with the Quaker bonnet as with every other garment the Quaker has ever worn—the cut originated in that centre of all ideas of fashion, and the abode of taste, Paris, while the expression of Quakerism lay simply in the absence of any superfluous adornments. In this one idea lies the secret of Quaker dress." Doubtless the author is right, but who can look upon even a picture of a Quaker bonnet without sighing for the superfluous adornments?

Although no rigid laws had been passed by the Quakers forbidding the use of gay colours, members of the sect were recommended to abstain from them, and soft grays, dull drabs, sage greens, and sombre browns were so generally worn by Friends that they were thenceforth associated with them. We read in many instances of the careful pains even the strictest of Friends took to match these solemn colours. Figure 250 is the portrait of a beautiful Quaker lady in a gown of sage silk.

* The Quaker, a Study in Costume.

"The Quaker simplicity of garb was but another name for the finest and costliest raiment that could be produced, the richest sombre coloured silks, the most delicate lawn, the finest broadcloth. A modest splendour which cost more thought and care than the ordinary habiliments which were denounced by the sect as pomps and vanities of the world," says that gentle historian, Mrs. Oliphant. But the use of sheer cambric in caps, handkerchiefs, and aprons gave to the dress of the Quaker maids and matrons a dainty air of unpretentious refinement for which they have ever been distinguished.

The cape in Figure 232 is of pale gray silk lined with white cambric. It is taken from an original garment of about 1775. The cap is of finest linen cambric sewed with the invisible stitches of early days and worn by that distinguished colonial dame of Pennsylvania, Deborah Norris Logan, at the close of the eighteenth century. The combination may at first seem an anachronism, but in point of fact the Society of Friends followed with reluctant footsteps the changes of fashion, and while caps of the style of Figure 232 were probably worn at the close of the century and even later, the cape is of a shape worn by Quaker dames as early as 1775 and as late as 1800.

A delightful instance of departure from Quaker costume on an especial occasion is thus told by Mrs. Gummere:*

"A Quaker Wedding.

"In the month of May, 1771, Isaac Collins of Burlington, New Jersey, married Rachel Budd, of Philadelphia, at the 'Bank Meeting' in that city. His wedding dress was a coat of peach blossom cloth, the great skirts of which had outside pockets. It was lined throughout with quilted white silk. The large waistcoat was of the same material. He wore small clothes, knee buckles, silk stockings, and pumps. A cocked hat surmounted the whole.

"The bride, who is described as 'lovely in mind and person,'

* The Quaker, a Study in Costume.

EIGHTEENTH CENTURY.

FIGURE 221.—Two pairs of stays
        Corded linen breeches
        Leather stock
        Bead bag and embroidered purse
        Quilted petticoat
        Three pairs of spectacles
        One silk shoe.
FIGURE 222.—Two silk calashes
        One velvet riding-cap with visor
        One Quaker bonnet
        One beaver hat
        Two pairs of men's gloves
        Embroidered muslin skirt.

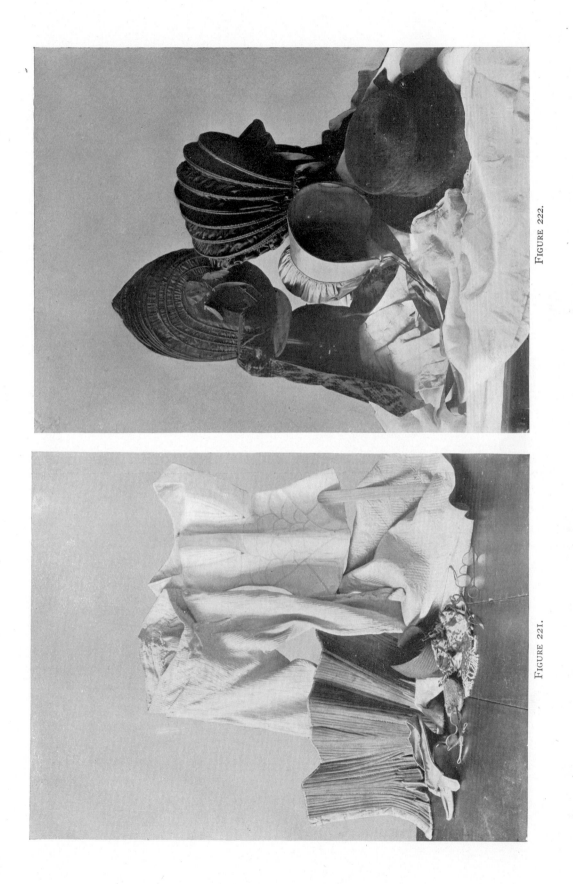

FIGURE 222.

FIGURE 221.

wore a light blue brocade, shoes of the same material, with very
high heels, not larger than a gold dollar, and sharply pointed at the toes." In Figure 263 a photograph of the original shoes worn on that occasion is given. "Her dress was in the fashion of the day, consisting of a robe, long in the back, with a large hoop. A short blue bodice, with a white satin stomacher embroidered in colours, had a blue cord laced from side to side. On her head she wore a black mode hood lined with white silk, the large cape extending over the shoulders. Upon her return from meeting after the ceremony, she put on a thin white apron of ample dimensions, tied in front with a large blue bow."

FIGURE 223.
Lady in Capuchin with Fur Trimmings and Muff,
1780. Reign of George III.

Cloaks for outdoor wear were used with some changes of form, under the successive names of "pompadours," "Roquelaures," "cardinals," and "capuchins," throughout the eighteenth century. "Umbrellas to keep off the rain were not known at this time, but a few people used quitasols, which were about the size of the present parasols. They were of oiled muslin, and were of various colours. They must, however, have been but rare, as they never appear in any advertisements," according to Mr. Watson, who is also responsible for the following statement:

"In those days dress was discriminative and appropriate, both as regards the season and the character of the wearer. Ladies never wore the same dress at work as on visits; they sat at home or went out in the morning in chintz, and brocades, satins and mantuas were reserved for evening wear or for dinner parties. Robes or negligées, as they were called (Figures 192, 204, and 207), were often worn in full dress. Muslin gowns were not worn at all."

During the reign of George III, women of fashion began to wear their hair high again. In 1775, it was worn absurdly high, rolled over a framework of wire and surmounted by a large cap, turban, or hat with tall feathers; this fashion was never quite as exaggerated in the Colonies as in England, but many ancestral portraits testify to its popularity. For instance, the portraits of Mrs. Duer and Mrs. Izard in "The Republican Court" show this extreme of fashion.

Virginia was always one of the gayest of the Colonies. In the Diary of Philip Fithian, this description of festivities in 1774 is given:

"A VIRGINIA BALL AND VIRGINIA BELLES (1774).

"Tuesday, January 18. Mrs. Carter and the young ladies came home last night from the ball, and brought with them Mrs. Lane. They tell us there were upward of seventy at the ball; forty-one ladies; that the company was genteel; and that Colonel Harry Lee, from Dumfries, and his son Harry, who was with me at college, were also there. Mrs. Carter made this an argument, and it was a strong one indeed, that to-day I must dress and go with her to the ball. She added also that she desired my company in the evening when

FIGURE 224.—Portrait of Mr. and Mrs. Ralph Izard of the Carolina Colony.
(By Copley, 1774.)
FIGURE 225.—Portrait of the West family. (By Benjamin West, 1799.)

FIGURE 224.

FIGURE 225.

she should come home, as it would be late.   After considering a while,
I consented to go, and was dressed.

"We set away from Mr. Carter's at two.   Mrs. Carter and the
young ladies went in the chariot, Mrs. Lane in a chair, and myself
on horseback.

"As soon as I had handed the ladies out I was saluted by Parson
Smith.   I was introduced into a small room where a number of gentlemen were playing cards (the first game I have seen since I left home)

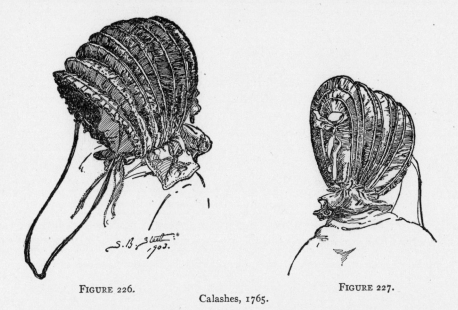

FIGURE 226.   FIGURE 227.

Calashes, 1765.

to lay off my boots, riding-coat, &c.   Next I was directed into the
dining-room to see young Mr. Lee.   He introduced me to his father.

"With them I conversed till dinner, which came in at half after
four.   The ladies dined first, when some good order was preserved.
When they rose, each nimblest fellow dined first.   The dinner was
as elegant as could be well expected when so great an assembly were
to be kept for so long a time.   For drink, there were several sorts
of wine, good lemon punch, toddy, cider, porter, &c.

"About seven, the ladies and gentlemen began to dance in the ball-room,—first, minuets, one round; second, jigs; third, reels; and last of all, country-dances. They struck up marches occasionally. The music was a French-horn and two violins.

"The ladies were dressed gay and splendid, and when dancing, their silks and brocades rustled and trailed behind them."

The minuet, from the French *menuet*,—so called from the small steps taken in it,—was invented in France about the middle of the seventeenth century, and throughout the eighteenth century was the favourite dance of all ceremonious occasions in the Colonies as well as in Europe.

The same diary also contains valuable items of contemporary costume and allusions to the fashionable deportment taught to the young ladies of the Colonies and absolutely essential to the proper setting off of the costumes then in vogue.

"Friday, June 24.—To-day Mr. Christian's* dance takes place here. He came before breakfast. Miss Jenny Washington came also, and Miss Priscilla Hale while we were at breakfast. Miss Washington is about seventeen. She has not a handsome face, but is neat in her dress, of an agreeable size, well proportioned, and has an easy winning manner. She is not forward to begin a conversation, yet when spoken to she is extremely affable, without assuming any girlish affectation, or pretending to be overcharged with wit. She has but lately had an opportunity for instruction in dancing yet she moves with propriety when she dances a minuet, and without any flirts or capers when she dances a reel or country-dance. Her dress is rich and well-chosen, but not tawdry, nor yet too plain. She appears to-day in a chintz cotton gown with an elegant blue stamp, a sky-blue silk quilt (Figure 213), and spotted apron. Her hair is a light brown, it was craped up, with two rolls at each side, and on the top was a small cap of beautiful gauze and rich lace, with an artificial flower interwoven. Her person and carriage at a small

* Mr. Christian was evidently a dancing master.

REIGN OF GEORGE III

1760-1776

FIGURE 228.—A house costume of light blue lutestring. The bodice is cut low in front and finished with tabs below the waist. The sleeves fit close to the arm and curve around the elbow; they are finished with a graduated ruffle of lace. This gown was worn by Mrs. St. Clair about 1760. The muslin cap and fichu are taken from a contemporary portrait.

FIGURE 229.—A suit of dark satin with a waistcoat of white satin embroidered in colours, which originally belonged to Robert Livingston of Clermont (third Lord of the Manor). The hair, copied from a contemporary portrait, is powdered and tied with a long black ribbon. The shoe-buckles in the picture are copied from a very beautiful Colonial pair of graduated stones (paste) set in wrought silver; unfortunately, the graceful design cannot be seen in the reproduction. These buckles belonged to Mrs. Jonathan Dickinson Sergeant, of Philadelphia.

FIGURE 230.—The white satin wedding gown of Mrs. St. Clair, who was married in 1760. It is made like the blue lutestring (Figure 228) and trimmed with lace in festooned flounces, or falbalas, edged with silver gimp according to the prevalent fashion. The powdered hair is copied from a contemporary portrait by Copley. A back view of this gown is given in Figure 218. The blue dress is just like it. These gowns are still owned by a direct descendant of Mrs. St. Clair.

FIGURE 231.—A suit of uncut velvet with waistcoat of quilted pale blue satin trimmed with silver galloon. The original costume belonged to Robert Livingston of Clermont, and is of a beautiful soft colour, a sort of warm old rose.

All the costumes on this plate were lent for the purpose of reproduction by descendants of the original owners.

FIGURE 228.   FIGURE 229.   FIGURE 230.   FIGURE 231.

distance resemble not a little my much respected Laura. But on close examination her features are something masculine, while those of Laura are mild and delicate. Mr. Christian very politely requested me to open the dance by stepping a minuet with this amiable girl. I excused myself by assuring him that I never was taught to dance. Miss Hale is about fourteen, and is a slim and silent girl. She has

black eyes and black hair and a good set of eyebrows, which are esteemed in Virginia essential to beauty. She looks innocent of every human failing, does not speak five words in a week, and I dare say from her carriage that her modesty is perfect. She is dressed in a white Holland gown, cotton, quilted very fine, a lawn apron, has her hair craped up, and on it a small tuft of ribbon for a cap. She is but just initiated into the school, and only hobbles yet. Once I saw her standing. I rose immediately and begged her to accept my chair. She answered most kindly, 'Sir, I thank you.' That was all I could extract from this wonder of the sex for the two days she staid, and I seemed to have an equal share in the favours of her conversation. So that in describing the mental faculties of Miss

FIGURE 232.
Quaker Cape and Cap, 1780.

Hale, it is sufficient to say that I think she is far removed from most of the foibles of women. Some time after these, came Colonel Lee's chariot with five young misses."

In England, in the first half of the eighteenth century, it was the custom of the noble patrons of the different theatrical companies to bestow their cast-off suits upon their favourite actors. As national distinction was utterly disregarded in dramatic productions of the day, and histories of costume were unknown, the heroes and heroines of classic lore, as well as of Shakespeare, were dressed in the fashionable garb of the passing hour. We hear of even Garrick appearing as Othello in a regimental suit of George II's body-guard, with a flowering Ramilie wig; and of Barry in the same rôle (in 1765) dressed in a full suit of gold-laced scarlet, a small cocked hat, and silk stockings.

More striking still must have been the Othello of James Quin in a large powdered major wig and a blackened face. Fancy Lady Macbeth in a hoop eight yards in circumference, which, as we read, was the costume Mrs. Yates assumed in the part.

Barton Booth, an actor of note in the early part of the century, took pains to encase the soles of his shoes in felt when acting the ghost in Hamlet, but Pope records of his impersonation of Addison's Cato in 1712:

> " Booth enters, hark the universal peal!
> But has he spoken? not a syllable.
> What shook the stage and made the people stare?
> Cato's long wig, flowr'd gown and lacquer'd chair."

Mrs. Cibber as Juliet, in a white satin gown with an enormous hoop, does not seem to have been thought unseemly attired.

Even John Kemble, the author of many reformations in stage effects, appeared as Hamlet in a modern court dress of rich black velvet with deep ruffles, with the pendent riband of an order on his breast, and mourning sword and buckles; his hair was powdered and, in the scenes of feigned distraction, flowed dishevelled in front over his shoulders.*

The first theatre in America was at Williamsburg, Virginia, which was inaugurated by the London Company of Comedians under the management of Mr. Lewis Hallam in 1752. The play was "The

* Annals of the English Stage, by Dr. Doran.

FIGURE 233.—Reticule made of the court gown worn by Mrs. Carroll of Carrollton, Maryland.

FIGURE 234.—Gloves made of soft doeskin, embroidered with flowers in colour. Worn by Mrs. Wentworth, of New Hampshire, about 1717.

FIGURE 235.—Bead reticule and paste buckles, about 1770.

FIGURE 236.—A bonnet of muslin made over reeds, worn about 1780.

FIGURE 237.—Crêpe shawl with flowers printed in colour, late eighteenth century.

FIGURE 238.—Linen pocket embroidered in colour, worn by Mrs. Wodkind of Massachusetts (1752). (From the original in the Essex Museum, Salem.)

FIGURE 239.—Paste shoe buckles worn by Elisha Lawrence, Esq., of Chestnut Grove, New Jersey, in 1720. Silver spoons and steel chatelaine owned by Mrs. Edward Pennington of Philadelphia, in 1754. Snuff-box of conch-shell with the Pennington coat-of-arms engraved on the lid and the date 1777. The lady's snuff-box is also of conch-shell. The monogram E. L. C. (Elizabeth Le Comte) is engraved on the silver cover.

FIGURE 240.—Slipper of green and white striped taffeta, worn by Mrs. Samuel Appleton, of Ipswich, Massachusetts, in 1758.

FIGURE 241.—Fan painted by Gamble, 1771.

FIGURE 233.

FIGURE 234.

FIGURE 235.

FIGURE 236.

FIGURE 237.

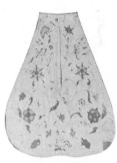

FIGURE 238.

FIGURE 239.

FIGURE 240.

FIGURE 241.

Merchant of Venice." The unfortunate Signor Antonio probably dressed in a ruffled shirt, knee buckles, long coat, and buttoned waistcoat, with a powdered wig, after the manner of Mr. Clarke at the Haymarket Theatre in London; while Shylock stood whetting his wicked knife in a very long-tailed coat and a falling band of linen, in imitation of Macklin, who was delighting English audiences with his representation of the part about that time. Opera glasses came into use early in this century (eighteenth).

Miss Sarah Eves, of Philadelphia, remarks in her journal (January 5, 1773): "The poor Doctor thought his clothes were not good enough to wait upon us in, therefore he delays his visit until he gets fitted up in the Macaronia taste I suppose." This was the popular name for a dandy at the time Miss Eves wrote, the Macaronis being a class of fops in London who introduced a particular style of dress in 1772. The name originated in the following manner. A number of young men of fashion who had visited Italy formed an association called "The Macaroni Club," in contradistinction to the "Beefsteak Club" of London. As the fashion of this time was to wear long waistcoats and coats with wide and heavy skirts, they wore theirs exceedingly short, and the whole dress of very close cut. Their wigs were remarkable for an enormous club, or turned-up bunch of hair behind. They had little cocked hats, swords dangling about their heels at the end of long straps, and sticks with large tassels. Their stockings were covered with coloured spots and their dress generally piebald in the same manner.

In 1773 an alteration took place in their dress, consisting chiefly in elevating the hair to an enormous height, with large curls ranging on each side of it, and in wearing immense bunches of flowers at the breast. They attracted much attention during the few years of their existence.*

* Fairholt's English Dress.

II

"Ye belles and beaus of London town,
    Come listen to my ditty;
The muse, in prancing up and down,
    Has found out something pretty.
With little hat, and hair dress'd high,
    And whip to ride a pony,
If you but take a right survey,
    Denotes a Macaroni.

"Five pounds of hair they wear behind
    The ladies to delight, O!
Their senses give unto the wind,
    To make themselves a fright, O!
Thus fashion who does e'er pursue
    I think a simple tony,
For he's a fool, say what you will,
    Who is a Macaroni."

This ballad was popular in the streets of London at this time, and was probably sung by the English soldiers in the Colonies. It suggests a close connection with the national air, "Yankee Doodle," which so many writers have attempted to explain without, however, settling the vexed question.

"Yankee Doodle came to town
    Riding on a pony
With a feather in his hat,
    Upon a Macaroni"

can be traced to the time of Charles I, and has been ascribed to the pen of a cavalier poet in derision of Cromwell. But this version does not seem any more palpable than other explanations, and "a feather in his hat" is not suggestive of Cromwell.

According to the Century Dictionary, it is said to have been first applied in the Colonies to a Maryland company of militia distinguished for its showy uniform.

The Lydia Fisher jig, sung to the same tune, runs:

"Lucy Locket lost her pocket
    Lydia Fisher found it,
Not a bit of money in it
    Only broidery round it."

We give a picture of a beautifully embroidered linen pocket, made by a colonial lady, which would be well worth finding even as empty as that of Lucy Locket (Figure 238).   This pocket was intended to be worn outside the dress, as the careful needlework proclaims. The original is in the Essex Institute at Salem, Massachusetts.   It was worked and worn by Mrs. Samuel Wodkind about 1750.   A similar pocket made of printed cotton is in the Museum of Memorial Hall, Philadelphia.

According to Fairholt, the Macaroni style of costume was quite the rage with the town (London).   Everything that was fashionable was *à la* Macaroni.   Even the clergy had their wigs combed, their clothes cut, "their delivery refined," *à la* Macaroni.   The shop windows were filled with caricatures and other prints of this tribe; there were portraits of "Turf Macaronis," "Parade Macaronis," "Macaroni Parsons," "Macaroni Scholars," and a variety of other species of this extended genus.   Ladies set up for female Macaronis. Their costume was scarcely so distinctive as that of the men; it was chiefly known by the high head-dress, large bunch of flowers, and an exceedingly wide and spreading sleeve hanging with deep ruffles from the elbow.

> "No ringlets now adorn the face,
>   Dear Nature yields to art,
> A lofty head-dress must take place,
>   Abroad in ev'ry part.
> Patch, paint, perfume, immodest stare,
>   You find is all the fashion.
> Alas, I'm sorry for the fair,
>   Who thus disgrace the nation."*

I have not met with a single notice of a female Macaroni in the Colonies.

The English country people of the eighteenth century were rather picturesque in costume.   When dressed for church or a country fair,

* Fairholt's Satirical Poems on Costume.

the young women wore flowered chintzes with muslin kerchiefs and aprons. The short skirts showed clocked stockings, usually of a bright colour. Their shoes were strong but not clumsy in pattern, and the little muslin caps they wore under their hats were extremely pretty and becoming.

On these occasions the men wore breeches to the knees, coats of homespun, waistcoats usually of some contrasting colour, buckled shoes, and cocked hats.

When at work, the damsels generally wore short skirts of a coarse woolen material tied round the waist over short sacques of calico, with kerchiefs about the neck. (Figures 247 and 259.)

The men wore knit jerkins or blouses of coarse linen, such as oznaburg or dowlas, leather boots pulled up over coarse woolen breeches, and Monmouth caps. Homespun linsey-woolsey was much in use for both sexes.

The domestics of a household were always clothed by their masters. A letter of Mistress Hannah Penn, written in 1700, requests that "ten yards of frieze for servants and some four or six skirts" be sent by barge from Philadelphia to Pennsbury, where she was preparing for her husband's return. The following items tell us what Washington ordered from England for the servants at Mt. Vernon in 1759:

8 doz. pairs of plaid hose sorted,
4   "   Monmouth caps,
25 yds. broadcloth to cost about 7s. 6d.
15   "   coarse double thick broadcloth,
6   "   scarlet broadcloth,
30   "   red shalloon,
12 doz. white washed waistcoat buttons,
20   "   "   "   coat   "
40 yds. coarse jean or fustian for summer frocks for negro servants,
1½ doz. pairs strong coarse thread hose fit for negro servants,
1   "   pairs coarse shoes and knee buckles,
1 postillion cap,
6 castor beavers.

The livery worn by his servants was of scarlet faced with white, the colours of the Washington coat-of-arms.

The following notices from newspapers of 1740 to 1772, show the usual dress of servants and slaves in the Colonies:

"Now in the custody of Thomas Smith, Sheriff of Cape County, a run-away negro man, who goes by the name Jupiter Hazard, is about twenty-seven years of age, but very black, of a middle size and well built. Had on when taken up, a flannel shirt, leather breeches with a fob in the waistband, shoes and stockings, both very good, the stockings of a blue colour, bathmetal buckles, a good felt hat and worsted cap. He speaks English like a country born negro who has lived some time among the Dutch.

"He had a bundle with him which contained two white shirts, a dimity jacket and breeches, a white handkerchief, a linen cap, a pocket-book with four dollars in it, and a pair of silver knee buckles marked N. S."

"Ran away on the 20th from Nathan Watson, of Mount Holly, an Irish servant man, named Christopher Cooney, a short well-set fellow, about twenty-six years of age, of a pale complexion, short brown curled hair, had lost one of his under fore teeth, and has had his right leg broke, and walks with his toe turned outward. Had on when he went away, a new castor hat, a red great coat, a light-coloured fustian coat and jacket, new copper coloured broadcloth breeches, lined with leather, new black and white yarn stockings, old shoes, newly soled. He was some time past a hostler at Jonathan Thomas's, in Burlington. Whoever takes up and secures said servant, so that his master may have him again, shall have forty shillings reward, and reasonable charges, paid by

NATHAN WATSON."

From the "Pennsylvania Gazette," 1773:

"Ran away from the subscriber, an English servant girl named Christina Ball, but calls herself Caty for shortness, about twenty years of age, brown skinned, black eyes, and hair lately cut short, a little stoop-shouldered. Her cloathes are very ordinary, a brown cloth petticoat, other coarse shifts and a striped calico short gown; any other cloathes uncertain. Whosoever takes her up, and confines her in any gaol within twenty miles of this city shall have twenty shillings reward, and three pounds if taken up at any distance further, paid by

HENRY NEILL."

The advertisements in the early newspapers in America are a valuable contribution to the history of costume. I will give a few from the leading papers of different parts of the Colonies early in the eighteenth century.

Among quaint and curious advertisements, we find this one of Thomas Peck's, advertising goods sold by him at the Hatt & Beaver, Merchant's Row, in Boston.

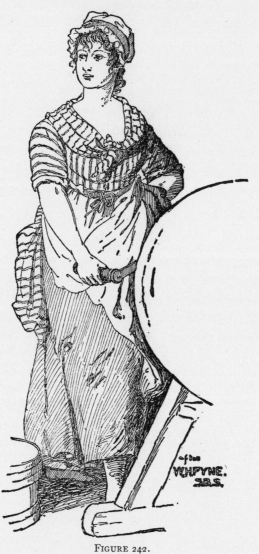

FIGURE 242.
Typical Dress of English Country Girl, 1780. (End of the Eighteenth Century.)

"A fresh assortment of Linen Linings, suitable for Beaver, Beaverett, Castor, and Felt Hatts, Tabby ditto, Mohair Lupings, Silk Braid ditto, flatt and round silk lace and Frogs for Button Lupes, plain and sash Bands, workt and plain Buttons, black Thread, Gold and Silver Chain, yellow and white Buttons, hard and light Brushes, Velures, Cards, large and small bowstrings, Looping Needles, Verdigrees and Coperas, a good assortment of mens and boys felt Hatts, Castor ditto.—He likewise sells logwood."

From the "New York Gazette" of May 9, 1737, we learn of a thief's stealing "one gray Hair wig, one Horse Hair Wig, not worn five times, marked V. S. E., one brown Natural Wig, one old wig of Goats Hair put in buckle." "Buckle" meant "to curl," and a wig was "in buckle" when it was rolled on papers for curling. Other advertisements tell of the dress-stuffs of the time with the weird names chilloes, betelles, deribands, tapsiels, that were familiar enough over the shop counters in colonial New York.

Here is another curious old advertisement:

"May 11, 1761. Imported by John and Thomas Stevenson and to be sold at their shop at the *Sign of the Stays*, opposite the South Side of the Town-House, Boston, at the very lowest prices, Viz.

"Lawns of all sorts, Strip'd and Flowr'd kenting Handkerchiefs, cotton and linen ditto; silk and gauze ditto; Cambricks, Calicoes and printed Linens—white and coloured Threads; silk, worsted, cotton and thread stockings, Women's silk and worsted Mitts—Broad-Cloths; German Serge—Thicksets; Fustians, Jeans, Pillows and Dimities—Broglios, Dorsateens, Venetian Poplins, flowr'd and plain Damasks, Prussianets, Serpentines, Tammies, strip'd stuff, Camblets, Callimancoes, Shalloons and Buckrams,—Worsted Caps, Garters, Needles and Pins—white brown and strip'd Hollands—white and checked Linnen Diaper, Bed-Ticks, Tartans, Plaids Breeches and Jackets Stocking Patterns, Cotton and silk gowns, Stock Tapes, Leather Breeches, Mens' and Women's Leather Shoes, &c., &c."

The following is also of interest:

"Just imported from London, and to be sold by
"DANIEL BOYER, Jeweller,
"At his Shop opposite the Governor's in Boston.
Best Brilliant and Cypher Earing and Button Stones, Binding

Wire, Brass and Iron ditto, Brilliant and cypher ring stones, Brass stamps, Garnets, Amethysts, and topaz. Buckle and ring brushes, Ring and buckle sparks, Money scales and weights, Locket stones & Cyphers, Small sheers & Plyers, Ruby and white foyle, Screw dividers, Coral beads, Blow pipes, Coral for Whistles, Shoe and knee Chapes, Draw plates, Moulding sand, Rough and smooth files, Crucibles and plack pots, Borax and Salt-Petre, Pommice and Rotten-stone, &c.

Where also may be had, some sorts of Jewellers and Goldsmith work, cheap for cash."

That Paul Revere was at one time a dentist, we learn from the following startling advertisement in the "Boston Gazette," December 19, 1768:

"Whereas many Persons are so unfortunate as to lose their Fore-Teeth by Accident, and otherways, to their great Detriment, not only in looks, but speaking both in Public and Private:—This is to inform all such that they may have them replaced with artificial ones, that looks as well as the Natural, and answers the end of speaking to all Intents, by Paul Revere, Goldsmith, near the head of Dr. Clarke's Wharf, Boston.

"All Persons who have had false teeth fixt by Mr. John Baker, Surgeon-Dentist, and they have got loose (as they will in time) may have them fastened by the above who learnt the Method of fixing them from Mr. Baker."

Here is an invoice of goods imported in 1771:

"Imported in the Neptune (Capt. Binney) and to be sold by Daniel Parker, Goldsmith, At his Shop near the Golden-Ball, Boston,

"An Assortment of Articles in the Goldsmith's and Jewellers Way, viz. brilliant and cypher'd Button and Earing Stones of all Sorts, Locket Stones, cypher'd Ring Stones, Brilliant Ring Sparks, Buckle Stones, Garnetts, Amethysts, Topaz, and Sapphire Ring Stones, neat Stone Rings sett in Gold, some with Diamond Sparks, Stone Buttons in Silver, by the Card, black ditto in Silver, best Sword Blades, Shoe and Knee Chapes of all sizes."

Another invoice by the same ship contains the following list:

"Broad Cloths, German Serges, Bearskins, Beaver Coating, Half Thick, red Shagg, 8 qr. Blankets, Shalloons, Tammies, Durants, Calimancoes, worsted Damasks, strip'd and plain Camblets, strip'd Swanskins, Flannell, Manchester Velvet, Women's ditto, Bombazeen, Allopeen, colour'd Duffels, Hungarians, Dimothy, Crimson and green China, Cotton Check, worsted and Hair Plush, Men's and Women's Hose, worsted caps, mill'd ditto, black Tiffany, Women's and Children's Stays, cotton Romalls, printed Linnen Handkerchiefs, black Gauze ditto, Bandanoes, Silk Lungee Romalls, Cambricks, Lawns, Muslins, Callicoes, Chintz, Buckrams, Gulick Irish and Tandem Holland, Men's and Women's Kid and Lamb Gloves, black and white Bone Lace, Capuchin Silk and Fringe, Gartering, Silk and Cotton Laces, strip't Ginghams, Yellow Canvas, Diaper, Damask Table Cloths and Napkins, Bedtick, Garlix, Soletare necklaces and Earings, Tapes, Women's Russel Shoes, sewing Silk, Looking Glasses, Ticklenburg, English and Russia Duck, English and India Taffety, Grograms, English and India Damask, Padusoys, Lutestrings, black and white Satin, Rich Brocade, Gauze Caps and Ruffles, Shades and handsome Silk Cloakes, &c., &c., &c."

Of interest, too, is this advertisement from the "Pennsylvania Gazette," 1773:

"JOHN MARIE
"Taylor from Paris.
Humbly acquaints the Gentry and Public that he has taken a house in Gray's Alley, between Walnut and Chestnut Streets, the fourth door from Second Street, and has provided good workmen. He has had the pleasure of pleasing some of the most respectable gentlemen in London, and hopes by the strictest attention and most particular punctuality to give general satisfaction.

"N. B. At said Maries', gentlemen's cloaths of all colours cleaned, all spots taken out, and made equal to new, without the tedious and disadvantageous method of ripping or washing them."

The following notice is rather amusing:

"WILLIAM LANG,
"Wig-Maker and Hair Dresser,
Hereby informs the Public, that he has hired a Person from Europe,
by whose assistance he is now enabled, in the several Branches of
his Business, to serve his good customers, and all others, in the most
genteel and polite Tastes that are at present in Fashion in England
and America. In particular, WIGS made in any Mode whatever,
such as may grace and become the most important Heads, whether
those of Judges, Divines, Lawyers, or Physicians, together with
all those of an inferior Kind, so as exactly to suit their Respective
Occupations and Inclinations. HAIR-DRESSING, for Ladies and Gentlemen, performed in the most elegant and newest Taste—Ladies
in a particular Manner, shall be attended to, in the nice, easy, genteel and polite Construction of ROLLS, such as may tend to raise
their Heads to any Pitch they may desire, also French Curls, made
in the neatest Manner. He gives Cash for Hair."

In the Museum at Memorial Hall, Philadelphia, are some jute
braids once worn under nets by women of the Colonies.

The following notices from various newspapers in different parts
of the Colonies, appearing at the dawn of the Revolution, prove
that the people of that day were not wholly given up to the vanities
of the world.

This, from a New England paper about 1768, is a proof of
the patriotic spirit of the dames of colonial days:

"In a large circle of very agreeable ladies in this Town, it was
unanimously agreed to lay aside the Use of Ribbons, &c., &c.,
&c. for which there has been so great a Resort to Milliners in times
past. It is hoped that this resolution will be followed by others
of the Sex throughout the Province—How agreeable they will appear in their native Beauty, stript of these Ornaments from the prevailing Motive of Love to their Country."

Another notice reads:

"We must after all our Efforts, depend greatly upon the Female
Sex for the introduction of Economy among us; and those who

have the Pleasure of an Acquaintance with them assure us that their utmost Aid will not be wanting.

"So strong is the Disposition of the Inhabitants of this Town to take of the Manufacturers that come from the Country Towns, especially Womens and Childrens Winter Apparel, that nothing is wanting but an Advertisement where they may be had in Town, which will be taken in, and published by the printers of this Paper gratis." *

Mrs. Caulkins tells us that "with the prospect of war with the Mother Country before them, many of the inhabitants of Boston decided upon a non-importation system, and a non-consumption of articles on which heavy duties were laid. It was the practice then, as it is at this day, in the Colonies as well as in England, to dress in black clothes on mourning occasions. It was decided to discontinue such dresses, and the custom of wearing black on these occasions was generally laid aside; the only sign made use of was a piece of black crape about the hat, which was in use before, and a piece of the same stuff around the arm.

"An agreement to this effect was drawn up and very generally signed by the inhabitants of the town, also by some members of the Council and Representatives. This would affect the sale of English goods, and none were to be purchased except at fixed prices. At the same time another agreement was very extensively signed to eat no lamb flesh during the year. This was to increase the sheep in the country, and consequently to encourage the manufacture of woolen goods, which were imported from England in large quantities.

"The practice of wearing expensive mourning dresses was soon very generally laid aside. It was further proposed 'to give no other gloves than are of the manufacture of the country in lieu of white ones, that are seldom drawn on a second time.' It was suggested

* The days of the Spinning Wheel in New England. Extracts from Colonial Papers.

to the glovers that, 'it might not be amiss if some peculiar mark were put upon them, as a bow and arrow, or pine tree, instead of the usual stitching on the back,' and a great number of the respectable tradesmen of the Town came into a resolution to wear nothing but leather for their working habits. Instead of the rich cloth Roquelaures, even the magistrate and the colonel were satisfied with cloaks of brown camlet lined with green baize, and the greatest lady in the land had her riding hood also of camlet. As the great struggle

FIGURE 243.
Night-rail.

for liberty gradually overshadowed the land, and the sacrifices necessary to consummate the Revolution began to be appreciated, a decided change took place in regard to dress, amusements, and display. Women discarded all imported ornaments, and arrayed themselves wholly in domestic goods. Fine wool and choice flax were in higher estimation than silk and laces, and the hearts of the patriots as well as the laudations of the poet were given to beauty in homespun garments. Gentlemen also that had been accustomed to appear in society in the daintiest costume, following the example first set by the women, discarded their shining stocks, their cambric ruffles, silk stockings, silver buckles, and other articles of foreign production, and went back to leather shoestrings, checked handkerchiefs, and brown homespun cloth.

"The encouragement of home manufactures and the rejection of all imported luxuries were regarded as tests of patriotism. Common discourse grew eloquent in praise of plain apparel and Labrador tea. The music of the spinning wheel was pronounced superior to that of the guitar and harpsichord. Homespun parties were given

FIGURE 244.—A picture of a gown of mauve crêpe, worn about 1795 by Madame Sartori, of New Jersey.

FIGURE 245.—A Watteau sacque, part of the wedding outfit of Mrs. William West, *née* Mary Hodge, of Hope Lodge, White Marsh, Pennsylvania, in 1752. Fawn-coloured silk, with flowers brocaded in colour.

FIGURE 246.—Picture of a gown of white embroidered muslin, worn in 1790.

FIGURE 247 is a calico short sacque, made without seams on the shoulder, worn in Pennsylvania late in the eighteenth century.

FIGURE 248.—A gown of buff glazed chintz, worn by Madame Chevalier, who came to Philadelphia from Martinique about 1795.

(Photographed from original garments.)

FIGURE 244.

FIGURE 245.

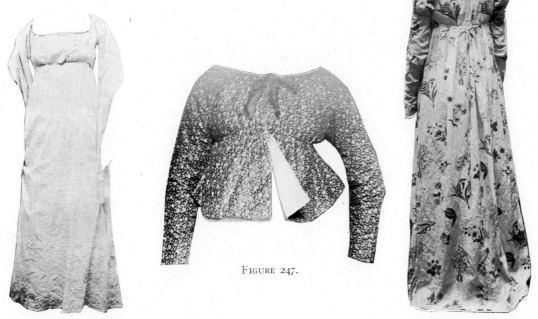

FIGURE 246.

FIGURE 247.

FIGURE 248.

where nothing of foreign importation appeared in the dresses or upon the table. Even wedding festivities were conducted upon patriotic principles." *

. After the Battle of Bunker Hill, the colonists everywhere were too seriously engaged to give much attention to the fashions, only the Tories, who persisted in shutting their ears to the spirit of Revolution now rife in the Colonies, and spreading in ever-widening circles about them, continued to import the fashionable novelties from England. On that July morning in 1776 when the Declaration of Independence was read to an eager crowd in the State House yard in Philadelphia, the colonial period of American history came to an end.

AFTER THE REVOLUTION

Philadelphia in the winter of 1777 was the scene of much gaiety. The Tories of the Colony, refusing even then to take a serious view of the situation, amused themselves and the British officers stationed there with Sir William Howe, by a series of dances and routs which had "an appropriate closing" in the famous Mischianza given by Major André and the other members of Howe's staff, probably with the desire to return some of the hospitality received, although Major André himself called it "the most splendid complimentary entertainment ever given by an army to their Commander." The splendour of this ball, preceded by a regatta on the Delaware and the absurd mock tournament, has been so often described that it is not necessary to dwell upon it here. The costumes of the knights and ladies were designed by André as well as the tickets of admission. The original drawing made for the ladies' costumes and one of the tickets for the occasion are in the possession of the Philadelphia Library Company.

During the Revolutionary period (1776–1783), and, in fact, for

* History of Norwich, Connecticut, by Frances Mainwaring Caulkins.

the remaining years of the eighteenth century, patriotic Americans who wished to be very fashionable imported their finery direct from Paris, and French taste prevailed both in furniture and dress.

Depreciation of the currency was one of the many trials entailed by the breach with England.

Speaking of the high prices during the Revolution, Mrs. Bache (Sarah Franklin), in writing to her father, says: "I have been obliged to pay fifteen pounds and fifteen shillings (£15 15s.) for a common calamanco petticoat without quilting, that I once could have got for fifteen shillings. I buy nothing but what I really want, and wore out my silk ones before I got this." (Philadelphia, 1778.)

A few months later she says: "A pair of gloves cost seven dollars. One yard of common gauze twenty-four dollars." *

The hoop skirt, which had held its own for so many years, went out of fashion in 1778.

About this time hair in Paris was worn extravagantly high, but as we do not notice the extreme of this or, in fact, of any of the French styles in the portraits of the day in this country, it seems more than likely that they did not find favour in American eyes.

A letter from Miss Franks, one of the reigning belles in American society, describes a new thing in bonnets to her sister, Mrs. Hamilton, living in the neighbourhood of Philadelphia: "I shall send you a pattern of the newest bonnet; there is no crown, but gauze is raised on wire and punched to a sugar loaf at the top. The lighter the trimming the more fashionable. (Figure 236.)

"Nancy Van Horn and myself employed yesterday morning in trying to dress a rag baby in the fashion, but could not succeed; it shall go, however, as it will in some degree give you an opinion on the subject.

"As to the jacket and the pinning in of the handkerchief, yours you say reaches to the arms. I know it, but it must be pinned up

* Letters to Benjamin Franklin from his Family and Friends.

to the top of the shoulders and quite under the arms as you would a girl's Vandyke (Figure 259).

"The fuller it sets, the handsomer it is thought. Nobody ever sets a handkerchief out in the neck, and a gauze handkerchief is always worn double and the longest that can be got; it is pinned round the throat, as Mrs. Penn always did, and made to set out before like a man's shirt. The ladies here always wear either a pin or a brooch as the men do."*

Chintz gowns were the usual wear for mornings at home, even when admiring British officers were about, for Sally Wister, writing from the country home of her father in 1778, says to Deborah Norris:

"I rose by or near seven, dress'd in my light chintz which is made gown-fashion, Kenton handkerchief and linen apron."† Quilted petticoats were still very fashionable at this time.

Caps of a great variety of shapes were worn on all occasions by the women of this period (Figures 200, 201, 202, and 219). A picture of one of a striking style is given (Figure 202) which was worn by Mrs. Nathaniel Appleton in Massachusetts, in 1784.

Many of the English memoirs and letters mention the "great-coat," which came into use in 1786, and so pleased Queen Charlotte that she commanded Miss Burney to celebrate it in verse. The result was not remarkable as a poem, but interesting as a note on popular costume.

"The garb of state she inly scorn'd
    Glad from its trappings to be free'd,
She saw thee humble, unadorn'd,
    Quick of attire,—a child of speed.

"Still, then, thrice honour'd Robe! retain
    Thy modest guise, thy decent ease.
Nor let thy favour prove thy bane
    By turning from its fostering breeze."

* Letter written from Long Island to Mrs. Hamilton of Woodlands near Philadelphia.
† Pennsylvania Magazine, vol. vii.

As Miss Burney speaks later of wearing a "white dimity great-coat as usual in the morning," it was probably another form of the negligée, the ancestress of our tea gown (Figure 161). Of the same nature, too, were the gowns which Maria Dickinson mentions; writing of an evening spent at Fairhill, the country-seat of Isaac Norris near Philadelphia, she says:

"It was the custom to disrobe and put on one of the soft warm gowns of green baize provided for each guest," then follows a charming description of innocent gossip over the fire. This letter is dated January 1, 1787.

Quaker dress was at this time noticeable for uniform simplicity of cut and sober colouring, although, as we see by the following extract from a letter, lilac satin was allowed on occasions.

"Phila. 23 Sept. 1783.

"We reached the antiquated building on Front street ere they made their appearance, and being seated very advantageously, we soon had the pleasure of seeing them enter. The bridegroom in a full suit of lead coloured cloth, no powder in his hair, which made him look tolerably plain. The bride was in lilac satin gown and skirt with a white satin cloak and bonnet. It would be needless to enumerate the variety of dresses which made their figures on this occasion. Suffice it to say that all looked much in the smartness especially neighbor G ———, who had procured an enormous large hat which made him the most conspicuous person present" (Figure 220).

For this amusing letter I am indebted to Miss Anne H. Wharton, the author of the delightful biography of Martha Washington, as well as other well-known books on the colonial period.

There are very few portraits of Quakers of this period; two, however, of old ladies in their muslin caps and plain silk gowns are reproduced in Figures 250 and 252. Mrs. Pennington, sister of the Mayor of Philadelphia, wears a dress of sage green under her kerchief. In the original painting the colouring is very attractive. The other portrait is copied from an engraving, but there is great charm in the delicate face. The white sheer cap is fastened with a white ribbon bow and the dress is probably of gray silk (Figure 252).

After the proclamation of peace with Great Britain, while Adams was Minister to the English Court, his wife wrote full accounts of the prevailing styles there for the benefit of her gay friends in the United States. In 1786 she wrote:

"To amuse you then, my dear niece, I will give you an account of the dress of the ladies at the ball of Comte d'Adhemar. There was as great a variety of pretty dresses, borrowed wholly from France, as I have ever seen; and amongst the rest, some with sapphire-blue satin waists, spangled with silver, and laced down the back and seams with silver stripes; white satin petticoats trimmed with black and blue velvet ribbon; an odd kind of head-dress, which they term the 'Helmet of Minerva.' I did not observe the bird of wisdom, however, nor do I know whether those who wore the dress had suitable pretentions to it. 'And pray,' say you 'how were my aunt and cousin dressed?' If it will gratify you to know, you shall hear. Your aunt, then, wore a full-dress court cap without the lappets, in which was a wreath of white flowers, and blue sheafs, two black and blue flat feathers (which cost her half a guinea apiece, but that you need not tell of), three pearl pins, bought for Court, and a pair of pearl earrings, the cost of them—no matter what; less than diamonds, however. A sapphire blue *demi-saison* with a satin stripe, sack and petticoat trimmed with a broad black lace; crape flounce, etc., leaves made of blue ribbon, and trimmed with white floss; wreaths of black velvet ribbon spotted with steel beads, which are much in fashion and brought to such perfection as to resemble diamonds; white ribbon also in the Vandyke style, made up the trimming, which looks very elegant; and a full dress handkerchief, and a bouquet of roses. 'Full gay, I think, for my aunt.' That is true, Lucy, but nobody is old in Europe. I was seated next the Duchess of Bedford, who

12

had a scarlet satin sack and coat, with a cushion full of diamonds, for hair she had none, and is but seventy-six neither. Well now for your cousin: a small white leghorn hat, bound with pink satin ribbon; a steel buckle and band which turned up at the side, and confined a large pink bow; a large bow of the same kind of ribbon behind; a wreath of full blown roses round the crown, and another of buds and roses within-side the hat, which, being placed at the back of the hair, brought the roses to the edge; you see it clearly; one red and black feather with two white ones, completed the head-dress. A gown and coat of Chamberi gauze, with a red satin stripe over a pink waist, and coat flounced with crape, trimmed with broad point and pink ribbon; wreaths of roses across the coat, gauze sleeves and ruffles."

As costumes similar to those described by Mrs. Adams may be

FIGURE 249.
A Riding Habit about 1785 (from a Contemporary Print).

FIGURE 250.—A portrait of Mrs. Pennington, showing the dress of a Quaker lady, 1780.

FIGURE 251.—A portrait of Catharine Schuyler Van Rensselaer, about 1795, showing collarette and cuffs of embroidered muslin. (From the original portrait.)

FIGURE 252.—A portrait of Mrs. Morris, showing the dress of a Quaker lady, 1785.

FIGURE 253.—Portrait of a Dutch lady of the New York Colony about 1765, showing a close-fitting cap and kerchief of sheer lawn edged with lace.

FIGURE 250.

FIGURE 251.

FIGURE 252.

FIGURE 253.

seen in Racinet, Pauquet, and other books of French costume, it is not necessary to give pictures of them here.

The small proportion of the people in America in the latter years of the eighteenth century who could truthfully be called gay lived, of course, in the large towns and cities; the majority lived quietly in the country on their large estates or plantations. The "History of Durham, Connecticut," * describes the home customs as well as the home costumes of rural New England from 1776 to 1800.

"The inhabitants were generally clad in fabrics manufactured, that is made by hand, in the family. There was woolen cloth spun in the house but fulled and dressed at the clothier's shop. There was brown tow cloth, and streaked linen for the males, with bleached linen for shirts. In the summer they generally wore brown tow or linen trowsers and frock; the latter being a kind of over shirt. The fulled cloth worn in the winter time though often coarse was warm. It was sometimes very decent in appearance when made of fine wool, well spun and well dressed. The females were clad in streaked linen or checked linen, on week days, and in chintzes and it may be muslins and silks on the Sabbath. The wedding gowns if not muslin were sometimes brocade or lutestring. Near the close of the last century silk was reeled and woven in Durham. For a considerable time the women wore cloaks of scarlet broadcloth. In the year 1800 women might be seen on the Sabbath riding or walking in the street or sitting at church having on these cloaks; a very comely and comfortable article of dress. Chaises were introduced into Durham about 1775 or '80. For some years there were only three chaises in the town. The people went to meeting on horseback, the women sitting behind the men on pillions. While this fashion continued every house had a horse-block. A characteristic of the houses built in the first half century after the settlement of Durham was the large kitchen fireplace, which in some cases was seven or eight feet in

* By Chauncey Fowler.

width, having sometimes one and sometimes two ovens in it, admitting back logs two or three feet in diameter, and three or four children into the chimney 'corners.' The large and steady fire on the hearth in such a fireplace shone on the faces of many a family circle, gathered together on a winter's evening. To many a large family of eight or ten children the hearth-stone was a load stone to draw them around it. There was knitting for the mother and the elder daughters. There were the slates for the older sons. There were apples and nuts for the younger children, or it may be a lesson in spelling. There were the two volumes from the Town Library for the father and others. There was story telling and song singing. There was the mug of cider enlivened by red pepper against cold. There was the family Bible and there was prayer before retiring to rest. In short, there were family government, family instruction, family amusement, and family religion."

FIGURE 254.
A Summer Costume, 1790–1795 (from a Contemporary Portrait).

REIGN OF GEORGE III AND FIRST YEARS OF THE REPUBLIC
1778–1790

FIGURE 255.—Copy of a suit worn at the Court of France by William West, Esq., of Philadelphia, in 1778. Coat and breeches are of uncut velvet of a delicate shade of mauve. The waistcoat is of white corded silk with a small embroidered figure scattered over it and a border of flowers in a contrasting colour.

FIGURE 256.—Costume of the prevailing French fashion so popular in the early days of our Republic, 1777–1779. The gown is of flowered silk or lawn looped over paniers; the underskirt of a plain colour, trimmed with a box plaiting of the same. The bodice is pointed sharply in front and laced with a silk cord through eyelet holes. In the back it is cut round about the waist without a point. The hair—still powdered in full dress—in this picture is arranged over a high cushion and finished with an embroidered muslin head-dress arranged like a turban and caught with a bunch of artificial flowers.

FIGURE 257.—Suit of drab cloth lined with green silk; waistcoat of striped silk. From a contemporary print, 1786.

FIGURE 258.—A muslin gown made with flowing skirt and a long-sleeved bodice. Kerchief is very bouffant and tucked into the dress in front. The large hat is of blue silk faced with green and has a soft puffed crown. The hair is powdered lightly after the fashion called "mouse colour," and hangs in the loose curls which were extremely fashionable at the time (1790) both in Europe and America.

FIGURE 255.   FIGURE 256.   FIGURE 257.   FIGURE 258.

On the occasion of the inauguration of Washington as President, in New York, his dress is described as of fine dark brown cloth of American manufacture, with white silk hose, shoes with silver buckles, and a dress sword. The ball which followed brought out all the finery the women of the young Republic could afford. This is the description given in "The Republican Court":

"NEW YORK, 1789.   INAUGURATION BALL.

"The costume of the time is very well illustrated by the portraits of the day, of which fortunately there are many, but some readers may be interested in the remarks on the dresses of the women which form a portion of Colonel Stone's description of the First Inauguration Ball. "Few jewels," he says, "were then worn in the United States, but in other respects the dresses were rich and beautiful, according to the fashion of the day. We are not quite sure that we can describe the full dress of a lady of rank in the period under consideration, so as to render it intelligible, but we will make the attempt. One favorite dress was a plain celestial blue satin gown with a white satin petticoat. On the neck was worn a large Italian gauze handkerchief, with border stripes of satin. The head-dress was a pouf of gauze, in the form of a globe, the *creneaux* or head piece of which was composed of white satin, having a double wing, in large plaits, and trimmed with a wreath of artificial roses, falling from the left at the top to the right at the bottom, in front, and the reverse behind. The hair was dressed all over in detached curls, four of which, in two ranks, fell on each side of the neck, and were relieved behind by a floating chignon. Another beautiful dress was a perriot made of gray Indian taffeta, with dark stripes of the same colour, having two collars, the one of yellow, and the other white, both trimmed with a blue silk fringe, and a revere trimmed in the same manner. Under the perriot was worn a yellow corset or bodice, with large cross stripes of blue. Some of the ladies wore hats *à l'Espagnole* of white satin, with a band of the same material placed on the crown, like a wreath of flowers on the head-dress above mentioned. This hat,

with a plume, a popular article of dress, was relieved on the left side, having two handsome cockades, one of which was at the top and the other at the bottom. On the neck was worn a very large plain gauze handkerchief, the end of which was hid under the bodice; after the manner represented in Trumbull's and Stuart's portraits of Lady Washington. Round the bosom of the perriot a fall of gauze, *à la Henri IV*, was attached, cut in points around the edge. There was still another dress which was thought to be very simple and pretty. It consisted of a perriot and a petticoat, both composed of the same description of gray striped silk, and trimmed

FIGURE 259.
Woman in Typical Working Dress, 1790–1800 (taken from Original Garment at Stenton, Philadelphia).

round with gauze, cut points at the edges in the manner of herrisons. The herrisons were indeed nearly the sole trimming used for perriots,

FIGURE 260.—White satin wedding slippers, 1800.

FIGURE 261.—Cups and saucers which belonged to Robert Treat Paine, one of the signers of the Declaration.

FIGURE 262.—Group of slippers, 1735, 1770, and 1780.

FIGURE 263.—Slippers of blue brocade worn by a Quaker bride in 1771.

FIGURE 264.—Wine-glasses and a piece of a point-lace ruffle belonging to John Wentworth, Governor of New Hampshire, from 1717 to 1730.

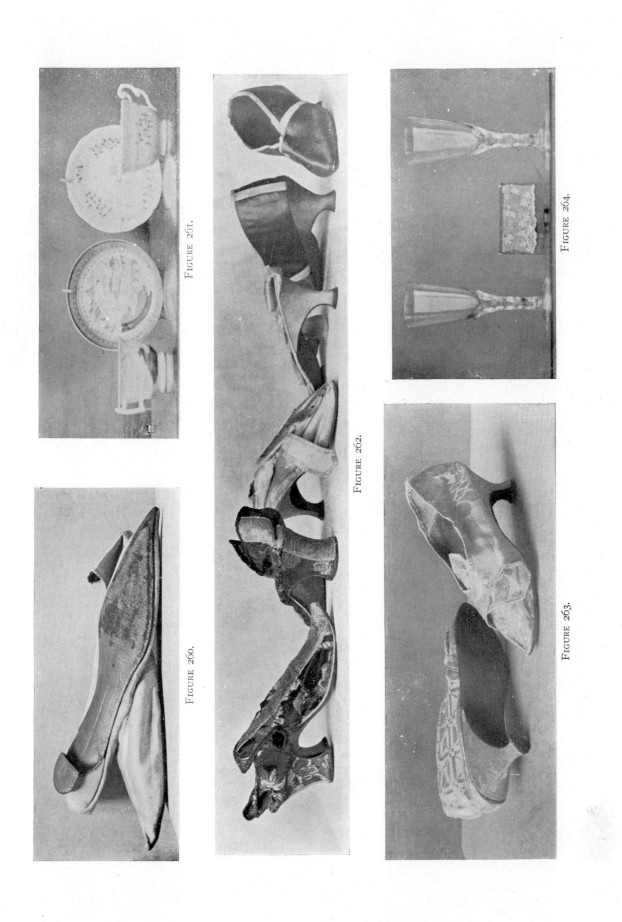

FIGURE 261.

FIGURE 264.

FIGURE 262.

FIGURE 260.

FIGURE 263.

caracos, and petticoats of fashionable ladies, made either of ribbons or Italian gauze. With this dress they wore large gauze handkerchiefs upon their necks, with four satin stripes around the border, two of which were narrow, and the other broad. The head-dress was a plain gauze cap, after the form of the elders and ancients of a nunnery. The shoes were celestial blue, with rose coloured rosettes. Such are descriptions of some of the principal costumes, and although varied in divers unimportant particulars, by several ladies, according to their respective tastes and fancies, yet as with the peculiar fashions of all other times, there was a general correspondence—the *tout ensemble* was the same."

A perriot was evidently an overdress. The name betrays the French influence, and as it is always mentioned in connection with a petticoat it probably opened in front like a polonaise or sacque.

It was so much the custom of the women of that time to write verses, that the following lines by Mrs. Warren * on the frivolities of 1790 have more interest on account of the theme than the literary style could possibly claim:

"Woman's Trifling Needs.

"An inventory clear
Of all she needs Lamira offers here;
Nor does she fear a rigid Cato's frown
When she lays by the rich embroidered gown,
And modestly compounds for just enough—
Perhaps, some dozens of more flighty stuff;
With lawns and lustrings, blond and Mechlin laces,
Fringes and jewels, fans and tweezer-cases;
Gay cloaks and hats of every shape and size,
Scarfs, cardinals, and ribbons of all dyes;
With ruffles stamped, and aprons of tambour,
Tippets and handkerchiefs, at least three score;
With finest muslins that fair India boasts,
And the choice herbage from Chinesan coasts;
(But while the fragrant Hyson leaf regales,

*Poems Dramatic and Miscellaneous.

Who'll wear the homespun produce of the vales?
For if 'twould save the nation from the curse
Of standing troops; or—name a plague still worse—
Few can this choice, delicious draught give up,
Though all Medea's poisons fill the cup.)
Add feathers, furs, rich satins and ducapes,
And head-dresses in pyramidal shapes;
Sideboards of plate and porcelain profuse,
With fifty dittos that the ladies use;
If my poor treacherous memory has missed,
Ingenious T——— shall complete the list.
So weak Lamira, and her wants so few,
Who can refuse?—they're but the sex's due.
In youth indeed, an antiquated page
Taught us the threatenings of an Hebrew sage
'Gainst wimples, mantles, curls, and crisping-pins,
But rank not these among our modern sins:
For when our manners are well understood,
What in the scale is stomacher or hood?
'Tis true, we love the courtly mien and air,
The pride of dress and all the debonair;
Yet Clara quits the more dressed negligee,
And substitutes the careless polanee;
Untill some fair one from Brittania's court,
Some jaunty dress or newer taste import;
This sweet temptation could not be withstood,
Though for the purchase paid her father's blood.

.   .   .   .

Can the stern patriot Clara's suit deny?
'Tis beauty asks, and reason must comply."

The portrait by Copley of Mercy Warren, reproduced as a frontis-piece to her biography in the popular series "Women of Colonial and Revolutionary Times," represents her in a brocade sacque richly trimmed with lace and a small fly cap, under which the hair is arranged low and without powder.

Mr. Wansey, the English traveller, describes a visit to the theatre in Philadelphia, which he said was "as elegant and convenient and large as Covent Garden. I should have thought myself still in England judging by the appearance of the company around me. The ladies wore small bonnets of the same fashion as those I saw in London—some of chequered straw; many had their hair full dressed, without caps, as with us, and very few had it in the French style. The younger ladies appeared with their hair flowing in ringlets on their shoulders (Figure 254). The gentlemen had round hats, coats with high collars, cut quite in the English fashion, and many coats of striped silk."

In 1795 a very decided change in women's dress is noted. Soft clinging materials superseded the stiff brocades and rustling silks. Gowns were made with narrow skirts and short bodices with long tight-fitting sleeves; the shoulders were generally uncovered, but muslin or gauze handkerchiefs were sometimes worn in the house, while for outdoor wear, long scarfs were put on around the shoulders and fell to the feet in front. Hair was worn in loose curls, generally caught up with a comb or knot of ribbon. Caps

FIGURE 265.
Back of Mauve Crêpe.

for elderly people were made in a variety of styles (Figures 224, 225, 253, 259).

In her memoirs, Elizabeth Bowne takes the trouble to describe just how the gowns of her day were made. In 1798 she writes to her family:

"The gown patterns I shall enclose, the one with a fan back is meant to just meet before and pin in the robings, no strings, belt or anything. The other pattern is a plain waist with strips of the same stitched on, and laced between with bobbin or cord. I have a muslin done so with black silk cord, which looks very handsome, and I have altered my brown silk into one like the other pat-

tern.   I was over at Saco yesterday and saw one Mary (King) had
made in Boston.   It was a separate waist, or rather the breadth did

not go quite up. The waist
was plain with one stripe of
cording let in behind and the
rest of the waist was perfectly
plain.   The skirt part was
plaited in box plaits three of a
side, which reached to the
shoulder straps and only enough
left to meet straight before, and
is one of the patterns I have
sent."

In Figure 341 the picture of
a dress is given which has an
interesting story connected with
it (Figure 265).

The owner, Mlle. Henrietta
Madeline l'Official de Wofoin
(afterwards Mrs. Sartori), was a
god-daughter of Queen Marie
Antoinette, her father being an
officer at the Court of Louis
XVI, who was sent to San
Domingo on official business
just before the outbreak of the
French Revolution.   Soon after
occurred the insurrection of the
Negroes against the whites in
San Domingo.   M. de Wofoin

FIGURE 266.
Pelisse of Sage-green Silk with Quilted Border
(from an Original Garment of 1797).

managed to escape to this country, but lost all traces of his daughter
in the excitement and knew nothing of her fate.   He made his way

Seventeenth Century Utensils.

Figure 267.—Charcoal foot-warmer
　　　　　　Four fat-oil lamps
　　　　　　One candle sconce
　　　　　　One tin lantern
　　　　　　One toaster.
Figure 268.—One sadiron
　　　　　　One charcoal tongs
　　　　　　Ladles, skimmer, and fork
　　　　　　Two trivets
　　　　　　Copper chopping-dish.

FIGURE 267.

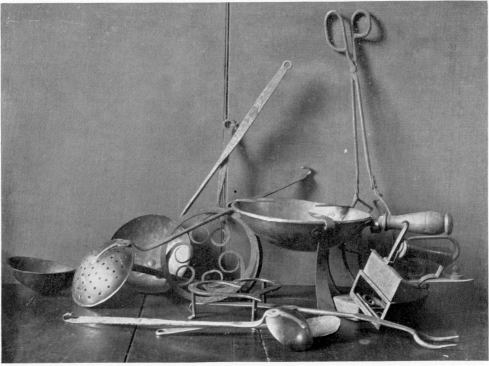

FIGURE 268.

to Trenton, New Jersey, and while there wandered one day into the market-place, where he met his daughter's old black nurse. She told him that she had brought "Mademoiselle" to America and also to Trenton. Shortly after young Sartori, who had been sent from Rome by his father to visit this country, arrived at Trenton and fell in love with Mademoiselle. They were married and lived at Lambertville, New Jersey. Mrs. Sartori died at the age of forty, having been the mother of fifteen children. The original gown from which this picture is taken has been most kindly lent to us for this book, by a direct descendant of the heroine of the story.

A dress of a quaint cut and of a fine glazed cotton unknown to-day came from Martinique with Madame Chevalier, who became a pensioner at Christ Church Hospital, Philadelphia, in the last years of the eighteenth century (Figures 248, 342).

This fashion of short waists and narrow skirts for women (Figures 341, 342, 344) and high-collared coats short at the waist for men marked the end of the eighteenth century.

CHILDREN'S GARMENTS
1700–1800

FINERY

In a frock neatly trimmed with beautiful lace,
And hair nicely dressed, hanging over her face,
Thus decked, Harriet went to the house of a friend,
With a large *little* party the evening to spend.

"Ah! how they will all be delighted, I guess,
And stare with surprise at my elegant dress";
Thus said the vain girl, and her little heart beat,
Impatient the happy young party to meet.

But alas! they were all too intent on their fun
To observe the gay clothes this fine lady had on;
And thus all her trouble quite lost its design,
For they saw she was proud, but forgot she was fine.

'T was Lucy, though only in simple white clad
(Nor trimmings, nor laces, nor jewels she had),
Whose cheerful good-nature delighted them more
Than all the fine garments that Harriet wore.

'Tis better to have a sweet smile on one's face
Than to wear a rich frock with an elegant lace,
For the good-natured girl is loved best in the main
If her dress is but decent, though ever so plain.

—J. T.

Children's Garments

1700–1800

HE clothes of the children of the eighteenth century were marvellously made and quaintly resembled the garments of their parents. From many authorities we learn that children wore stays in Colonial times, and one interesting specimen, of which a picture is given in Figures 280 and 281, has been most kindly lent for this book. This particular pair of stays was evidently worn by a child of about two years old. One little gown of which I cannot learn the exact history, although it belonged to the family of James Logan, is made with elbow sleeves and square neck, the bodice evidently to be worn over stays, and the skirt opening over a petticoat. This is made of flowered chintz. (Figure 271.) Another child's dress is made in the same style, but the bodice opens over a sort of stomacher in front, and the material is of heavy damask linen. The sleeves of this gown are finished at the cuffs with three tiny buttons, worked over with linen thread (Figure 272).

Dresses of a little later period, probably 1750, are made with even greater skill, of fine white cambric with low necks and short sleeves fastened up with buttons and loops of narrow tape on the shoulder. They are ornamented with groups of the very tiniest tucks, with cording and tambour embroidery.   Caps, which babies wore both by day and night, are also of exquisite needlework.   Socks, worked with the initials of the baby, were knitted of fine white silk.   One little pair of this kind is owned by the Pennsylvania Society of Colonial Dames, which was worn in babyhood by Isaac Norris, Speaker of the Continental Congress.   Little mitts of linen were worn by these babies too.   The pictures given here are of mitts worn in Pennsylvania by babies of the Norris and Logan families (Figures 272, 277). One minute pair is marked in red silk with the initials J. L. in monogram.   A quaint little gown of buff chintz with flowers in different colours scattered over it is given in Figure 276.   This was worn by a child of two years in the West family.

In the Museum of Memorial Hall, Philadelphia, there is a child's quilted hood of about 1760 made of dark blue silk, and some charming little gowns and caps of even earlier date may be seen in the Museum of the Colonial Dames at Stenton, Philadelphia (Figures 271, 272).

Very interesting are the infant dress and cap shown in Figure 286, not only on account of the skilled needlework, but also for the history associated with them.   The baby for whom these clothes were made so beautifully grew in time to be a patriotic doctor in New York, and being called upon one day, in 1789, to apply a fly blister to the chest of our great Washington, he mounted the poultice on a piece of white kid and decorated the edges with a pattern in gold leaf.   As he was in the act of placing the plaster the illustrious patient startled him by the question, "Will it draw any better for the decoration, young man?"   We are told that the doctor finished his work in great confusion, but he lived to be proud of the opportunity which has lent an additional interest even to his baby clothes.   It must be confessed that our picture fails to show the exquisite drawn-work where the threads of sheerest muslin have been drawn at intervals to form a stripe of open work and a delicate pattern embroidered

REIGNS OF QUEEN ANNE, GEORGE I, II AND III
1702-1790

FIGURE 270.—A girl in a red stuff gown and muslin cap, about 1730.

FIGURE 271.—Child in a printed gown and embroidered cap taken from a genuine little costume preserved in the Logan family, date about 1710.

FIGURE 272.—Child in a gown of white damask linen with mitts and embroidered cape, date about 1720. This and the costume shown in Figure 271 can be seen at Stenton, Philadelphia.

FIGURE 273.—Little boy in a suit of blue silk, lace ruffles, and powdered wig, date 1740.

FIGURE 274.—Little boy in brown velvet suit and cocked hat, about 1760.

FIGURE 275.—Boy in a blue ribbed silk suit lined with green, which is copied from an original costume now in the Colonial Museum in Independence Hall, Philadelphia. The coat has filigree silver buttons. He has on a waistcoat of flowered dimity. The hair is tied in a queue and is not powdered, date about 1756.

FIGURE 276.—Child in a buff printed cambric dress, with thin muslin kerchief and cap. This is also an original gown, date about 1760.

FIGURE 277.—Child in sheer muslin gown trimmed with tambour embroidery with cap to match, about 1790.

FIGURE 278.—Little girl in cloak, muff, and hat, after Sir Joshua Reynold's picture—1780.

FIGURE 279.—Young girl in a muslin gown trimmed with a very elaborate pattern of embroidery in white cotton. This is from an original garment of 1790.

FIGURE 270.   FIGURE 271.   FIGURE 272.   FIGURE 273.   FIGURE 274.

FIGURE 275.   FIGURE 276.   FIGURE 277.   FIGURE 278.   FIGURE 279.

on the filmy mesh (Figure 286).   A simple everyday slip of printed cotton, white ground with a pin dot of red, belonged to the same baby.*

Until the latter part of the eighteenth century it was customary to dress children exactly like their parents.   This we learn from old portraits, and very uncomfortable must the powdered wigs and lace stocks have been at a Royal Juvenile Party such as Queen Caroline

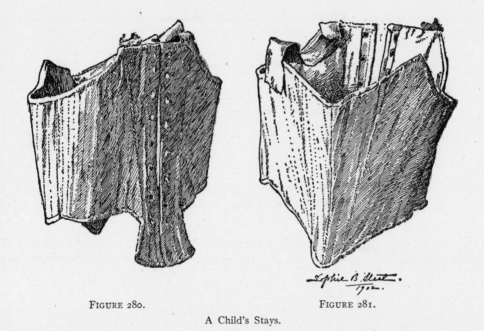

FIGURE 280.   FIGURE 281.

A Child's Stays.

delighted in giving for the diversion of her large family of prince-lings, where the children were dressed in miniature copies of their parents' court costumes.†

In the Colonies the dress of the children was strangely elaborate.

In the collection of Washington's manuscripts (edited by Ford) are two lists of clothes ordered for the Custis children at the tender ages of four and six, which would startle a modern nursery.   Washington

* Samuel Holden Parsons Lee, born in Connecticut, 1771.

† Chronicles of Fashion.

ordered for young Custis, his stepson (aged six), the following outfit from England in 1759:

> One piece Irish Holland at 4s
> Two yards fine cambric at 10s
> Six pocket handkerchiefs small and fine
> Six pairs gloves
> Two laced hats
> Two pieces India Nankeen
> Six pairs fine thread stockings
> Four pairs coarser thread stockings
> Six pairs worsted stockings
> Four pairs pumps
> One summer suit of clothes to be made of something light and thin
> One piece of black hair ribbon
> One pair handsome silver shoe and knee buckles
> One light duffel cloak with silver frogs

And for little Nellie Custis, then at the age of four, the following articles were ordered:

> Eight yards fine printed linen at 3s 6d
> One piece Irish Holland at 4s
> Two ells of fine Holland at 10s
> Eight pairs kid mits
> Four pairs gloves
> Two pairs silk shoes
> Four pairs Calamanco shoes
> Four pairs leather pumps
> Six pairs fine thread stockings
> Four pairs fine worsted stockings
> Two fans
> Two masks
> Two bonnets
> One stiffened coat of fashionable silk made to pack thread stays
> One-half piece of flowered Dimity
> Two yards fine cambric at 10s
> Two caps
> Two pairs ruffles
> Two tucker bibs and aprons, if fashionable.

In addition to this order for suitable clothing and materials, the great man, under whose beneficent care it was the good fortune of the

FIGURE 282.—A portrait of a young girl in Philadelphia, about 1760.

FIGURE 283.—A portrait of Miss Hill of Philadelphia, about 1756.

FIGURE 284.—A portrait of a child in the New York Colony, about 1700.

FIGURE 285.—Picture of a girl in New York Colony early in the eighteenth century—Christiana Ten Broeck.

FIGURE 282.

FIGURE 283.

FIGURE 284

FIGURE 285.

Custis children to come, added 10s. worth of toys, six little books for children beginning to read, one fashionably dressed baby, 10s. 1d., and other toys, 10s.

In New England, too, children were most richly attired; and we read with amazement of a boarding-school outfit provided for two maidens of Norwich.

"The daughters of General Huntington were sent successively at the ages of twelve and fourteen years to finish their education at a boarding-school in Boston. The lady who kept the establishment was of high social standing, and made a point of taking her pupils often into company, that their manners might be formed according to the prevailing codes of politeness and etiquette. Of course the

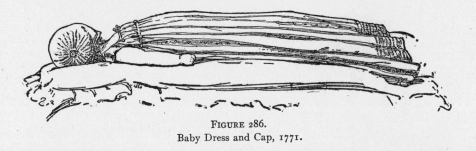

FIGURE 286.
Baby Dress and Cap, 1771.

wardrobe prepared for the young ladies was rich in articles of ornament and display. One of the daughters who had been carefully fitted out with twelve silk gowns, had been but a short time in Boston when her instructress wrote to her parents requesting that another dress should be procured for her, made of a certain rich fabric that had recently been imported, in order that her appearance in society might be equal to her rank. A thirteenth robe of silk of an exquisite pattern was therefore immediately procured and forwarded." *

"Little misses at a dancing-school ball (for these were almost the only *fêtes* that fell to their share in the days of discrimination) were dressed in frocks of lawn or cambric. Worsted was then thought

* History of Norwich.

dress enough for common days,"* the famous annalist tells us, in speaking of Philadelphia children in the Revolutionary period.

Marie Antoinette was the first mother to disregard the established court fashion. She had a simple suit of jacket and trousers made for the Dauphin, but the Chronicle of Fashion assures us that "even this, probably the most sensible of all the ill-fated Queen's innovations in dress, was reviled as if the paraphernalia of full dress was a moral obligation."

FIGURE 287.
Boy in Ordinary Dress, 1790.

In the portraits of English children in the latter part of the century, we become familiar with costumes at once simple and picturesque, as in Figures 269, 277, 278, 279, 287. Copley's well-known family group, and the picture of his family by Benjamin West (Figure 225), are satisfactory evidence of the adoption of these appropriate fashions for the children of the Colonies.

Figures 284 and 285 are photographed from portraits of two little girls in the New York Colony during the reign of Queen Anne, in gowns so stiff and so unsuitable they would have baffled even the graceful brush of a Reynolds or a Romney.

* Watson's Annals.

FIGURE 288.—Picture of a garment called a "flying Josie," made of white cambric and worn in Pennsylvania late in the eighteenth century.

FIGURE 289.—Back view of the same.

FIGURE 290.—A suit of blue silk, with buttonholes of silver thread, worn by a little boy in Pennsylvania, about 1756.

FIGURE 291.—Picture of a child's dress, buff chintz with coloured flowers, worn in Pennsylvania about 1710.

FIGURE 292.—Picture of a white shift, the sleeves of which are laid in fine plaits, to be worn under a gown with elbow sleeves and square neck. The ruffle at neck is of very fine linen cambric, and made to turn down over the dress, as in Figure 195.

FIGURE 293.—A child's dress of damask linen, with linen mittens, worn in Pennsylvania about 1720.

(Photographed from original garments.)

FIGURE 288.

FIGURE 289.

FIGURE 290.

FIGURE 291.

FIGURE 292.

FIGURE 293.

MEN'S APPAREL

1700–1800

During the Time of
Queen Anne, George I, II, and III of England,
Presidents Washington and Adams
of the United States

GOVERNOR WENTWORTH.

"A portly person, with three-cornered hat,
A crimson velvet coat, head high in air,
Gold-headed cane and nicely powdered hair,
And diamond buckles sparkling at his knees,
Dignified, stately, florid, much at ease.
For this was Governor Wentworth, driving down
To Little Harbour, just beyond the town,
Where his great house stood, looking out to sea,
A goodly place, where it was good to be.
It was a pleasant mansion, an abode
Near and yet hidden from the great highroad;
Sequestered among trees, a noble pile,
Baronial and Colonial in its style!

Within, unwonted splendours met the eye,
Panels and floors of oak, and tapestry;
Carved chimney pieces, where, on brazen dogs,
Revelled and roared the Christmas fire of logs;
Doors opening into darkness unawares,
Mysterious passages and flights of stairs;
And on the walls, in heavy gilded frames,
The ancestral Wentworths, with old Scripture names.
Such was the mansion where the great man dwelt.

He gave a splendid banquet served on plate
Such as became the Governor of the State
Who represented England and the King,
And was magnificent in everything."
                            —"*The Poet's Tale.*"

Men's Apparel

1700–1800

FIGURE 294.

ERIWIGS and cocked hats were the characteristic features of the dress of men in the first half of the eighteenth century.

REIGNS OF QUEEN ANNE AND GEORGE I

Under Queen Anne the hats worn by men were smaller and were regularly cocked on three sides, and the cuffs of the coats were very wide and long, reaching almost to the wrist. The broad sword belt had vanished, and the sword hilt could be seen beneath the stiffened skirt of the square-cut coat (Figure 163). Blue or scarlet silk stockings, with gold or silver clocks, were much worn, as were also shoes with red heels and small buckles (Figure 163); velvet garters were worn over the stockings below the knee, being fastened on one side by small buckles (Figure 163). Campaign wigs imported from France now became popular. They were made very full with long curls hanging towards the front (Figure 163). When human hair was scarce, a little horsehair supplied the place, in the part least in sight.

In 1706 a peculiar cock of the hat came into fashion called the Ramilie, and a long plaited tail to the wig with a great bow at the top and a small one at the bottom known as the Ramilie wig (Figure 299).

Those who did not wear powder and who objected to the

299

enormous expense or weight of the fashionable wigs, wore their own hair in long curls to resemble them, but the long popularity of the uncomfortable fashion of the periwig is indeed astonishing.

Dr. Granger in his Life of Charles II, speaking of the fashion when it first came into vogue, says: "It was observed that a periwig procured many persons a respect and even veneration which they were strangers to before and to which they had not the least claims from their personal merit," and he quotes the amusing anecdote of a country gentleman who employed a painter to place periwigs upon the heads of several of Vandyke's portraits. Large wigs were worn until the middle of the eighteenth century. A plain peruke imitating a natural head of hair was called a short bob.

A facetious barber in London had the following rhyme painted on the sign over his door:*

"Oh Absolom, Oh Absolom,
Oh Absolom my son,
If thou hadst worn a periwig
Thou hadst not been undone."

The ridiculous long wigs of 1710 were decidedly expensive. One is mentioned in "The Tatler" costing 40 guineas.

We read that in Philadelphia early in the eighteenth century men were wearing "cocked hats, and wigs, coats with large cuffs, big skirts, lined and stiffened with buckram. The coat of a beau had three or four large plaits in the skirt, wadded almost like a coverlet to keep them smooth, cuffs very large up to the elbows, the collars were flat and low, so as readily to expose the close plaited neck-stock of fine linen cambric and the large silver stock-buckle on the back of the neck, shirts with hand ruffles, sleeves finely plaited, breeches close fitted, with silver, stone or paste buckles, shoes or pumps with silver buckles of various sizes and patterns, thread, worsted and silk stockings. The very boys often wore wigs, and their clothing in general was similar to that of the men."

* Hone's Every Day Book.

FIGURE 295.—Portrait of Kiliaen Van Rensselaer, Second Patroon and First Lord of the Manor of Rensselaerwyck, 1663–1719, showing coat worn in the reign of Queen Anne. (From the original painting.)

FIGURE 296.—Jan Baptist Van Rensselaer, Director of the Manor of Rensselaerwyck, showing a coat with cuffs reaching above the elbow, in reign of George I. (From the original painting.)

FIGURE 296.

FIGURE 295.

In the year 1719 Jonathan Dickinson, a Friend, in writing to London for his clothes, says, "I want for myself and my three sons, each a wig—good light bobs."

The reign of George I offers no distinctive changes for remark. Wigs held their ground, and in 1720 white hair for the manufacture of them "brought a monstrous price."

Heavy cloaks or Roquelaures were still worn by men and were often trimmed with fur. Mention is made in letters from New England about 1720 of a striped camlet cloak lined with a plain colour. Drugget was also used for the purpose (Figure 297).

The ordinary costume of gentlemen during the reigns of Queen Anne and George I is thus briefly summed up by M. Planché in his "History of British Costume." He says: "Square cut coats and long flapped waistcoats with pockets in them, the latter meeting the stockings, still drawn up over the knee so high as entirely to conceal the breeches, but gartered below it; large hanging cuffs and

FIGURE 297.
Taken from a Genuine Roquelaure, Middle of the Eighteenth Century.

lace ruffles.　The skirt of the coat stiffened out with wire or buckram from beneath which peeped the hilt of the sword deprived of the cord and splendid belt in which it swung in the preceding Reigns. Blue or scarlet silk stockings with gold or silver clocks.　Lace neck-cloths, square-toed, short quartered shoes, with high red heels and small buckles; very long and formally curled perukes (or periwigs), black riding wigs, and night cap wigs; small three cornered hats laced with gold or silver galloons, and sometimes trimmed with feathers comprised the habit of the noblemen and gentlemen from 1702 to 1724."

As in all ages and all climes, variations of the prevailing style were indulged in by gay young men about town.　The pet extravagance at this period was beautiful lace in ruffles and neckties.

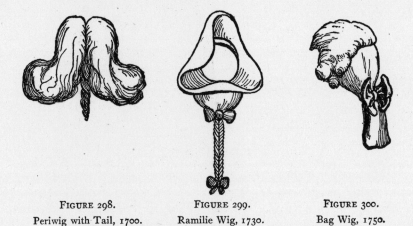

FIGURE 298.　　　　FIGURE 299.　　　　FIGURE 300.
Periwig with Tail, 1700.　Ramilie Wig, 1730.　Bag Wig, 1750.

Queen Anne had a zealous care for the English church in America and took personal pleasure in sending beautiful services of silver to parishes in all her colonies.　Many of these may be seen to-day with an historic inscription and the Queen's initials engraved in the simple script of her time.　In her reign the dress of the English clergyman was inconspicuous but distinctive, and with slight modifications was worn by the majority of clergymen in America.　Knee-breeches fitting close, buckled shoes, long black coats, and wigs were the prevailing characteristics in everyday life.　In connection with the portrait

FIGURE 301.—Portrait of William Penn, Proprietor and Governor of Pennsylvania Province. (By Benjamin West.)

FIGURE 302.—Portrait of George Washington, First President of the United States. (By Gilbert Stuart, 1797.)

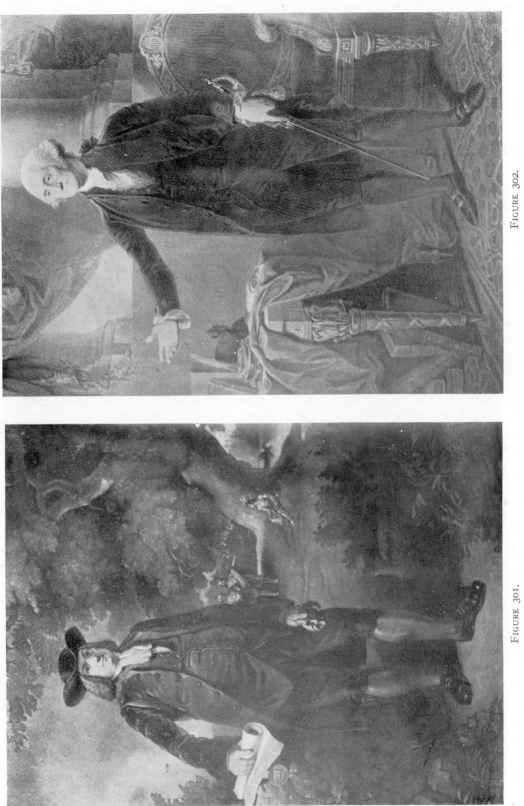

FIGURE 302.

FIGURE 301.

of Bishop White of Pennsylvania given in Figure 358, it is interesting to recall the story told by himself of his appointment as chaplain to the Continental Congress. He was riding with a friend when a messenger from Congress overtook him. He hesitated for a few moments, realizing the danger of enrolling himself with the cause of the patriots, but after a short deliberation he turned his horse's head and accompanied the emissary to General Washington's headquarters before Yorktown.* It was a brave step which he never regretted, and his name has ever been associated with the early sessions of our Congress in Philadelphia. Bishop White was consecrated at Lambeth Palace in 1787, and, despite his republican partisanship, amid many tokens of good will on the part of the king and others.

REIGN OF GEORGE II

There are numerous authorities for the costume of George II's reign, but the versatile genius of Hogarth † alone has furnished us with sufficient material for a study of the dress of all classes and conditions of the English men and women of his day. His "Five Orders of Periwigs" gives us the favorite varieties of that style of head-gear, which was certainly a very expensive fashion, for in 1734 we read that in the Colonies periwigs of light gray human hair were four guineas each. Light grizzle ties were three guineas, and other colours in proportion, down to twenty-five shillings. Light gray human hair cue-perukes were from two guineas to fifteen shillings each, and bob perukes of the same material a little dearer, real gray hair being most in fashion, and dark of "no estimation."

The court dress of noblemen in 1735 is described as a coat made of coloured velvet or fine cloth laced with gold or silver, breeches to match; waistcoat of rich flowered silk of a large pattern on a white ground. Wigs were still worn with large curls standing up from the forehead (Figure 296).

* Simpson's Lives of Eminent Philadelphians. † Born 1697; died 1764.

Fairholt in his "History of English Dress" says: "By the cock of the hat, the man who wore it was known; and they varied

from the modest broad brim of the clergy and country-man to the slightly upturned hat of the country gentleman or citizen, or the more decidedly fashionable cock worn by merchantmen, and would-be-fashionable Londoners; while a very pronounced *à la militaire* cock was affected by the gallant about the court." All of these styles may be seen in the pictures of Hogarth. These hats were usually made of soft felt with a large brim caught up by three loops of cord to a button on the top. Being soft, they could be crushed under the arm and each flap could be let down at pleasure in case of

FIGURE 303.

Back View of Figure 229, Middle Eighteenth Century (from the Original Costume).

wind, or rain, or sun. Mr. Wingfield speaks of a hat "unlooped although it doth not rain," and observes that in one of Cibber's

FIGURE 304.—Portrait of Rev. George Whitefield, showing the gown and wig worn in New England by a clergyman of the English church in the latter half of the eighteenth century.

FIGURE 305.—Portrait of Rev. Jacob Duché, D.D., showing a gown and close wig worn in Pennsylvania late in the eighteenth century.

FIGURE 306.—Portrait of Dr. Ezra Stiles, in periwig and gown worn in New England late in the eighteenth century.

FIGURE 307.—Portrait of Rt. Rev. Richard Challoner, Vicar Apostolic of the English Colonies in America, 1756, showing that wigs were worn by the priests of the Roman Catholic Church of that date.

FIGURE 308.—Portrait of Jonathan Edwards, showing the plain coat and bands of a Presbyterian minister, second half of the eighteenth century.

FIGURE 309.—Portrait of Rt. Rev. Samuel Provoost, D.D., First Bishop of New York, showing the white wig, full sleeves, and black gown, late eighteenth century.

FIGURE 304.

FIGURE 305.

FIGURE 306.

FIGURE 307.

FIGURE 308.

FIGURE 309.

comedies we find a footman "unlooping his hat to protect his powdered head from the wet."

To use the snuff-box gracefully was an accomplishment considered necessary to the young man of fashion on his entrance into the gay world of the eighteenth century. Made of every sort of metal, adorned with precious stones or costly miniature paintings, the snuff-box was in great demand, and considered as indispensable on occasions of full dress as the fan. Many of these boxes which were used in the Colonies have been preserved. In Figure 239 is given a picture of one owned by Madame Le Comte, for the fashion of using snuff was not confined to men.

A beau of this time is spoken of as "appearing in a different style of wig every day, and thus perplexing the lady to whom he was paying his addresses, by a new face every time they met during the first months of their courtship. Hats could be moulded in so many different cocks as to change the whole appearance of the wearer." *

Hats had broader brims (Figure 197) and "were cocked triangularly, and pulling them off by way of salutation was invariably the fashion for all who had any breeding," according to a famous letterwriter of that day. Boots were worn for riding, with large broad tops which reached half-way up the thigh.

The fashionable costume for men in the Colonies, identical with the prevailing style in England, was not subject to quite as many changes as the dress of the women.

In 1740 a "jockey coat" was ordered from Boston of fine cloth with waistcoat and breeches to match. It is "to be trimmed plain, only with a button of the same sort as that of the waistcoat but proportionately bigger." The same gentleman ordered "as much three pile black velvet as is made for men's wear, and the best that can be had for the money, as much as will make a complete suit." In

* The Spectator.

14

addition to this he desires a night-gown of a deep crimson Genoa damask lined with the same colour.

About this time there was a slight change in shoes. Square toes went out of fashion and were replaced by pointed toes for both sexes. (See Figures 229, 231.) Buckles became the ambition of all classes, and were worn of every size and shape.

Claret coloured cloth was at that time considered the correct thing for suits, and light blue with silver button-holes and silver garters at the knees, was also very fashionable between 1740 and 1751.

Pigtails came into fashion about the middle of the eighteenth century.

> "'But pray what's that much like a whip,
> Which with the air does wav'ring skip
> From side to side, and hip to hip?'
> 'Sir, do not look so fierce and big
> It is a modish pigtail wig.'"

Instead of swords, many of the gay young sparks carried long oak sticks with ugly faces carved on the handles.

One of the marked characteristics of the men of fashion in the eighteenth century was a mincing air. We read of Horace Walpole that "he always entered a room with that style of affected delicacy which fashion had made almost natural; with *chapeau-bras* between his hands as if he wished to compress it, or under his arm; knees bent, and feet on tip-toe as if afraid of a wet floor."*

About 1740 the large cocked hat and full-bottomed wig went out of style, and the lace cravat with long ends, which had been in fashion for about thirty years, gave place to a small black cravat worn with a ruffled shirt front (Figure 197.) There was a change in the coat also. A broad collar which turned back round the neck contrasted strangely with the total want of collar in the earlier style, while the cuffs became very deep, reaching above the elbows and not very wide at the wrists. The coat itself fitted close to the body with skirt reaching to the calf of the leg. This change of style did not

* Miss Hawkins' Memoirs.

FIGURE 310.—Back view of a coat of light brown velvet figured in red and green, showing the very full tails of George II's reign.

FIGURE 311.—Front view of the same. Worn by Robert Livingston, Esq., of Clermont Manor, New York Colony.

FIGURES 312 and 313—Front and back views of a coat of brown twilled cotton jean, typical summer garment of a Friend.

(Photographed from original garments.)

FIGURE 310.

FIGURE 311.

FIGURE 312.

FIGURE 313.

long remain popular even in England. In prints of 1744 we again notice the wide cuffs and wider hat brims of a few years before.

About 1750 muff-tees, or little woolen muffs of various colours, were used by men in the Colonies. They were "just big enough to admit both hands and long enough to screen the wrists, which were then more exposed than now; for they wore short sleeves to their coats on purpose to display their fine plaited linen shirt sleeves with their gold cuff buttons and on occasions ruffles of lace." (Figures 182, 214.)

In the summer season men often wore calico morning gowns at all times of the day in the street as well as at home. A damask banyan was much the same thing by another name.

We can hardly

FIGURE 314.
Gentleman in Banyan and Cap.

wonder that in Virginia and the southern colonies the hot wigs and cumbrous petticoats prescribed by fashion were often found too uncomfortable for daily wear, and we read with a certain sense of relief, of a negligée costume of banyans and nightcaps adopted by the planters and their wives.

The climate must be remembered as a potent inducement to go without the long curled wigs and wadded coats; and, alas, the discomfort of stiff stays and voluminous petticoats in an American summer!

REIGN OF GEORGE III

In 1760, when wigs were powdered, they were frequently sent for that purpose in a wooden box to the barber to be dressed on his blockhead. "Brown wigs," for which a brown powder was used, were worn, but were less fashionable than "the white disguise."

On ceremonious occasions, if wigs were not worn, the hair was craped, curled, and powdered by barbers.

About 1770, when wigs went out of favour and the natural hair was preferred, it became the fashion to dress it in a queue, or to wear it in a black silk bag tied with a bow of black ribbon (Figures 303, 318, 352, 353, 354, 355).

With the queues belong frizzled sidelocks, and toupées formed of the natural hair, or in the absence of a long tie a splice was added to it (Figures 352, 353, 354, 355). Such was the general passion for the longest possible whip of hair, that sailors and boatmen used to tie theirs in eel skins to aid its growth.

A curious silhouette of Washington by Folwell represents him with what is supposed to be a fine net worn over hair and queue to keep the powder in place (Figure 357).

A colonial item of interest is gleaned from Washington's manuscripts. In 1759 he ordered from England for his own use:

"A New-market great coat with a loose hood (Figure 364) to it, made of Blew Drab or broadcloth with straps before, according to the present taste—let it be made of such cloth as will turn a good shower of rain."

FIGURE 315.—Portrait of John Penn, Colonial Governor, showing fur-trimmed coat.

FIGURE 316.—Portrait of Thomas Penn, Colonial Governor.

FIGURE 317.—Portrait of Patrick Gordon, Colonial Governor.

FIGURE 318.—Portrait of James Hamilton, Lieutenant Governor of Pennsylvania, 1783.

FIGURE 315.

FIGURE 316.

FIGURE 317.

FIGURE 318.

"A light summer suit of Duroy by the measure,
Four pieces best India nankeen,
Two best plain beaver hats at 20s.
One piece of black satin ribbon,
  1 sword belt, red morocco or buff, no buckles or rings,"

are also ordered on the same date.

In Watson's "Annals of Philadelphia" we read: "Coats of red cloth were considerably worn, even by boys, and plush breeches and plush vests of various colours, were in common use. Everlasting, or durant, made of worsted, was a fabric of great use for breeches, and sometimes for vests which had great depending pocket flaps, and the breeches were very short above the stride because the art of suspending them by suspenders was unknown. It was then the test of a well-formed man, that he could by his natural form readily keep his breeches above his hips, and his stockings without gartering, above the calf of the leg.

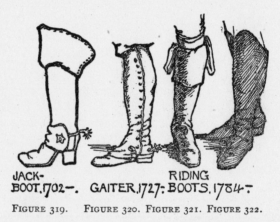

JACK-   RIDING
BOOT.1702-. GAITER.1727: BOOTS.1784:

FIGURE 319.   FIGURE 320. FIGURE 321. FIGURE 322.

"In the time of the Revolutionary war many of the American officers introduced the use of Dutch blankets for great coats (Figure 364). Large silver buttons worn on coats and vests were a mark of wealth. Some people had the initials of their names engraved on each button. Sometimes they were made out of real quarter dollars, with the coinage impression still retained; these were used for the coats, and the eleven-penny-bits for vests and breeches. One old gentleman wore an entire suit decorated with conch shell buttons, silver mounted."

In New England before the Revolution, "powdered wigs full and curled were worn by clergymen and other dignitaries (Figures 304,

306, 307, 308, 317, 326, 329). A full-dress suit for a gentleman was usually made of silk, with trimmings of gold and silver lace, the waistcoat often richly embroidered."* Roquelaures and great coats were worn of cloth or camlet in all the colonies.

Mr. Sydney George Fisher, the historian, despite his Quaker ancestry, exclaims with unwonted enthusiasm: "Those were brave days when the judges on the bench wore scarlet robes faced with black; when the tailor shops, instead of the dull-coloured woolens which they now offer, advertised, as in the New York Gazetteer of May 13, 1773, 'scarlet, buff, green, blue, crimson, white, sky blue, and other coloured superfine cloths'; when John Hancock, of penmanship fame, is described in his home in Boston with a red velvet skull-cap lined with white linen which was turned over the edge of the velvet about three inches deep, a blue damask dressing-gown lined with silk, a white stock, satin embroidered waistcoat, black satin breeches, white silk stockings to his knees, and red morocco slippers."†

The first umbrellas to keep off the rain were of oiled linen, very coarse and clumsy, with rattan sticks. Before their time some physicians and ministers used an oiled linen cape hooked round their shoulders, looking not unlike the big coat-capes now in use. They were only used for severe storms, like modern water-proofs.

We believe it was about the year 1771 that the first efforts were made in Philadelphia to introduce the use of umbrellas in summer as a protection from the sun. "They were then scouted in the public 'Gazette' as a ridiculous effeminacy. On the other hand, the physicians recommended them to keep off vertigoes, epilepsies, sore eyes, fevers, etc."

Watches were worn in fob pockets with seals attached by a ribbon, but they were not in common use until the end of the century.‡

* History of Norwich, by F. M. Caulkins.
† Men, Women, and Manners of Colonial Days.
‡ Watson's Annals.

FIGURE 323.—Portrait of James Logan, showing white wig and judicial robe, worn in Pennsylvania, 1745.

FIGURE 324.—Portrait of Fisher Ames, showing a plain costume of the middle of the eighteenth century.

FIGURE 325.—Portrait of John Jay in his robes as First Chief Justice of the United States.

FIGURE 326.—Portrait of Nathaniel Appleton of Boston, showing white wig with puffs at side. (By Copley.)

FIGURE 327.—Portrait of Henry Laurens. (By Copley.)

FIGURE 323.

FIGURE 324.

FIGURE 325.

FIGURE 326.

FIGURE 327.

Of New York in the eighteenth century we read: "Whether it be in the journals of visitors or in private correspondence, we always get the impression of a lively and cheerful town, where people like to come and from which they are sorry to go away. In the old days, indeed, there was a restful sense of leisure which the rapid pace of modern life has ruthlessly destroyed."*

Although the style of living in colonial New York was comfortable, with little display, when we come to the subject of dress, we find the case was very different. Early in the eighteenth century the streets of New York were gorgeous with elaborate costumes.

Gay masculine garments are described in inventories: Green silk breeches, flowered with silver and gold, silver gauze breeches, yellow fringed gloves, lacquered hats, laced shirts and neck-cloths.

From 1760 to 1770, gentlemen in Massachusetts were wearing "hats with broad brims turned up into three corners with loops at the sides; long coats with large pocket-folds and cuffs, and without collars.

FIGURE 328.
Working Garb, Middle Eighteenth Century, 1750.

* Dutch and Quaker Colonies, by Fiske.

(Figures 327 and 334.) The buttons were commonly plated, but sometimes of silver, often as large as a half-dollar. Shirts had bosom and wrist ruffles; and all wore gold or silver shirt-buttons at the wrist united by a link. The waistcoat was long, with large pockets; and the neckcloth or scarf was of fine white linen or figured stuff broidered and the ends hanging loosely on the breast. The breeches fitted close, with silver buckles at the knees. The legs were covered with gray knitted stockings which on holidays were exchanged for black or white silk. Boots with broad white tops, or shoes with straps and large silver buckles, completed the equipment."* It seems strange indeed that, during the eighteenth century when men had so much fighting on hand, they should have paid such attention to dress and fashion, but abundant proof exists in the letters and diaries of the day that every detail, the width of the cuff, the length of the cravat, the size even of the button-holes, was to the masculine mind a matter of grave import. Apparently the sword knot received as much attention as the sword. Even "the greatest American," in his youthful days, paid exact attention to details.

"Memorandum: To have my coat made by the following directions; to be made a frock with the lapel breast, the lapel to contain on each side six button-holes, and to be about five or six inches wide all the way, equal, and to turn as the breast of the coat does, to have it made very long waisted and in length to come down below the bend of the knee. The waist from the arm-pit to the fold to be exactly as long or longer than from thence to the bottom, not to have more than one fold in the skirt and the top to be made to turn in, and three button-holes, the laps at the top to turn as the cape of the coat, and bottom to come parallel with the button-holes, the last button-hole in the breast to be right opposite to the button on the hip."† At this time Washington was only a boy of fifteen.

* History of Lynn, Mass., by Lewis and Newhall.
† The writings of George Washington, edited by W. C. Ford.

FIGURE 329.—Portrait of John Hancock, Governor of the Massachusetts Colony, showing coat with a turned-down collar and double pocket-flaps, reign of George III.

FIGURE 330.—Portrait of Samuel Shoemaker, Mayor of Philadelphia, in a bob-wig, and his son, who wears his natural hair long on the shoulders and cut in a straight bang across the forehead (from a portrait painted in 1789).

FIGURE 331.—Showing the plain but handsome costume of a gentleman in Pennsylvania at the outbreak of the Revolution.

FIGURE 332.—Showing a cocked hat worn by a Quaker gentleman of Pennsylvania, 1774.

Figure 329.

Figure 330.

Figure 331.

Figure 332.

We learn that English tradesmen were apt to take advantage of their colonial customers, and that Washington had occasion to protest against things being sent to him from London that were unfashionable and inferior in quality. We give his letter of September 28th, 1760:

"And here gentlemen, I cannot forbear ushering in a complaint of the exorbitant prices of my goods this year all of which are to come to hand. For many years I have imported goods from London as well as other ports of Britain, and can truly say I never had such a penny-worth before. It would be a needless task to enumerate every article that I have cause to except against. Let it suffice to say that woolens, linnens, nails, etc., are mean in quality but not in price, for in this they excel indeed, far above any I have ever had.

"Let us beseech you gentlemen to give the necessary directions for purchasing of them upon the best terms. It is needless for me to particularize, the sorts, quality or taste I would choose to have them in, unless it is observed. And you may believe me when I tell you that instead of getting things good and fashionable in their

FIGURE 333.
Sporting Dress, Middle Eighteenth Century (after Highmore).

several kinds, we often have articles sent us that could only have been used by our forefathers in the days of yore. 'tis a custom I have some reason to believe with many shopkeepers and tradesmen in London, when they know goods are bespoke for exportation, to palm sometimes old and sometimes very slight and indifferent goods upon us, taking care at the same time to advance 10, 15 or perhaps 20 per cent. upon them. My packages, per the 'Polly,' Capt. Hooper, are not yet come to hand, and the Lord only knows when they will without more trouble than they are worth."

According to Fairholt, the costume of the ordinary classes during the greater part of the eighteenth century was exceedingly simple, consisting of a plain coat, buttoned up the front, a long waistcoat reaching to the knees, but having capacious pockets with great overlapping flaps, a plain bobwig, a hat slightly turned up, and high quartered shoes.

We read that, in 1746, flat cocked hats were worn by English sailors, and twenty years later, hats of glazed leather or of woolen thrums, closely woven, and looking like rough knap; and their "small clothes," as we would say now, were immense wide petticoat-breeches, open at the knees, and not extending below them. Labouring men wore ticklenberg linen for shirts, and striped ticken breeches, and in winter heavy coats of gray duroy. The leathern breeches worn by men and boys were made without any opening flaps, and, according to Watson, were so full and free in girth that the wearers ordinarily changed the rear to the front if any signs of wear appeared. Aprons of leather were used by all tradesmen and workingmen.

In a paper of 1771, a reward of ten pounds is offered for the arrest of a man named William Davis who robbed the church at Wilmington of its hangings and had a green coat made of them. Green was very fashionable at this period.

AFTER THE REVOLUTION

At his second inauguration, in Philadelphia, 1793, Washington's costume was "a full suit of black velvet," cut in the fashion of Figure 302, "his hair powdered and in a bag; diamond knee buckles and a light sword with gray scabbard. Behind him was Jefferson, gaunt, ungainly, square-shouldered, with foxy hair, dressed in a blue coat,

Figure 334.—A suit of velvet with raised figures, worn by Robert Livingston of
    Clermont Manor, New York, 1770.
Figure 335.—Pistols with silver mounting, about 1765.
Figure 336.—Cap worn by Governor Taylor of New York, about 1730.
Figure 337.—A waistcoat of buff silk trimmed with shaded brown ribbon, 1780.
Figure 338.—A double-breasted waistcoat of figured silk, 1790.
    (Photographed from original garments.)

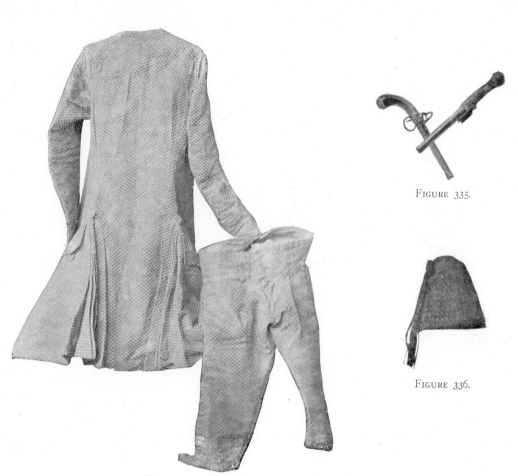

FIGURE 335.

FIGURE 336.

FIGURE 334.

FIGURE 337.

FIGURE 338.

small clothes, and vest of crimson; near by was pale, reflective Madison and burly, bustling Knox." Unfortunately for us, their dress on that occasion is not described. Adams was clad in a full suit of fine gray cloth.

Powder, worn for a hundred years, went out of fashion in 1794, but the hair was still worn in a queue tied with a black ribbon.

The following list of a gentleman's outfit gives an insight into a fashionable wardrobe at this time:

"A light coloured broadcloth coat, with pearl buttons; breeches of the same cloth; ditto, black satin; vest, swansdown buff striped; ditto, moleskin chequer figure; ditto, satin figured; ditto, Marseilles white; ditto, muslinet figured; undervest, faced with red cassimere; two

FIGURE 339.
A Workingman in the Last Half of the Eighteenth Century
(from a Contemporary Print).

ditto, flannel; one pair of flannel drawers; one ditto; cotton ditto; one pair black patent silk hose; one ditto; white ditto; one ditto; striped ditto; ten or a dozen white silk hose; three pair of cotton hose; four pair of gauze ditto; twelve neckerchiefs; six pocket handkerchiefs, one of them a bandanna; a chintz dressing gown; a pair of silk gloves; old kid ditto."

Coats for men became shorter in the waist and all the garments were worn fitting more closely to the figure. The tails of the coats were cut away in front and were quite long in the back. Although a few people might have been seen wearing cocked hats after 1800, a soft, low-crowned straight-brimmed hat came into fashion in 1794. At that time waistcoats were cut low over ruffled shirt fronts. Soft stocks were worn around the neck, finished with a bow and ends under the chin.

Inventory of the wearing apparel of a gentleman in Connecticut at the end of the eighteenth century:

1 Great Coat	3 pr. Old Breeches
1 do do	16 Cotton & Linen Shirts
1 Black Coat	4 pr. Worcested Hose
1 Common do	4 Linen & Cotton do
5 Old Coats	2 pr. plaited do
4 pr. black Breeches	2 pr. black silk do
5 pr. velveteen do	1 Morning Gown
3 worcested waistcoats	3 pr. Cotton breeches
1 velvet do, 1 buff	5 pocket Handkerchiefs
1 Eider down do	1 pr. Gingham Trowsers
1 plaid Gown	7 waistcoats
1 Coatee	3 Neck handkfs.
2 Hats	1 White waistcoat
7 pr. Woolen Hose	3 Under Waistcoats
1 pr. Boots	2 pr. leather mittens
4 pr. Shoes	1 pr. woolen do
1 pr. overalls	1 pr. linen and leather Gloves

A great-coat of blue camlet with several short capes, long of waist and large of button, was the popular garment in severe weather. Trousers of leather and leggings of deer-skin supplemented the coat as a protection against storms. An extra pair of stocking legs well tucked into the low shoes was a homely substitute for leggings, and

THE REPUBLIC UNDER WASHINGTON AND ADAMS

1790–1800

FIGURE 340.—Man in brown broadcloth, from an original suit worn by Mr. Johnson of Germantown about 1790. The coat is of the cut called shad-belly worn by Friends in Pennsylvania until long after 1800.

FIGURE 341.—A mauve crêpe gown trimmed with groups of tucks and a fold of silk of same colour inserted between. The head-dress is from a contemporary picture. The history of Mrs. Sartori, the owner of this dress, is given on page 274.

FIGURE 342.—A dress of fine glazed cambric made very simply with long sleeves and high waist, owned by Madame Chevalier, end of eighteenth century. The hair is copied from a contemporary portrait of 1797.

FIGURE 343.—Man in style of 1800. High collar and short-waisted coat of changeable plum-coloured silk. Nankeen breeches. Hat of felt with rather high crown.

FIGURE 344.—Muslin dress trimmed with tambour embroidery, worn by Deborah Logan of Philadelphia, 1797. The original dress may be seen at Stenton, Philadelphia.

The pictures on this plate are all from original garments lent for this book.

FIGURE 340.   FIGURE 341.   FIGURE 342.   FIGURE 343.   FIGURE 344.

overshoes of very heavy leather were sometimes worn over the ordinary shoes.

LEGAL DRESS IN THE EIGHTEENTH CENTURY

Martin mentions a portrait of James Logan as Chief Justice of the Province of Pennsylvania which represents him in gown, bands, and wig. The original colour of the gown is hard to determine in the portrait. In shape it represents an academic gown, and may have been worn in more than one capacity, as that distinguished colonist played many parts in his day. The dignified garment in question would equally become the governor and the chief justice. (Figure 323.)

In his diary, under date of 1787, Manasseh Cutler, describing a visit to the State House, says: "In this Hall the Courts are held and as you pass the aisle you have a full view of the Court. The Supreme Court was now sitting. This bench consists of only three judges. Their robes are scarlet, the lawyers' black. The Chief Judge McKean sitting with his hat on, which is the custom, but struck me as being very odd and seemed to derogate from the dignity of a judge."*

Among other customs brought over from England by the legal profession is the practice still in use of carrying briefs and papers in bags. "Lawyers' bags," an English authority asserts, "were, until a comparatively recent date, green, but leaders of the chancery and common law bars carried red bags. Chancery juniors, it is stated, were permitted to carry blue bags, etiquette forbidding them to carry bags of the same colour as their leaders." †

In those days (latter half of the eighteenth century) it was the custom of the Supreme Court to hold sessions in the various counties. When the Supreme Court came to Harrisburg (1777–78) to hold court, numbers of the citizens of the place—as many as two hundred

* Life, Journals and Correspondence of Rev. Manassah Cutler, LL.D.
† The King's Peace, by Inderwick.

people at a time—would go out on horseback to meet the judges and escort them to town. The sheriff with his rod of office and other public

FIGURE 345.
A Doctor of Civil Law, End of the Eighteenth Century (from an Old Print).

officers and members of the bar would attend on the occasion, and each morning while the Chief Justice was in town the sheriff and

FIGURE 346.—A summer coat of dark-blue changeable silk with nankeen breeches, worn late in the eighteenth century.

FIGURE 347.—Back view of a brown broadcloth coat, worn by a Quaker gentleman in Germantown about 1790.

FIGURE 348.—Front view of same suit over a nankeen waistcoat.

FIGURE 349.—A coat of brown twilled cotton worn by a Quaker gentleman of Germantown; a white silk embroidered waistcoat and brown satin knee breeches worn in Philadelphia about 1790.

(Photographed from original garments.)

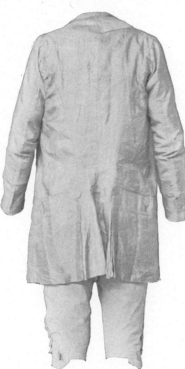

FIGURE 346.

FIGURE 347.

FIGURE 348.

FIGURE 349.

constables escorted him from his lodgings to the court-room. When on the bench, he sat with his hat on and was dressed in a scarlet gown.

A "Grand Federal Procession" took place in Philadelphia on the Fourth of July, 1788, which is described at length in the "Pennsylvania Gazette," July 9, 1788. A great ship on wheels represented the Constitution, and in it was seated Chief Justice McKean in his robes of office, and the judges of the Supreme

after W.H.PYNE. S.B.S.

FIGURE 350.
A Judge in Scarlet Robe, End of the Eighteenth Century (from an Old Print).

Court in their robes of office. Had there been any decided change prescribed for the robes of the judges and lawyers in the framing of the Constitution it would have surely been emphasized in the procession, but as a matter of fact among the printed articles in Congress on the subject of the Judiciary, not a word regarding robes or etiquette is given. The portrait of Chief Justice McKean, which hangs in the Law School of the University of Pennsylvania, depicts him in a scarlet gown. It is a recent portrait, but was painted under the direction of the family. The red robe of the English Court was evidently worn throughout the eighteenth century in America.

John Jay, the first Chief Justice of the Supreme Court of the United States, was appointed to that office by Washington in 1789. The full-length portrait of him in his robe is reproduced in Figure 325. According to a contemporary authority, this robe is the black silk gown with facings of salmon-coloured satin with a white edge, given with his degree of Doctor of Laws by Columbia University and worn by the Chief Justice during the term of his high office under the Government.*

UNIFORMS IN AMERICA
1775–1800

The history of the American Navy, according to good authority, dates from the twenty-second of December, 1775, and the history of its uniform from the fifth of September, 1776, when the Marine Committee of the Continental Congress made the following regulations regarding it:

Captains—A blue coat with red lapels, slashed cuffs, a stand-up collar, flat yellow buttons, blue breeches and a red waistcoat with yellow lace.

Lieutenants—A blue coat with red lapels and round cuffs faced, a stand-up collar, yellow buttons, blue breeches, and a plain red waistcoat.

Masters—A blue coat with lapels, round cuffs, blue breeches, and a red waistcoat.

Midshipmen—A blue coat with lapels, round cuffs faced with red, a stand-up collar, red at the buttons and buttonholes, blue breeches, and a red waistcoat.

* Life and Works of Gilbert Stuart.

Marines—A green coat faced with white, round cuffs, slashed sleeves and pockets, with buttons round the cuffs, a silver epaulet on the right shoulder, skirts turned back, buttons to suit the facings, white waistcoat, breeches edged with green, black gaiters and garters.

The men were to have green shirts if they could be procured.

Common sailors and seamen wore loose breeches and short square-cut jackets, according to Watson and other authorities. (Figure 351.)

The British troops established in America had been kept continually on the alert at different points to protect the inhabitants from the dreaded onslaught of the Indians, but a time of comparative quiet gave the commanders an opportunity to observe a certain hostile attitude the citizens had evinced toward the soldiery. This new phase of feeling in the Colonies was duly mentioned in official despatches, but was so little heeded that England felt a slight shock of alarm at the news of the bold measures of the colonists in

FIGURE 351.
Dress of an Ordinary Seaman, 1775.

Boston in 1768, and the spreading discontent which was becoming manifest in all directions. General Gage was ordered in June to send a force "sufficient to assist the magistrates and revenue officers in enforcing the law." Under Colonel Dalrymple the 14th and 29th

15

Foot* and one company of artillery with five guns arrived at Boston and demanded quarters in the town, which the citizens flatly refused to grant, and Gage, feeling the throbbing pulse of rebellion, withdrew the command and found quarters for the troops at the King's expense.   Shortly after this the 64th and 65th regiments were sent as reinforcements, but they were not able to awe the "mob of Boston," which devoted every spare moment to drilling.   They found an opportunity to practise the skill thus acquired under their leader, Samuel Adams, in the riots of 1770, which resulted in the withdrawal of both British battalions from the city.   The tax on tea and its consequences on the sixteenth of December, 1773, proved a harbinger of the coming trouble.   Gage returned from a visit to England, where his chief object had been to explain the tension of affairs in America, with more troops and the title of Governor of the Province of Massachusetts.   Ten thousand men were then ordered to America instead of the twenty thousand asked for by Gage.

Meanwhile the Provincial Congress had met at Cambridge and passed resolutions for the collection and manufacture of arms, and General Gage, hearing that a quantity of powder and ammunition had been stored at Concord, sent the flank company of his garrison to seize it.   This was the nineteenth of April, 1775, forever memorable in American history.

Paul Revere's gallant ride had not been in vain.   The British troops found a body of militia drawn up on the village green at Concord to protect the stores, and after a fierce skirmish the Redcoats were obliged to retreat, followed for about fifteen miles by the Provincials, whose numbers were augmented at every point on the road by "patriots in homespun."   This battle of Lexington brings us to the organization of the Continental army, which was strongly urged by the Provincial Congress.   The militia troops before Boston had already shown

* For the uniforms of these British regiments, see Her Majesty's Army, by Walter Richards, with coloured plates.

FIGURE 352.—Portrait of Washington, drawn from life, showing hair in pigtail queue.

FIGURE 353.—Portrait of Henry Laurens, Jr., drawn from life, showing hair in side puffs and pigtail queue.

FIGURE 354.—Portrait of W. H. Drayton, Esq., drawn from life, showing hair arranged in puff on top and queue.

FIGURE 355.—Portrait of Gouverneur Morris, drawn from life, showing smooth hair and queue.

FIGURE 352.

FIGURE 353.

FIGURE 354.

FIGURE 355.

good metal in their composition; many of them had fought in the French and Indian War. The Continental army began to drill and manœuvre with redoubled energy, although in the eyes of the British army "their equipment was deficient and their discipline very faulty indeed."

Contemporary letters written from Boston before the Revolution give a vivid picture of the situation.

"The people in England have been taught to believe that five or six thousand regular troops would be sufficient to humble us into the lowest submission to any parliamentary act, however tyrannical. But we are not so ignorant in military affairs and unskilled in the use of arms as they take us to be. A spirit for martial skill has strangely catched from one to another throughout at least the New England colonies. A number of companies in many of our towns are already able to go through the military exercises in all its forms with more dexterity and a better grace than some of the regiments which have been sent to us, and all our men from twenty to sixty years of age are either formed or forming into companies and regiments with officers of their own choosing, to be steadily tutored in the military art. It is not doubted but by next spring one hundred thousand men will be well qualified to come forth for the defense of our liberties and rights should there be a call for it. We have besides in the New England Colonies alone a number of men who, in the last war, were made regulars by their services over your troops now in Boston. I cannot help observing to you here that we have in this town a company of boys from about ten to fourteen years of age who in the opinion of the best judges can go thro' the whole military exercises with more dexterity than a great part of the regulars have been able to do since they have been here."*

An interesting description of the dress and arms of the famous Minute Men is given in the History of Woodbury.†

* Extract from a letter of Charles Chauncey to Richard Price, Boston, January 10, 1775. Massachusetts Historical Society Proceedings, Boston, 1903.

† History of Ancient Woodbury, Connecticut, by William Cothren.

"As the militia rallied on the several calls and detachments, at a minute's or an hour's warning, in whatever clothes they happened to have on, with whatever weapons of war came first to hand, or had descended to them from their fathers, they often presented a very grotesque appearance. They wore small-clothes, coming down and fastening just below the knee, and long stockings with cowhide shoes, ornamented by large buckles, while not a pair of boots graced the company. The coats and waistcoats were loose and of huge dimensions, with colours as various as the barks of the oak, sumach, and other trees of our hills and swamps could make them, and their shirts were all made of flax, and, like every other part of the dress, were homespun. On their heads were worn large round-top and broad-brimmed hats. Their arms were as various as their costumes; here and there an old soldier carried a heavy queen's arm, with which he had done service at the conquest of Canada, twenty years previous, while by his side walked a stripling boy with a Spanish fuzee, not half its weight or calibre, which his grandfather may have taken at Havana, while not a few had old French pieces, that dated back to the reduction of Louisburg. Instead of the cartridge-box, a large powder-horn was slung under the arm, and occasionally a bayonet might be seen bristling in the ranks. Some of the swords of the officers had been made by our province blacksmiths, perhaps from some farming utensil; they looked serviceable, but heavy and uncouth. Such was the appearance of the Continentals, to whom a well-appointed army was soon to lay down their arms."

It is more than likely that the hardest fighting of the war of the Revolution was done by men dressed in hunting shirts of dressed leather, with leather breeches and buckskin shoes. At Bunker Hill the British regiments engaged were the flank companies of the 4th, 10th, 18th, 22nd, 23rd, 35th, 59th, 63rd, and 65th, the entire strength of the 5th, 38th, 42nd, 47th, and 52nd, and two battalions of marines;*

* History of the British Army, by J. W. Fortescue.

FIGURE 356.—Silhouette of John Randolph of Roanoke.

FIGURE 357.—Silhouette of Washington, showing fine net over the hair and queue. (Reproduced through the kindness of Dr. S. Weir Mitchell, who owns one of the few copies of this portrait.)

FIGURE 358.—A silhouette of Bishop White in the knickerbockers worn by English churchmen.

FIGURE 359.—Silhouette of Alexander Hamilton.

FIGURE 360.—A silhouette of James McClellan of Connecticut, showing the queue worn in the last year of the eighteenth century.

FIGURE 356.

FIGURE 357.

FIGURE 358.

FIGURE 359.

FIGURE 360.

these men, in the splendid uniforms of the British regulars, formed a striking contrast to the oddly dressed Continentals. General Washington, who had been chosen unanimously for the Commander-in-Chief of the Continental Army, July 2, 1775, took command of the strangely assorted company before Boston, and later of the three thousand men from Pennsylvania, Virginia, and Maryland.

A few of the provincial regiments were equipped with uniforms, notably the New Jersey Infantry, under Colonel Schuyler, which went by the name of the Jersey Blues, from their coats of blue cloth faced with red; gray stockings and buckskin breeches completed the costume. The Virginia Infantry, of which Washington was colonel, adopted the Whig colours, blue and buff; coats of dark blue faced with buff, with waistcoats and breeches of buff. This was Washington's uniform when he took command of the army at Cambridge. (July, 1775.)

From the "History of the First Troop City Cavalry," which on many occasions had the honour of escorting the Commander-in-Chief, the following account is taken:

FIGURE 361.
Uniform of the Light-Horse Troop of Philadelphia.

"UNIFORM OF THE LIGHT-HORSE OF THE CITY OF PHILA-
DELPHIA. *

"A dark brown short coat, faced and lined with white; white
vest and breeches; high-topped boots; round black hat, bound with
silver cord; a buck's tail; housings brown, edged with white, and
the letters L. H. worked on them." And arms: "A carbine, a pair
of pistols and holsters, with flounces of brown cloth trimmed with
white; a horseman's sword; white belts for the sword and carbine."

In the early part of this year (1775), Captain Markoe presented
to the Troop a handsome silken standard. It is of great historic
interest as being the first flag which bore upon it the thirteen stripes,
symbolizing the thirteen colonies then asserting their rights and
ultimately struggling for their independence. Its first recorded duty
brought the Troop early into the notice of General Washington, who
passed through Philadelphia June 23, 1775, and was escorted by
the Troop as far as New York, on his journey to the camp at Cambridge, Massachusetts.

In order that reliable descriptions of the uniforms worn by the
soldiers from 1775 to 1800 may be had, extracts from contemporary
official papers, reprinted under the supervision of the Quartermaster-
General of the United States (Washington, 1895), are quoted verbatim.

Resolved. That thirteen thousand coats be provided.............
and one thereof be given to each non-commissioned Officer and
Soldier of the Massachusetts forces.

Resolved. That each coat be faced with the same kind of cloth of
which it is made; that the coats be made in the common, plain way,
without lappels, short and with small folds. (Proceedings of Massachusetts Provincial Congress, July 5, 1775.)

Resolved. That the Committee of Supplies...................
are to cause all the coats to be buttoned with pewter buttons, and that
the coats for each Regiment, respectively, have buttons of the same

---

* Afterwards known as First Troop Philadelphia City Cavalry.

FIGURE 362.—A portrait of Commodore Barry of the United States Navy.

FIGURE 363.—Portrait of Paul Jones, Commodore of the United States Navy.

FIGURE 364.—Picture of the Camp at Valley Forge, showing military cloak and great coat worn by the officers and the Dutch blankets worn by the private soldiers.

FIGURE 362.

FIGURE 363.

FIGURE 364.

number stamped on the face of them.—(*Amer. Archives*, Vol. II, 4th series, p. 1486.)

To prevent mistakes the General Officers and their Aids de Camp will be distinguished in the following manner: The Commander-in-Chief by a light blue ribband, worn across his breast, between his coat and waistcoat; the Majors and Brigadiers General by a pink ribband worn in like manner; the Aids de Camp by a green ribband. (General Orders, Headquarters, Cambridge, July 14, 1775.)—(*Amer. Archives*, Vol. II, 4th series, p. 1662.)

.... every Major of Brigade will be distinguished by a green ribband. ....
(General Orders, Headquarters, Cambridge, July 20, 1775.)—(*Amer. Archives*, Vol. II, 4th series, p. 1710.)

As the Continental Army have unfortunately no uniforms, and consequently many inconveniences must arise from not being able always to distinguish the commissioned Officers from the non-commissioned, and, the non-commissioned from the privates, it is desired that some badges of distinction may be immediately provided; for instance, that the field Officers may have red or pink colored cockades in their hats; the Captains yellow or buff, and the subalterns green.

The sergeants may be distinguished by an epaulette or stripe of red cloth sewed upon their right shoulders; the Corporals by one of green. (Gen. Orders, Headquarters, Cambridge, 23 July, 1775.)—(*Amer. Archives*, Vol. II, 4th series, 1775, p. 1738.)

It being thought proper to distinguish the Majors from the Brigadiers General by some particular mark, for the future the Majors General will wear a broad *purple* ribband. (Gen. Orders, Headquarters, Cambridge, 24 July, 1775.)—(*Amer. Archives*, Vol. II, 4th series, 1775, p. 1739.)

The General also recommends it to the Colonels to provide *Indian* boots or leggings for their men, instead of stockings,............

especially as the General has hopes of prevailing with the Continental Congress to give each man a hunting shirt.......................... (General Orders, Headquarters, Cambridge, August 7, 1775.)—(*Amer. Archives*, Vol. III, 4th series, p. 248.)

The enlisted men of the 1st Virginia Regiment of Infantry were, however, in the year 1775, uniformed at their own expense in hunting shirts, leggings, and white bindings on their hats.—(*Amer. Archives*, Vol. IV, 4th series, p. 92.)

Resolved. That when the *Green Mountain Boys* are raised, each of them shall be furnished with a coat, and.................be requested to purchase green cloth for that purpose, and red cloth sufficient to face these coats. .... (New York Prov. Congress, Aug. 15, 1775.)—(*Amer. Archives*, Vol. III, 4th series, p 530.)

Resolved. That Clothing be provided for the new Army by the Continent and paid for by stoppages out of the soldiers wages......... That as much as possible of the cloth for this purpose be dyed brown and the distinctions of the Regiments made in the facings.—(Res. Congress, Nov. 4, 1775.)—(*Amer. Archives*, Vol. III, 4th series, p. 1907.)

The Colonels upon the new establishment to settle as soon as possible with the Quartermaster General the uniform of their respective Regiments that the buttons may be properly numbered and the work finished without delay. (General Orders, Headquarters, Cambridge, Nov. 13, 1775.)—(*Amer. Archives*, Vol. III, 4th series.)

It is recommended to those Corps which are not already supplied with uniforms, to provide hunting shirts for their men. (General Orders, Headquarters, New York, May 6, 1776.)—(*Amer. Archives*, Vol. VI, 4th series, p. 426.)

The General being sensible of the difficulty and expense of providing Clothes, of almost any kind, for the Troops, feels an unwillingness to recommend, much more to order, any kind of Uniform; but

FIGURE 365.—General Warren, in the dress of a minute-man.
FIGURE 366.—General Daniel Morgan in a buckskin coat of the Virginia rangers.
FIGURE 367.—Comte de Rochambeau, showing dress of a French officer, 1791.

FIGURE 367.

FIGURE 366.

FIGURE 365.

as it is absolutely necessary that men should have Clothes, and appear decent and tight, he earnestly encourages the use of Hunting Shirts, with long breeches made of the same cloth, gaiter fashion about the legs, to all those yet unprovided. (General Orders, Headquarters, New York, July 24, 1776.)—(*Amer. Archives*, Vol. I, 5th series, p. 677.)

Resolved that, for the further encouragement of the non-commissioned Officers and soldiers who shall engage in service during the war. A suit of Clothes be annually given to each of said officers and soldiers; to consist, for the present year, of two linen hunting shirts, two pairs of overalls, a leathern or woolen waistcoat with sleeves, one pair of breeches, a hat or leather cap, two shirts, two pair of hose and two pair of shoes. (Continental Congress, Oct. 8, 1776.)—(*Amer. Archives*, Vol. II, 5th series, p. 1392.)

.... the Congress of the United States have .... further resolved to give .... annually to each man one complete suit of clothing, which, for the present year, is to consist of two linen hunting shirts, two pair of stockings, two pair of shoes, two pair of overalls, a leathern or woolen jacket with sleeves, one pair of breeches, and one Leathern cap or hat. (General Orders, Headquarters, October 24, 1776.)—(*Amer. Archives*, Vol. III, 5th series, p. 331.)

In 1777, and subsequently, the uniform for the four regular regiments constituting the Corps of Artillery was a blue or black coat reaching to the knee, and full trimmed, lappels fastened back, with ten open-worked button-holes in yellow silk on the breast of each lappel, and ten large regimental yellow buttons, at equal distances, on each side; three large yellow regimental buttons on each cuff, and a like number on each pocket-flap. The skirts to hook back, showing the red lining, bottom of coat cut square, red lappels, cuff linings, and standing capes; single-breasted white waistcoat, with twelve small yellow regimental buttons, white breeches, black half gaiters, white stock, ruffled shirt, and at the wrists, and black cocked hat bound with yellow; red plume and black cockade, gilt-handled small sword and gilt epaulettes.—(*Mag. Amer. Hist.*, Vol. I, p. 473.)

Congress, by resolution of March 23, 1779, "authorized and directed the Commander-in-Chief, according to circumstances of supplies of Clothing, to fix and prescribe the uniform as well with regard to color and facings as the cut or fashion of the Clothes to be worn by the troops of the respective States and regiments, woolen overalls for winter and linen for summer to be substituted for the breeches."

In accordance with the above Resolution, the following General Order, dated Headquarters, Moore's House, 2 Oct., 1779, was promulgated by General Washington:

"The following are the uniforms that have been determined for the troops of these States respectively, so soon as the state of the public supplies will permit of their being furnished accordingly; and, in the meantime, it is recommended to the Officers to endeavor to accommodate their uniforms to the standard, that when the men come to be supplied, there may be a proper uniformity.

NEW HAMPSHIRE, MASSACHUSETTS, RHODE ISLAND and CONNECTICUT.

Blue, faced with white; buttons and linings white.

NEW YORK and NEW JERSEY.

Blue, faced with buff; white linings and buttons.

PENNSYLVANIA, DELAWARE, MARYLAND and VIRGINIA.

Blue, faced with red; buttons and linings white.

NORTH CAROLINA, SOUTH CAROLINA and GEORGIA.

Blue, faced with blue; buttonholes edged with narrow white lace or tape; buttons and linings white.

ARTILLERY and ARTILLERY ARTIFICERS.

Blue, faced with scarlet; scarlet linings; yellow buttons, yellow-bound hats. Coats edged with narrow lace or tape, and buttonholes bound with same.

LIGHT DRAGOONS.

The whole blue, faced with white; white buttons and linings."

MILITARY UNIFORMS IN AMERICA

1775–1785

FIGURE 368 shows the uniform recommended by Washington in the early part of the Revolution. A hunting shirt of thick linen cloth or buckskin, according to the season, with ruffled strips of the same material round the neck, on the shoulders, and about the knees; breeches to match and gaiters made of tan cloth steeped in a tan vat until it reached the colour of a dry leaf. Large hat unlooped, black stock, and pigtail queue.

FIGURE 369 represents a minute-man in the ordinary costume of the day. Suit of blue cloth, waistcoat of buff, cocked hat.

FIGURE 370.—A member of the 1st Co. Governor's Foot Guard (Connecticut) in scarlet cloth coat, faced with black, trimmed with gold braid and buttons. Buff cassimere waistcoat and breeches, leggings of brown leather. Bearskin hat with scarlet pompon at one side.

FIGURE 371.—Pennsylvania Regiment of the Continental Line, First Pennsylvania Infantry. Brown coat faced with buff. Overalls instead of breeches and gaiters.

FIGURE 372.—Second Pennsylvania Infantry. Blue coat faced with red, black stock. Cocked hat with tape binding, and buckskin overalls.

FIGURE 373.—Uniform directed by the Minister of War, 1785. Blue faced and lined with white for the infantry, and blue faced and lined with red for the artillery. Buff waistcoat and breeches; half leggings of leather.

FIGURE 374.—Light Infantry in 1782. Blue coat, white facings. white waistcoat and breeches, high leggings, black stock, round hat ferretted, and pigtail queue.

FIGURE 375.—Front view of Figure 373.

FIGURE 368. FIGURE 369. FIGURE 371. FIGURE 372.

FIGURE 370. FIGURE 373.

FIGURE 374.

FIGURE 375.

Resolved. That the following articles be delivered as a suit of Clothes for the current and every succeeding year of their service to the Officers of the line and staff, entitled by any Resolution of Congress to receive the same, viz: one hat, one watch coat, one body coat, four vests, one for winter and three for summer, four pairs of breeches, two for winter and two for summer, four shirts, six pair of stockings, three pair thereof worsted and three of thread, four pair of Shoes.—(*Journals of Congress*, Nov. 25, 1779.)

As it is at all times of great importance both for the sake of appearance and for the regularities of service that the different military ranks should be distinguished from each other, and more especially at present:—

The Commander-in-Chief has thought proper to establish the following distinctions and strongly recommends it to all the Officers to endeavor to conform to them as speedily as possible.

The Major Generals to wear a blue coat with buff facings, yellow buttons, white or buff underclothes, two epaulettes, with two stars upon each and a black-and-white feather in the hat.

The Brigadier Generals, the same uniform as the Major Generals with the difference of one star instead of two and a white feather.

The Colonels, Lieutenant Colonels, and Majors, the uniform of their regiments, and two epaulettes.

The Captains, the uniforms of their regiments and an epaulette on the right shoulder.

The subalterns, the uniform of their regiment and an epaulette on the left shoulder.

The Aides de Camp, the uniforms of their ranks and Corps, or if they belong to no Corps, of their General Officers.

Those of the Major Generals and Brigadier Generals to have a green feather in their hat. Those of the Commander-in-Chief a white and green.

The Inspectors, as well Sub as Brigade, the uniform of their ranks and Corps, with a blue feather in the hat.

The Corps of Engineers and that of Sappers and Miners, a blue coat with buff facings, red lining, buff undercloaths, and the epaulettes of their respective ranks.

Such of the Staff as have Military rank, to wear the uniform of their ranks and of the Corps to which they belong in the line. Such as have no military rank to wear plain coats, with a cockade and sword.

All officers, as well warrant as commissioned, to wear a cockade and side arms either a sword or genteel bayonet. (Headquarters, Short Hills, Sunday, June 18, 1780.)

As it is much wished to establish uniformity in the corps; the officers are directed not to make any changes in the dress of themselves or their men 'till orders are given for a general rule.

The feathers directed to be worn by Major Generals are to have the white below, the black above; it will be best to have one feather the upper part black. It is recommended to the officers to have black and white cockades, a black ground with a white relief, emblematic of the expected union of the two armies. (Headquarters, Precaness, July 19, 1780.)

As nothing adds more to the beauty and appearance of a Corps, than exact uniformity of dress, the General recommends it thus early to the "Field Officers" newly arranged to fix upon a fashion for the regimental clothing of the officers of their respective corps (if it is not already done), confining themselves to the ground, facing, linings and buttons already assigned to the States to which they belong.

The General sees with concern the difficulties which the Officers labor under in procuring Cloth. It is not therefore his wish that those who are already furnished should run themselves to the expense of new uniforms, if their old are not exactly conformable, but that they should in future comply strictly with the regimental fashion and, if possible, get their old clothes altered to it. It has a very odd appearance especially to Foreigners to see the same corps of officers each differing from the other in fashion of the facings, sleeves and pockets of their coats.

An attention to these minutiæ has been thought proper in all services; it becomes peculiarly so in ours at this time as we shall more than probable take the field next campaign in conjunction with

FIGURE 376.—A portrait of Major-General Pinckney.
FIGURE 377.—A portrait of Major-General St. Clair.
FIGURE 378.—A portrait of General O. H. Williams.
FIGURE 379. –A portrait of General Andrew Pickens.

FIGURE 376.

FIGURE 377.

FIGURE 378.

FIGURE 379.

our Allies, composed of the first troops in Europe, who will receive impressions and form opinions from the first view ....

Strict attention is to be paid to the order of the 18th of June last, distinguishing the rank of officers by their badges. (Headquarters, Totoway, Nov. 15, 1780.)

ORDERS FOR THE MASSACHUSETTS LINE.

January 5th, 1781.

The Committee of Officers appointed to fix upon the fashion of the Massachusetts' uniform, have reported thereupon, and it is as follows:—

The color of the coats, waistcoat, linings and buttons, to be agreeable to the General Orders of the 2nd of October, 1779.

The length of the coat, to the upper part of the knee-pan, and to be cut high in the neck. As 3 is to 5, so is the skirt to the waist of the coat; or divide the whole length of the coat into 8 equal parts, take 5 for the waist and 3 for the skirts.

The lappel, at the top of the breast, to be 3 inches wide, and the bottom $2\frac{3}{10}$ inches; the lappel to be as low as the waist, and its wing to button within an inch of the shoulder seam with a small button on the cape. The epaulette to be worn directly on the top of the shoulder joint on the same button with the wing of the lappel. A round and close cuff, three inches wide, with four close worked buttonholes. The cape to be made with a peak behind, and its width in proportion to the lappels. The pocket flaps to be scollopped, four buttonholes, the two inner close worked, the two outer open worked, and to be set on in a curved line from the bottom of the lappel to the button on the hip. The coat to be cut full behind, with a fold on each back skirt, and two close worked buttonholes on each.

Ten open worked buttonholes on the breast of each lappel, with ten large buttons, at equal distance; four large buttons on each cuff, four on each pocket flap, and four on each fold. Those on the cuffs and pocket flaps to be placed agreeable to the buttonholes; and those on the folds, one on the hip, one at the bottom, and two in the centre, at an equal distance with those on the lappel. The coat is to button or hook as low at the fourth buttonhole on the breast, and is to be

flaunt at the bottom with a genteel and military air. Four hooks
and eyes on the breast as low as the coat is allowed to button. The
skirts to hook up with a blue heart at each corner, with such device
as the Field Officers of each Regiment shall direct. The bottoms
of the coat to be cut square. The waistcoat to be single-breasted,
with twelve buttons and holes on the breast, with pocket flaps, four
close worked buttonholes and four buttons, which shall appear below
the flaps. The breeches are to be made with a half fall; four buttons
on each knee. The small buttons on the waistcoat to be of the same
kind with the large ones on the coat. The number of the Regiment
is to be in the centre of the button, with such device at the Field
Officers shall direct. The epaulettes to be worn agreeable to his
Excellency the Commander-in-Chief's orders of June 18, 1780.

A fashionable military cock'd hat, with a silver button loop, and
a small button with the number of the Regiment. To wear a black
stock when on duty and on the *parade*.

No edging, vellum lace, or indeed any other ornaments which are
not mentioned, to be added to the uniform. No officer is to be permitted, at any time, to wear any other uniform than that of his Regiment.—(*Review Orders*, by H. Whiting, p. 164.)

The clothier is, if practicable, to obtain worsted *shoulder knots*,
for the non-commissioned officers; the sergeants are to be distinguished by one on each shoulder; and the corporals by one on the
right shoulder; and in the meantime it is proposed that a piece of
white cloth should be substituted by way of distinction. (General
Orders, Headquarters, Newburgh, May 14, 1782.)

FIGURE 380.—Portrait of General Montgomery, showing a black silk stock, hair in queue.

FIGURE 381.—General Francis Marion, showing coat with high collar and peculiar waistcoat.

FIGURE 382.—General Israel Putnam, showing uniform of a Continental trooper.

FIGURE 383.—General Philemon Dickinson, showing high cut coat.

FIGURE 384.—General John Sullivan, showing cocked hat edged with braid and a gorget.

FIGURE 383.

FIGURE 384.

FIGURE 382.

FIGURE 380.

FIGURE 381.

BRIGADE ORDERS, WEST POINT.

June 17, 1782.

The Honorable Brigadier-General Paterson, having expressed his wish that some honorary mark of distinction should be worn by each Non-commissioned Officer or Private in his Brigade, who has served in the Army of the United States a certain length of time; and has also made a present of materials for that purpose:—

The Commandant thinks proper to direct, that each Non-Commissioned Officer and Private, who has served four years in any Continental Regiment, shall be entitled to wear one stripe of white tape, on the left sleeve of his regimental coat, which shall extend from seam to seam, on the upper part of the sleeve, three inches from and parallel with the shoulder seam, so that the tape may form a herring-bone figure.

That none presume to wear the badge of distinction, but by the immediate permission of the Colonel or Commandant of the Regiment, who, on its being made to appear to his full satisfaction, that the man who applies for the badge has served four years, as above, will please to order this honor publicly conferred on him. The Commandant further directs, that when any Non-Commissioned Officer or Soldier shall complete eight years service, he shall have the addition of another stripe set on one inch below the first.

As emulation is essential to promote discipline, the Commandant wishes, by all laudable measure, to kindle the flame in every breast; and considers that punishment, as well as reward, is absolutely necessary in all government; to promote which design, he directs that these marks of distinction, in the first instance, be for all who have actually served as above, without discrimination of character; but, that after the publication of this order, none who shall commit a crime for which they are punishable by a Court Martial, shall be entitled to this honorary badge for four years from the time they were found punishable; and should any one who is honored with the badge be so lost to a sense of honor, which every soldier ought to possess, as to fall under the sentence of a Court Martial, he is to be divested of this badge of honor at the head of the Regiment, and excluded

from wearing it until he shall retrieve his character, by four years'
unblemished service.   (*Review Orders*, by Henry Whiting, p. 220.)

Honorary Badges of distinction are to be conferred on the veteran
non-commissioned officers and soldiers of the Army, who have served
more than three years with bravery, fidelity and good conduct, for
this purpose a narrow piece of white cloth, of an angular form is to
be fixed to the left arm on the uniform coats.   Non-commissioned
officers and soldiers who have served with equal reputation more
than six years, are to be distinguished by two pieces of cloth, set on
parallel to each other in a similar form .... whenever
any singularly meritorious action is performed, the author of it shall
be permitted to wear on his facings, over the left breast, the figure
of a heart in purple cloth or silk, edged with narrow lace or binding.
(Headquarters, Newburgh, Aug. 7, 1782.)

In order to prevent misapplication of the honorary badges of distinction to be conferred on the non-commissioned officers and soldiers
in consequence of long and faithful service, through any mistake or
misapprehension of the orders of the 7th inst., the General thinks
proper to inform the Army that they are only attainable by an uninterrupted series of faithful and honorable services.

The badges which non-commissioned officers and soldiers are
permitted to wear on the left arm as a mark of long and faithful
service, are to be of the same color with the facings of the corps they
belong to and not white in every instance as directed in the orders
of the 7th instant. (General Orders, Headquarters, Newburgh,
Aug. 11, 1782.)

The Honorable Secretary of War having been pleased to direct
that the uniforms of the American Cavalry and Infantry shall in future
be blue ground with red facings and white linings and buttons: The
General gives this early notice that provision may be made accordingly
before the Army shall receive their clothing for the present year.

The Corps of the Artillery is to retain its present uniform, and the Sappers and Miners will have the same. (Headquarters, Newburgh, Dec. 6, 1782.)

The non arrival of the clothing imported from Europe renders the greatest economy in that article doubly necessary. The Commander-in-Chief therefore recommends that the business of turning and repairing the coats of last year should now be considered as a primary object, in doing which a certain model as to the fashion and length, (for the coats ought to be made something shorter than at present) will be established by the commanding officer of the corps, from which there must be no deviation.........................

It is expected scarlet cloth for cuffs, capes and perhaps half facings will be furnished. (Headquarters, Newburgh, Feb. 24, 1783.)

Notwithstanding the proposed alteration in the uniforms of the Infantry and Cavalry it appears necessary from inevitable circumstances that all the Light Infantry companies should be cloathed in blue coats faced with white until further orders. (General Orders, Headquarters, Newburgh, March 3, 1783.)

The regiments which have not turned and repaired their coats are to draw lots for the scarlet cloth which arrived yesterday. (General Orders, Newburgh, April 14, 1783.)

When the Revolutionary War ended, one regular regiment of Infantry .... and two companies of the corps of artillery were retained in service. (General Orders, Headquarters, West Point, 23 Dec., 1783.) The Uniform of the infantry regiment was dark blue, with white facings, white linings, black cocked hats, white hat bindings, white worsted shoulder knots, white buttons, silver epaulettes for Officers, white cross belts, black stocks, white under dress, black gaiters, and black plume. The artillery uniform remained as heretofore; dark blue faced with scarlet, scarlet linings, yellow buttons, yellow binding for black felt cocked hat, and yellow edging of buttonholes; white under dress, gold epaulettes for Officers; and yellow worsted shoulder knots for non-commissioned officers and

16

buff belts, white cravats and black plume, with red top.—(*Mag. Amer. Hist.*, Vol. I, p. 482.)

The coats of the musicians remained red with blue facings, blue waistcoats and breeches, silk epaulettes for Chief Musician. (General Orders, War Dept., N. Y., 30 Jan., 1787.)—(*Mag. Amer. Hist.*, Vol. I, p. 482.)

The Infantry Officers were now required to wear half boots, white pantaloons and white vests, double breasted. (General Orders, Headquarters, Loftus Heights, 19 January, 1791.)

During the period of the confederation the troops retained substantially the revolutionary uniforms. The cavalry had brass helmets with white horsehair. (Secty. War to Q. M. Genl. Saml. Hodgden, 4 Aug., 1792.)—(*Mag. Amer. Hist.*, Vol. I, p. 483.)

Their swords were "long horseman's sword, steel mounted." Officers of Artillery and Infantry had swords of sabre form respectively yellow mounted and steel mounted, two feet six inches in length for each company officer, and three feet in length for each field officer.—(*Mag. Amer. Hist.*, Vol. I, p. 483.)

The officers being arranged to the four sub-legions it now becomes expedient to give those Legions distinctive marks, which are to be as follows, viz:

The first Sub-legion, white binding upon their caps with white plumes and black hair.

The second Sub-legion, red binding to their caps, red plumes with white hair.

The third Sub-legion, yellow binding to their caps, yellow plumes and black hair.

The fourth Sub-legion, green binding to their caps, green plumes and white hair. (General Orders, Headquarters, Pittsburgh, 11 Sept., 1792.)

The Officers will wear plain cocked hats with no other distinctive marks, but the plumes of their respective Sub-legions, except in actual service or action, when they will wear the same caps with the non-commissioned officers and privates of their respective Sub-legions. (Gen. Orders, Headquarters, Pittsburgh, Sept. 12, 1792.)

The following Select Corps shall be immediately drafted from the Legion .... the respective pay-masters will deliver to the Captains or officers commanding companies ....Two pairs linen overalls, two pairs of shoes and two shirts for each non-commissioned officer and private. .... (Gen. Orders, Headquarters, Greenville, June, 30, 1794.)

Paymasters ....will also furnish the commanding officers of each troop of Dragoons with two shirts and two pairs of linen overalls per man ....
The garrison duty men will parade for Review tomorrow...... fresh shaved and well powdered ...... All such as have five months and upwards to serve will be furnished with two pair of linen overalls, two shirts and two pairs of shoes per man. Those whose term of service will expire on or before the 1st of December next with one pair of shoes, one pair of overalls, and one shirt per man .... (Gen. Orders, Headquarters, Greenville, July 1, 1794.)

The Deputy Quartermaster will issue all the bearskins to the Sub-legionary Quartermasters for the use of the Battalion Companies. (Gen. Orders, Headquarters, Greenville, July 9, 1794.)

In 1794 the artillery received helmets, with red plumes. (Secty. War to Quartermaster Genl. Saml. Hodgden, 14 July, 1794.)—(*Mag. Amer. Hist.*, Vol. I, p. 484.)

The commanding officers of the respective Sub-legions, will make out a particular return to the Adjutant General of the number of Non-commissioned officers and soldiers......entitled to summer clothing, and who have not already been furnished........that the whole of the troops may appear in the most soldierly condition. On the 4th July......the Commanding Officers of Corps will cause the uniforms to be repaired, and the Hats and Caps properly decorated. The Acting Quartermaster will procure bearskins for covering the hats and caps. (General Orders, Headquarters, Greenville, June 26, 1795.)

The following uniform for the officers of Infantry is to be observed and adopted until otherwise regulated. Coats reaching to the knee and full trimmed, scarlet lappels, cuffs and standing capes, white buttons and trimmings, lapels and cape two inches, and cuffs three inches wide. Vests and breeches white, the former with short flaps and three buttons. Black stocks or cravats, Cocked Hats, and full boots with black tops. (General Orders, Headquarters, Greenville, 16th Feb., 1796.)

In 1799 the white plume was again prescribed for the Infantry ....(Gen. Orders, Headquarters, Loftus Heights, 2 Jan., 1799.)—(*Mag. Amer. Hist.*, p. 485.)

The uniform of the Commander-in-Chief to be a blue coat, with yellow buttons, and gold epaulettes, each having three silver stars, with lining, cape and cuffs of buff—in winter buff vest and breeches; in summer, a white vest and breeches, of nankeen.

The coat to be without lappels, and embroidered on the cape and cuffs and pockets; a white plume in the hat, to be a further distinction. The Adjutant General, the aids and secretaries of the Commander-in-Chief, to be likewise distinguished by a white plume.

The uniform of the other General Officers to be a blue coat, with yellow buttons, gold epaulettes, linings and facings of buff —the underclothes the same with those of the Commander in Chief.

The Major generals to be distinguished by two silver stars in each epaulet, and except the Inspector General, by a black and white plume, the black below.

The Brigadier to be distinguished by one silver star on each epaulet, and by a red and white plume, the red below.

The Aids, of all general officers, who are taken from regiments, and the officers of inspection, to wear the uniform of the regiments from which they are taken.

The aids to be severally distinguished by the like plumes, which are worn by the general officers, to whom they are respectively attached.

The uniforms of the aids of the commander in chief when not taken from regiments, to be a blue coat with yellow button, and gold epaulet, buff lining and facings .... the same under-clothes with the commander-in-chief.

The Inspector General, his aids, and the officers of inspection generally, to be distinguished by a blue plume. The Quartermaster General and other military officers in his department, to be distinguished by a green plume.

The uniform of the Infantry and artillery to be a blue coat with white buttons and red facings, white underclothes and cocked hats .... the length of the officers coats to reach the knees, the coats of the Infantry, to be lined with white, of the artillery with red. The uniform of the Cavalry, to be a green coat, with white buttons, linings and facings; white vest and breeches and helmet caps.

Each Colonel to be distinguished by two epaulettes; each Major, by one epaulet on the right shoulder, and a strap on the left. All the Field Officers, (except as above) and the Regimental Staff, to wear red plumes .... the Officers of companies are to wear red plumes.

Captains to be distinguished by an epaulet on the right shoulder; Lieutenants by one on the left shoulder; cadets by a strap on the right shoulder. The epaulets and straps of the regimental officers to be of silver.

Sergeant Majors and Quartermaster Sergeants, to be distinguished by two red worsted epaulets; Sergeants by a like epaulet on the right shoulder; Corporals by a like epaulet on the left shoulder; the flank companies to be distinguished by red wings on the shoulders.

The coats of the Musicians to be of the colors of the facings of the corps to which they severally belong. The Chief Musician to wear two white worsted epaulets. All the Civil staff of the Army, to wear plain blue coats, with yellow buttons, and white underclothes. No gold or silver lace, except in the epaulets and straps to be worn.

The commissioned officers, and cadets to wear swords.

All persons belonging to the Army to wear a black cockade with a small white Eagle in the centre. The cockade of non-commissioned officers, musicians, and privates to be of leather, with Eagles of tin. The regiments to be distinguished from each other, numerically. The number of each regiment to be expressed in the buttons. (War Office, Philadelphia, 9 January, 1799.)

FIGURE 385.
Uniform of an American Officer, 1796.

From "The Uniform of the Army of the United States" (Washington, 1895) is taken the following description of the uniform of an officer from 1776 to 1799: "A blue coat, with red facings and white bindings and white buttons and button-holes, white waistcoat and breeches, white gloves, white epaulettes. Cocked hat bound with

white, black pompon. Powdered hair in queue tied with narrow
black silk ribbon. High black silk stock, ruffle of white shirt showing at neck and wrists." (Figure 385.)

The short-waisted coats and high collars which marked the end
of the eighteenth century were specially noticeable in the uniforms,
both military and naval, and form a very striking contrast to the long-
waisted garments which characterized the close of the seventeenth
century.

For uniforms of the French officers in America during the Revolutionary period see
Our French Allies, by Edwin M. Stone. For uniforms of the French troops at this period, see
Racinet, Costumes Historiques, vol. v.

The uniforms of a Hessian dragoon and of the Brunswick Troopers in America during
the Revolutionary period are given in American History from German Archives, by Mr. J. G.
Rosengarten.

GLOSSARY

Glossary

Adonis wigs.—Made of fine white hair, were very fashionable and very expensive in the early part of the eighteenth century.

Aggrapes.—From the French *agrape*, "a clasp or buckle"; also "hooks and eyes."

Aiglet or **Aiguillette.**—A metal tag or point to a lace.

Aigret or **Egret.**—A tuft of feathers worn on the head. Fly caps with egrets were advertised in Boston, 1755.

Alamode.—A plain soft glossy silk often mentioned in advertisements in Colonial newspapers under various spellings—"elamond," "alimod," "olamod," "alemod," "arlimod," "allamode," and "ellimod," are some of the variations. It was used throughout the eighteenth century.

Allapine.—A strong woolen stuff spelled often "ellapine," "allpine," and "alpine," and very popular for men's wear during the first half of the eighteenth century.

Amazeen.—(under various spellings)—A strong corded silk in use from the time of Elizabeth to George III. Often advertised in Colonial papers.

Aprons.—First worn for use by the careful housewife as well as servants and workingmen, the apron became by some unaccountable freak of fashion late in the sixteenth century an article of full dress. In 1659 we read that green aprons went out of fashion. Aprons were worn in 1744 so long that they nearly touched the ground.

Artois.—A long cloak made with several capes and used by men and women in 1790.

Atlas.—A soft silk with satin surface, made in the East.

Baise, Baize, or **Bayes.**—A coarse woolen cloth made at Colchester in the days of Queen Elizabeth. Advertised in Colonial papers in all colours, and used for the clothing of servants and negro slaves.

Balandrans or **Balandranas.**—Cloaks with armholes.

Band.—A collar of lace or linen stiffened with starch or underpropped with wire. When allowed to fall upon the shoulders, it was termed a falling band.

Band-box.—Originally made to hold bands—whence the name.

Bandekyn.—A fabric of silk and gold thread.

Bandileers.—Cases of wood or tin, each containing a charge of powder, strung round the neck of a soldier.

Band-strings.—Were usually of ribbon or of cord finished with tassels; the latter were often decorated with pearls and other jewels.

381

Banyan.—Originally an Anglo-Indian name for a loose coat. A morning gown or wrapper worn by both sexes, usually of bright-coloured cloth or damask. We read that these garments were much worn in Virginia, and were sometimes lined with a rich material, and thus could be worn either side out.

Barlicorns.—A dress fabric used in the Colonies. "Check'd barlicorns" were advertised in 1755.

Barragon or **Barracan.**—A corded stuff suitable for summer wear. Made originally in the Levant, of camel's-hair.

Barratine.—A stuff, probably of silk, used for petticoats, stomachers, and "forehead clothes" as early as 1697.

Barrow-coat.—A form of swaddling cloth wrapped about an infant's body and turned up and fastened at the bottom to keep the feet warm.

Barry or **Barrie.**—An under-skirt or petticoat.

Barvell.—A coarse leathern apron used by workingmen.

Batts.—Heavy low shoes laced in front. Sent to the New England Colonists in 1636 and after.

Beard-boxes.—Were made of pasteboard and worn at night over a beard to keep it in shape.

Bearer.—A roll of padding placed like a bustle at either hip to raise the skirt.

Bearing cloth.—Old name for a Christening blanket.

Bell-hoops.—Stiffened petticoats in the shape of a bell were fashionable in 1731.

Biggin.—Probably a corruption of *beguine*, "a nun," and sometimes spelled "begin." It was a close cap worn always by young children and sometimes by grown people before 1700.

Binder.—A band of flannel worn by babies under the shirt, sufficiently tight to give some support to the back.

Birdet.—A silk stuff made in China or India. "Strip'd and plain birdet" was advertised in New England in 1737.

Bishop.—A sort of bustle stuffed with horsehair.

Blodins.—(Old English)—Sky-blue.

Bob-wig.—A short close wig worn by men and boys of all classes on ordinary occasions from about 1725 to 1780.

Bodice or **a paire of Boddies.**—A sort of stays, an article of apparel worn often by dandies and in general use by women in the seventeenth century.

Bodkin.—A large pin for the hair, usually of gold or silver.

Bombards.—Padded breeches.

Bombazin, Bomberzeen, or **Bombax.**—A mixture of silk and cotton, frequently advertised in old papers.

Bone-lace.—Usually of linen thread made over bobbins of bone, whence the name.

Bonnet.—We read of silk bonnets as early as 1725 in New England, and in 1760 of satin bonnets, quilted bonnets, and Kitty Fisher bonnets, also of Quebeck and Garrick bonnets, but they do not appear in the portraits of the day, and were probably not as fashionable as hoods and hats until late in the eighteenth century.

Bonnet-paper.—A stiff pasteboard used for the frames of bonnets and hats.

Bosom-bottle.—A small flat glass bottle, sometimes covered with silk to match the gown, concealed in the stomacher of the dress to hold water for flowers, so generally worn by ladies in the last half of the eighteenth century.

Brawls or **Brouls.**—A blue and white striped cotton cloth made in India, advertised in newspapers 1785 to 1795.

Breast Knot or **Bosom Knot.**—A dainty touch of coloured ribbon worn from 1730 and for the remainder of the century.

Breeches.—Were worn by the early Colonists, of dressed leather, but afterward they were made of every material. At first the shape was loose, fastened in at the knee and waist, but before the end of the eighteenth century they were worn skin-tight.

Breeches-hooks.—A device upon which the breeches were hung to keep them in shape, mentioned in the middle of the eighteenth century.

Brigandine.—A plate coat.

Broadcloth.—A fine woolen cloth with a smooth surface, mostly used for men's garments, and always regarded with respect by the lower classes.

> Ye wha are fain to hae your name
> Wrote in the coney Book of Fame
> Let merit nae pretension claim
>   To laurelled wreath!
> But hop ye weel, baith back and wame
>   In gude Braid claith!
> Braid claith lends fock an unco heese!
> Makes many kail-worms butterflies!
> Gives mony a Doctor his degrees
>   For little skaith.
> In short you may be what you please,
>   Wi gude Braid Claith!
> —*Robert Ferguson.*

Buff-coat.—A leather outer garment made exceedingly strong, sometimes ⅛ of an inch in thickness. Much used in the Civil Wars in England and by the Colonists of that period.

Buffin.—A coarse cloth first made in Elizabeth's reign.

Buffonts.—A piece of gauze or lace worn over or round the neck, and puffed out over the breast like a "pouter pidgeon." In New England papers of 1771 "Gauze Buffons" were advertised.

Bugles.—Glass beads used in trimmings very early in the Colonies.

Burgoigne.—The front part of a head-dress next the hair.

Caddis or **Cades.**—A woolen tape, often woven into garters, and in common use in the seventeenth century.

Calash.—From the French *calêche*, a hood made to pull over the head, introduced into England in 1765 by the Duchess of Bedford and very popular in the Colonies. Possibly a revival of the old fashion seen in the recumbent effigies of the sixteenth and seventeenth centuries.

Calico.—Originally Calicut, from the town in India whence it was imported; later the name was applied to a cotton fabric in general wear at the time of the Revolution. Towards the end of the century calico was worn by people of all conditions. The French calicoes imported were very fine and delicate in colouring, and were often used for trimming plain materials.

Calks.—Clogs with spiked soles to keep one from slipping on the ice.

Callimanco.—According to Fairholt, a glazed linen fabric showing a pattern on one side only, but described by some writers as a fashionable woolen material with a fine gloss. It was undoubtedly popular in the Colonies. "Callimanco gounds" are mentioned in America in 1666.

Callot.—A plain cap or coif.

Camlet or **chamlet.**—A fabric made of wool or silk, sometimes of both, much used for cloaks and petticoats in all the Colonies. The name is derived from the place of its manufacture on the banks of the River Camlet in England.

Campaign-wigs.—Were very fashionable at the end of the seventeenth and beginning of the eighteenth centuries. They were full and curled towards the front.

Cannons.—Garters or breeches-fasteners.

Canvas.—A stiff woven cloth of flax or hemp.

Cap.—The general name for a popular head covering of both sexes.

> "Any cap whate'er it be
> Is still the sign of some degree."

Capuchin or **Capucine.**—A cloak with hood like a Capuchin monk's, fashionable in the early part of the eighteenth century.

Carcanet.—A necklace set with stones or strung with pearls.

Cardinal.—Cloak with a hood like the mozetta worn by cardinals which came into use early in the eighteenth century.

Casket-girls.—Name given to the girls sent out by the French Government to Louisiana, each provided with a small trunkful of clothing.

Cassock.—A loose coat, like a jerkin, worn by men.

Catgut.—A cloth woven in cords and used for lining and stiffening garments.

Cathedral Beard.—According to Randle Holmes, this style of beard was worn by dignitaries of the Church.

It was cut square and broad at the ends.

Caul.—A net to confine the hair. The back part of a wig or a woman's cap is sometimes called a caul.

Caushets.—Corsets.

Cherridary.—An Indian cotton stuff like gingham. (1712 and after.)

Chicken-skin.—Chicken skin gloves were worn in bed to keep the hands white as late as the reign of George III.

Chin-band or **chin-cloth.**—A muffler of lace worn by ladies of the time of Charles I.

Chints or **chintz.**—(From the Hindoo "chint," *i. e.*, spotted cloth)—cotton printed in several colours.

Clocks.—The plaits of a ruff, also ornaments on stockings.

Clogs.—Overshoes of various materials worn in the Colonies throughout the eighteenth century.

Cloth of Bodkin.—A rich cloth interwoven of silk and gold. The name is a corruption of Baldach, the ancient name of Bagdad, whence it was brought.

Clout.—A coarse kerchief worn on the head.

Cockers, Cocurs, Cocrez.—Laced high shoes or half-boots; also thick stockings without feet.

Coif or **Quoif.**—A close-fitting cap.

Colbertine, Colberteen, or **Colbatteen.**—A lace resembling network, named for Monsieur Colbert, superintendent of the French King's manufactories. Randle Holmes describes it as "an open lace with a square grounding." It ultimately became cheap and unfashionable.

Swift, in "Cadens and Vanessa," says:

"The difference between
Rich Flanders lace and Colbertine."

Collaret.—A puff made of soft ribbon worn around the throat ending in a bow beneath the chin.

Commode.—A lady's head-dress made on a frame of wire two or three tiers high fitted to the head and covered with tiffany or other thin silk. It came into fashion in England during the reign of William and Mary.

Copatain.—A sugar-loaf hat, "a capped crown hat."

Cordevan.—A leather of goatskin, originally from Cordova, Spain; sometimes spelt "cordewayne," whence "cordwainer" or "cordiner," a shoemaker.

Cornet.—A cap, apparently a Dutch fashion.

Corselet.—A light body armour.

Cote.—In old English was a woman's gown.

Cravat.—A neck-cloth and often a very costly article of dress. Governor Berkeley of Virginia ordered one from England in 1660 which was to cost five pounds.

Cremesyn.—Crimson velvet.

Criardes.—Name given to paniers of stiffened linen, which creaked with every movement.

Crocus.—A coarse stuff worn by slaves and working people.

Crosscloth.—A part of a woman's head-dress worn across the forehead. Worn in Maryland in 1642 and Massachusetts in 1647.

Cue de Paris.—According to Watson, a sort of bustle padded with horse-hair.

Cuirass.—Armour for the breast and back (name derived from *cuir*) made of leather or of metal fastened with leather thongs.

Curch or **Curchef.**—A plain close-fitting cap worn by women in the Colonies.

Curli-murli.—A fantastic curl or twist.

Cypress, Cyprus, Sipers, Sypress, or **Syphus.**—The material, found under all these spellings, is described in 1678 as a fine curled stuff, part silk, part hair, and of a cobweb thinness. It was used like crape for mourning.

Dag-wain.—A rough material used for coverlets for beds, tables, or floors.

Damask or **Damascus.**—A fabric woven in elaborate patterns of silk, wool, or linen. Wool damask was used for curtains and bed hangings in Colonial days.

"Damask white and azure blewe
Well diapered with lilies new."
—"*The Squire of Low Degree.*"

Dauphiness.—A certain style of mantle advertised in Boston in 1755.

Deriband or **Deribund.**—A thin material made in India.

Desoy or **Sergedesoy.**—A coarse silken material used in the eighteenth century for men's clothing.

Dimity, Dimothy, or **Demyt.**—This is a fine ribbed cotton fabric made first in Damietta, used throughout the Colonial period and until the present day.

Dornex.—A heavy coarse linen, like canvas.

Doublet.—A garment usually made of two thicknesses of stuff, whence its name.

Dowlas.—A heavy linen originally from Brittany.

Drawers.—Summer breeches.

Drugget.—A fabric of wool used for heavy coats, etc.

Ducape.—A heavy corded silk of plain colour mentioned in inventories from 1675. It was durable and very popular.

Duck.—A strong linen fabric without a twill.

Duffels or **Duffals.**—A woolen stuff originally made in Flanders, used in the Colonies in 1672 and after.

Durant.—A woolen fabric, sometimes called "everlasting."

Dussens.—A sort of kersey. The Massachusetts Bay Colonists were supplied with "100 sutes of Norden dussens."

Embroidery.—Variegated needlework used for decoration of dress. From the French *broder.*

> "Embroidered was he, as it were a mede
> All of fresh flowers, white and red."
> —*"Canterbury Tales."*

Engageants.—Deep double ruffles hanging down to the wrist.

> "About her sleeves are engageants."
> —*"Mundus Muliebris,"* 1690.

Eschelles or **Echelles.**—A stomacher laced or ribboned in the form of a ladder.

Face-painting.—Portrait painting.

Falbalas or **Furbelows.**—Rows of plaiting or puffs, fashionable in the time of William and Mary. A puckered flounce.

Falding.—A kind of coarse cloth—like frieze.

Fall.—A falling band, a large collar, worn in the sixteenth and seventeenth centuries.

Fallals.—Full soft ruffles used for trimming.

Farthingale.—The under supporter of the wide gown or petticoat worn in the time of Elizabeth and James I. Made like a circular cushion stuffed with hair, and worn just below the waist-line.

Farthingale Breeches.—Stuffed out like a farthingale, supposed to be a protection from poniard thrusts and for that reason encouraged by James I.

Favourite.—A lock dangling on the temples.

Felt.—A fabric of wool and hair. Felt hats were first made in England in the days of Henry VIII.

Firmament.—An encircling ornament for the head set with gems.

Fly-fringe.—A very popular trimming made of tufts of silk to match or contrast with the gown. In fashion all through the Georgian Era.

Follette.—A very light fichu.

Fontange.—A knot of ribbon worn on the head-dress, so called for Mlle. Fontange, who first wore it. Sometimes confused with the Commode, on top of which it was usually worn.

Fote or **Foot-mantel.**—An outer skirt worn by a woman on horseback to keep her gown clean.

French Fall.—A sort of shoe.

Frieze.—A thick and warm woolen cloth in use since the fourteenth century.

Frilals.—Borders of ornamental ribbon.

Frontlet.—A piece of stuff worn under the hood and projecting beyond it over the forehead.

Furbelows.—An ornamental trimming for women's gowns, described as a puckered flounce.

Fustian.—A species of cloth, originally made at Fusht on the Nile, used for jackets and doublets as early as the fifteenth century. It had a warp of linen thread and a woof of thick cotton.

Fygury.—An old name for silk diapered with figures of flowers and fruit.

Galloon or **Galon.**—A kind of lace made of silk woven with cotton, gold, or silver, or of silk only.

Gamoshes.—High boots worn about 1688.

Garters.—The New England Colonists were furnished with Norwich garters. In the time of James I garters were small sashes of silk tied in a large bow.

Gauze.—A transparent silk texture invented at Gaza in Palestine, whence its name.

Gelofer or **Gillofer.**—The old name for carnation pinks.

Gloves.—Were worn on all occasions of ceremony by both sexes in early Colonial Days. They were often embroidered in gold or silver. We read of perfumed gloves in England in 1631.

> "One gives to me perfumed gloves, the best that he can buy me.
> Live where I will, I will have the loves of all that come nigh me."
> —"*A Fayre Portion for a Fayre Maide.*"

Glove Tightens.—To keep the long gloves in place, were made of plaited hair as well as of ribbon.

Goffering.—The mode of ironing the plaits of a ruff over heated poking or goffering sticks.

Golosh.—A shoe with soles of wood or leather kept on by straps over the instep.

Gorget.—An ornamental neckband which was full and broad in front, worn as early as 1642 in the Col-

onies. Metal gorgets were worn with armour.

Grain.—Scarlet (a colour).

Grassets or **Grazzets.**—A dress stuff in use from 1712 to 1768.

Greaves.—Armour worn to protect the front part of the legs.

Gridelin.—A soft blue gray colour fashionable in the eighteenth century.

Grogram.—A rough fabric of silk and wool with a diagonal weave. Country women wore gowns of it in the sixteenth and seventeenth centuries in England and it was much used in the Colonies.

Hair-clasps.—Worn to keep the back hair in place, made of various metals, and often set with pearls, etc.

Hair-lace.—A fillet for the hair, much worn in the eighteenth century.

Haling-hands.—Mittens for sailors and workingmen. The palms were often lined with leather.

Hanaper or **Hamper.**—A wicker basket.

Hand-ruffs.—Ruffles for the wrist.

Hanger.—A small sword worn by gentlemen with morning dress in the seventeenth century.

Hatch.—A locker in which clothing was kept and which generally stood at the foot of the bed and was used as a seat.

Hive.—A sort of straw bonnet shaped like a bee-hive.

> "Upon her head a platted hive of straw which fortified her visage from the sun."

Hoods.—(from the Anglo-Saxon *Hood*) —Were worn with great variations of fashion by both sexes from the eleventh to the eighteenth century Replaced by caps and hats in the reign of George II.

17

Hookers.—The name given to certain sects who eschewed the use of buttons. Mennonites or Dunkers.

Hoops.—In the Colonies followed all the English changes of shape, and were worn by old and young. (1712–1778.)

Hum-Hum.—A coarse cotton fabric brought from India, used for lining coats, etc., 1750–1770.

Inkle.—A woolen tape or braid. Used as a trimming and sewed on in patterns.

Iron-pot.—Familiar name of the iron head-piece worn by Cromwell's soldiers.

Isabella colour.—Dirty white.

Jack-boots.—Were introduced in the seventeenth century.

Jacket.—A popular garment worn in the Colonies from 1641 and after.

Jean.—A twilled cotton cloth used both for underwear and for outer garments. Summer suits for men were often made of jean in the Colonies.

Jerkin.—Another name for jacket or doublet.

Jerkinet.—A similar garment for women.

Joseph.—A lady's riding-habit buttoned down the front. When worn open this garment was popularly called a " flying Josie."

Jumps.—A loose bodice for women, also a loose coat or jacket for men, reaching to the thighs, buttoned down the front, with sleeves to the wrist.

Kendal.—A green woolen cloth or baize first made at Kendal in England.

Kenting.—A fine linen fabric.

Kersey.—(under various spellings)—A fine woolen material.

Kincob or **Kinkhaib.**—A rich Indian stuff of silk, brocaded in flowers and large figures.

Kirtle.—A loose gown or tunic.

Kist.—A chest.

Knop.—A button.

Lace.—A lacing cord (the name came from *lacier*, "to fasten"). In the earlier days, trimming woven with gold and silver thread and put on in flat rows. In its later sense signifying that delicate and beautiful fabric which is one of the most admirable ornaments of costume. Mechlin, a favourite lace in the Colonies, was made in Flanders; pointlace or French point, also much worn, was made in Alençon.

"Your snowy wrists do Mechlin pendants grace;
And do the smartest wigs adorn thy face?"
—"*The Test of Love,*" *Nicholas Amherot.*

Lappets.—The lace pendants of a lady's cap or head-dress. Very fashionable in the last half of the eighteenth century.

Lawn.—A delicate fabric used as early as Elizabeth's day.

Leno.—A thin linen fabric used for caps.

Levite.—Another name for a polonese, and made of dimity and muslin, often bordered with chintz or callimanco.

Linset.—The stool on which a woman sat when spinning.

Linsey-wolsey.—A coarse woolen stuff first made at Linsey in Suffolk, England, and very popular in the Colonies.

Liripipes.—Long streamers of gauze or ribbon attached to a head-dress and often hanging to the feet.

Loo masks.—Half masks covering the face to the nose only.

Loretto.—A silk material used for waistcoats.

Love-lock.—A long ringlet of hair worn on the left side of the head.

Lustring.—A soft silk, plain or flowered, in general wear for many years.

Macaroni.—Nickname for a London fop. Whence arose the use of the word in the contemporary doggerel of Yankee Doodle and its application as a name in the American Revolution to a body of Maryland troops remarkable for showy uniforms. (1770–1775.) (Century Dictionary.)

Mandillion.—An outer garment. The New England Colonists wore them lined with cotton and fastened with hooks and eyes.

Mantee.—A coat with sleeves which hung open from the throat showing the stomacher and petticoat beneath.

Mantua.—A form of sacque for outdoor wear, sometimes name of material for making sacques. We read, for instance, of yellow mantua silk in 1741.

Masks.—As a protection from the sun and wind, were worn by women and children in all the colonies.

Mercury.—The name for a certain kind of cap for women in fashion about 1760 in Boston and elsewhere.

Mittens.—Were made of heavy cloth and of dressed skins as well as knitted of wool.

Mitts.—Fingerless gloves made of kid or silk and often of lace-work for summer wear. Mitts made of cotton or linen like the dress were buttoned to the shoulder of the gown and were in fashion after the Revolution.

Mode.—A contraction of "alamode," a thin silk. A mantle with a hood fashionable in the eighteenth century was also called a "mode."

Modesty-piece.—A piece of lace worn across the upper part of the stays.

Monmouth Cap.—A popular headgear mentioned in the outfits of the Colonists. Made originally in the old parts of the town of Monmouth, which is still known as the Capper's town.

Monteroe or **Mountero Cap.**—Made with a low crown and flap which could be turned down for protection.

Morion.—A head-piece of armour introduced from Spain and worn by English soldiers in the latter half of the sixteenth century.

Mouches.—Black patches were thus called because they looked like flies.

Muffetees or **Wristlets.**—Were worn when the coat sleeves were short, by men and women in the time of William and Mary.

Muffs.—Have been in use from early in the seventeenth century to the present day. For many years they were carried by both men and women and made of woolen stuff, fur, and feathers. We read that Judge Dana of Boston carried one until after the Revolution.

Murry.—Mulberry colour.

Nabob.—A thin East India stuff.

Nankeen.—A cotton cloth of a yellow colour imported from China and named for Nankin, where it was made.

Neck-cloths.—Worn by both men and women in the Colonies.

"Before your glass each morning do you
  stand
And tie your neck-cloth with a critic's
  hand."

Neckstock.—A stiffly folded cravat

worn close to the throat, finished with a buckle at the back.

Negligée.—A loose gown or sacque open in front over a handsome petticoat; and, in spite of its name, was not only in high fashion for many years, but was worn in full dress.

Night-rail.—A dress unconfined at the waist and closed only at the neck—literally night-gowns, which the ladies adopted as a morning costume.

"Three night-gowns of rich Indian stuff."
—"*Mundus Muliebris.*"

None-so-Prettys.—Fancy tapes.

Orange-butter.—A pomade used in the Dutch Colonies.

Orrice.—A lace or gimp trimming woven with gold and silver thread.

Oxford Gown.—The academic gown worn usually on public occasions by men in authority, chiefly as a badge of office in the Colonies.

Oznaburg.—A coarse linen made in Hanover and named for a province of that name.

Paduasoy.—A rich smooth silk made originally at Padua.

Palisade.—A wire sustaining the hair next to the first knot. Part of the commode head-dress.

Paniers.—Were made of hoops of straw, cane, or whalebone fastened together by tapes.

Paragon.—A stuff used for common wear in the seventeenth century.

Patches.—First introduced towards the end of the reign of Charles I and varied into all manner of shapes.

Pattens.—A sole of wood on iron rings fastened to the foot by leather straps.

Pelerine.—A small cape with long ends in front.

Penistone.—(under various spellings)—A coarse woolen stuff made in England in the seventeenth and eighteenth centuries.

Pennache.—A bunch of tassels or narrow ribbons.

Perpetuana, Petuna, or **Perpets.**—A glossy woolen stuff like lasting worn by the Puritans in 1629 and after.

Persian.—A thin silk used for linings of cloaks and hoods or for summer gowns. Sold in New England in the eighteenth century.

Petticoat.—(Originally petty-coet)—A garment worn universally and made of every sort of material. Quilted petticoats were advertised as early as 1720 in the Colonies.

Philomot.—Colour of a dead leaf.

Pig-tail Wig.—Wig with a plaited tail tied with a ribbon, worn very generally in the middle of the eighteenth century.

Pilgrim.—A cape or ruffle fastened to the back of a bonnet to shield the neck; usually made of thin silk.

Pillion.—The extension of a saddle on which a woman rode before the days of side-saddles.

Pinner.—Usually a child's bib or apron and mentioned often in the seventeenth century, but caps fastened on with pins were also called pinners in the eighteenth century.

Pins or **Pinnes.**—Were sold for one shilling and four pence a thousand in the early Colonial days.

Plumpers.—Very thin round and light balls to plump out and fill up hollow cheeks.

Points.—Ties or laces of ribbon or leather decorated with tags and used instead of buttons to fasten garments together. They were in general use until late in the seventeenth century, both for armour and civilian's dress.

Polonese.—A long-sleeved coat-like garment for women opening down the front, finished often with a large hood at the back of the neck.

Pomander.—A perforated ball or box filled with perfumes, used to prevent infection.

Pompadour or **Pompadore.**—Was a word in constant use in the eighteenth century. We read of Pompadore shoes, laces, caps, aprons, sacques, stockings, and head-dresses.

Pompon.—An ornament made of artificial flowers, feathers, tinsel, etc.

Pretintailles.—Large cut-out patterns laid on a dress as trimming. Introduced in the time of William and Mary.

Prunella.—A close woolen stuff like lasting.

Puce Colour.—Colour of a flea. Name given by Louis XVI.

Pug.—A short cape with hood attached and usually made of silk, velvet, or cloth.

Pump.—A shoe with a thin sole and low heel, first mentioned in the sixteenth century.

Purl.—A species of edging used on caps, collars, cuffs, etc.

Qualitie.—A coarse tape for strings or binding, used in all the Colonies between 1700 and 1800.

Rail or **Rayle.**—A loose garment (old English), but later applied only to night-gowns.

Ramall or **Romall.**—A neckerchief or small shawl to be worn over the shoulders.

Ramilie.—A wig bushy at the sides, a braided tail in the back with a large bow at top and small bow at the end. (1708 and after.)

Rash.—A wool fabric of inferior quality.

Ratteen.—A heavy woolen material something like drugget.

Rayonné.—A species of hood.

Robings.—The ornamental part of a gown, such as lapels, reveres, etc.

Rocket or **Rochet.**—A long woolen mantle trimmed with fringe. Brought from Devon or Cornwall.

Roquelaure or **Roquelo.**—A cloak for both men and women, named for the Duke of Roquelaure, mentioned in New England papers of 1730. Made of all heavy materials and generally of bright colours. Often two small capes of the same material finished the garment on the shoulders.

Roses.—Ornaments in the form of roses made of ribbons, lace, and even jewels. One of the pet extravagances of the seventeenth century. Worn on shoes, garters, and hatbands. We read of an English gallant who paid 30 pounds for a pair.

Round-cord Cap.—A cap which was tied on with a fine cord back of the ears.

Ruffles.—Of lawn and lace were worn in the sleeves and in the front of the shirts until after 1800.

Russel or **Russet.**—A twilled woolen stuff like baize, much worn in the Colonies.

" Our clothing is good sheepskins
Gray russet for our wives
'Tis warmth and not gay clothing
That doth prolong our lives."
—"*Coridon's Song.*"

Safeguard.—An outside petticoat worn over the dress as a protection from mud or dust in riding by women in the Colonies. (1650 and after.)

Sagathy or **Sagathie.**—A durable woolen stuff.

Samare or **Semnar.**—A lady's jacket. Originally a Dutch garment. "It had a loose body and side flaps, or skirts which extended to the knee, the sleeves short to the elbow, turned back and faced" (Randle Holmes). The samare was often made long and was worn opening over a petticoat and waistcoat very much like the English sacque.

Sarsnet, Sarsenet, or **Sarsinet.**—A thin silk still in use, but dating from the thirteenth century.

Satin Jean.—A thick cotton cloth with a glossy surface used for shoes and similar purposes.

Say or **Soy.**—(from the French *soie*)—Originally a silk and wool material. It is mentioned in Colonial lists from 1629 to 1768.

Serge.—A twilled fabric of either wool or silk, often of both.

Shades.—A head covering, or a stuff suitable for headgear. We read in 1766 of "painted lawns and chequer'd shades."

Shadow.—A sunshade either worn on the head or held in the hand. (1580–1647 and after.)

Shag.—A heavy woolen cloth with a long nap. (1632 and after.)

Shagreen.—An untanned leather with a granular surface often made of sharkskin and dyed green.

Shalloons.—A woolen fabric not unlike the modern challis and made in Chalons, France.

Sherry-vallies.—A sort of legging worn in riding, to protect from mud, buttoned up outside the trousers.

Shift.—A shirt or chemise, usually of fine linen. This undergarment was in Colonial days often made with long sleeves which were laid in fine plaits with a knife when laundered.

Shoepack.—A shoe shaped like a moccasin, without a separate sole, made of tanned leather and much worn during the Revolution.

Skilts.—Short full trousers reaching just below the knee, full half a yard wide at the bottom. Worn during the Revolution by the country people.

Slyders or **Slivers.**—Overalls.

Smock.—A shirt of heavy linen worn by farm labourers and workingmen. Before 1700 a shift was often called a smock. In "Mundus Muliebris" we read:

"Twice twelve day-smocks of Holland fine
 Twelve more for night, all Flanders lac'd."

Snuff.—Came into general use in England in 1702.

Snuff-boxes.—Were carried by both men and women for the greater part of the century.

Solitaire.—A broad black ribbon introduced from France in the time of Louis XV worn close around the throat, apparently to protect the coat from the powdered wig. Sometimes it was tied to the back of the wig and brought round and tucked in the shirt ruffle. According to advertisements in the American newspapers, it was much worn in the Colonies.

Sorti.—A knot of small ribbon peeping out between the pinner and bonnet.

Spagnolet.—A gown with narrow sleeves, *à l'Espagnole.*

Spanish Paper.—A red colour with

which the ladies of Spain painted their faces. It was made up into little books and a leaf was torn out and rubbed upon the cheeks, the vermillion powder which covered it being transferred to the face. It was in use at the end of the eighteenth century.

Stamin or **Stammel.**—A heavy cloth like linsey-woolsey.

Startups or **Startop.**—A sort of buskin for ordinary wear worn in the sixteenth and seventeenth centuries by country folk.

Stayhooks.—Small ornamental hooks stuck in the edge of the bodice on which to hang an *étui*.

Steinkirk.—A cravat folded with careless grace. Name given by the French to commemorate the battle in 1692.

Stirrup-hose.—Were worn on horseback to protect the nether garments. They were wide at the back and fastened with straps to the girdle.

Stock.—A stiff neck-cloth buckled at the back of the neck, successor to the cravat.

Stock-buckle.—Buckle which fastened the stock.

" The stock with buckle made of plate
Has put the cravat out of date."

Strap Cap.—A cap which fastened with flaps under the chin.

Sultane.—A gown caught up with buttons and loops.

Swanskin.—A fleecy cloth like Canton flannel, used for linings, etc.

Tabby.—A sort of watered silk.

Tabinet or **Tabaret.**—Another name for poplin, used for petticoats, and also for covering furniture.

Taffeta.—A rich cloth used first in the sixteenth century and considered a luxury in the Colonial days.

Taminy.—A woolen stuff like alpaca, made in Norfolk, 1653 and after.

Tassets.—Splints of steel fastened to the corselet as a protection for the thighs. Worn until late in the seventeenth century.

Thrum.—The extremity of a weaver's warp, often about nine inches long, which cannot be woven. Caps and hats knitted of this material were called thrums.

"And her thrum'd hat and her muffler too."

Tiffany.—A heavy silk fabric. (1792 and after.)

Tippets.—A neck covering made of a variety of materials worn for ornament, of gauze and tissues, and for warmth, of fur.

Tongs.—Overalls of coarse cotton or linen.

Tufftaffeta.—A taffeta with a chenille stripe, worn in New England.

Tuly.—A shade of red.

Turban also **Turbin.**—A head-dress for women made of gauze and trimmed with feathers, very fashionable in the Colonies. (1760 and after.)

Trollopee.—Another name for negligée.

Vambrace.—The piece of armour which protected the forearm from elbow to wrist.

Vampay.—A short hose or sock of wool.

Veil.—One of the most ancient articles of female attire, the *couvre chef* of the Anglo-Saxon ladies and an important part of the conventual costume, but retaining its place in the wardrobes of women to-day.

Whisk.—A collarette or cape to cover the neck and shoulders, usually made of muslin trimmed with lace and worn with low-cut gowns, in the seventeenth and eighteenth centuries. We read of Tiffany whisks in 1660.

Whitney.—A heavy coarse stuff used for coats, cloaks, and petticoats, 1737 and after.

Whittle.—A blanket shawl with fringe, worn in 1665 and after, in the Colonies.

Worsted.—A woolen cloth first made at Worstead in England in the reign of Henry I.

INDEX

Index

ABLETTES, 72
Acadian exiles, 36
Actors in America, 238
Adams's, Mrs. Abigail, letter from England, describing the fashions, 259
Adventurers, 33, 43
Advertisements in colonial newspapers, 245–251
André, Major, 255
Andros, Sir Edward, 136
Aprons, 53, 68, 71, 100, 130, 195, 202
Armour, 56, 59, 60, 99
Arquebusiers, 27
Artificial flowers, 213
Artisans, 33
Attitude of the Colonists in New England towards the English Church, 113, 114

BABY-CLOTHES, 283
Back boards, 196
Bacon's Rebellion, anecdote of, 71
Baize, gowns of, 258
Baldricks, 51
Baltimore, Lord, 56
Bandoliers, 99, 103
Bands, 51, 64
Banyans, 315
Barbadoes, 63
Basquinas, 28
Bath bonnets, 222
Bayard, Nicholas, costume of, 144
Bayard, Madam, costume of, 147
Beards, 44
Beaver hats, 190, 214
Berkeley, Sir Wm., Governor of the Virginia Colony, 48, 60, 61
Bishops, 222
Blacksmith, 53
Boarding-school outfit, 291
Bobs, 300, 303
Bodices, coloured, 33
Bodices, pair of, 190
Bonnets, 202, 214, 222, 225, 256, 273
Boots, 64, 312, 324
Bowne's, Elizabeth, descriptions of dress in 1798, 273
Breeches, 53, 61, 67, 143

Bricklayer, 53
Bridal veil, 206, 209
Bridge spectacles, 193
Bridling, 196
Brigade Orders, West Point, 369
Broad-brimmed hats, 95, 312, 323
Buccaneers, 27, 28
Buckle, 247
Buckles, 311
Buckskin breeches, 346
Buckskin shoes, 346
Buff coats, 59, 60, 107
Burney, Miss, verses on a great-coat by, 257
Burroughs, Anne, 47
Buttons, 64, 67, 109, 324

CALASH, 214, 222, 233
California, 26, 31
Campaign wig, 147, 299
Canes, 205
Cannons or breeches fastenings, 99
Capes, 34
Capotes, 34
Caps for women, 100, 193, 214, 217, 257
Capuchins, 229
Cardinal, 140, 193, 194, 229
Carpenters, 53
Cavalier, Robert, Sieur de La Salle, 32, 33
Cavaliers, 63
Chaises, 263
Chapeau bras, 312
Chatelaines, 133
Chief justice, robe of a, 335
Children, dress of, 17th century, 47, 52, 113, 135
Children, dress of, 18th century, 283, 292
Chintz gowns, 257
Church services, 17th century, 54
City troop, uniform of the, 350
Cleaning establishment, 249
Clergymen, dress of, 17th century, 54, 114, 115
Clergymen, dress of, 18th century, 304, 307
Cloaks, 100, 103, 193, 217, 229, 252, 263
Clogs, 34, 186, 217
Coats, 17th century, 61, 109, 143
Coats, 18th century, 312, 332
Cockades, 376

397

Cocked hats, 143, 299, 328, 332
Cocking the hat, various forms of, 308, 311
Coif of a Dutch matron, 130, 136
Coifs, men, 152, 156
Coifs, women, 164
Colebatteen ruffles, 147
Colonial militia, 99
Colonial period, end of, 255
Commode, 108, 147, 181
Connecticut settlers, 84, 85
Continental soldiers, uniform of, 359
Cordovan leather, 26
Corselets, 99
Countryman, 17th century, 54
Cravats, 312
Creedon, Captain, 61
Cue de Paris, 222
Cuffs, 143, 202
Cuirass 60
Curli-murlis, 195
Curls, 194
Curtsey, 199
Curwen, Judge, 103
Cushions for the hair, 214, 217
Custis children, clothes ordered for, 288

Dances, 234
Delany, Mrs., 193
Delaware settled, 136
Delaware, Swedes on the, 136
Dentists, 248
Deportment, 196
Dickinson, Maria, letter quoted, 258
Discriminative dress, 230
Domestics, 244, 246
Doublets, 28, 44, 51, 59, 61, 96, 109
Drake, Sir Francis, 26
Drummer, 53
Dutch babies, 129, 130
Dutch bridal crown, 130
Dutch bride, 130
Dutch children, dress of, 135
Dutch merchants, 121
Dutch peasant women, dress of, 126
Dutch settlers, 121
Dutchman, working dress of, 129
Dyes, 122, 133

Earrings, 52
Encouragement of home manufactures, 252
English gentleman, dress of, 17th century, 44, 51, 52, 139, 143
English gentleman, dress of, 18th century, 299
English gentlewoman, dress of, 17th century, 52, 139, 143
English gentlewoman, dress of, 18th century, 177
English rule in all the Colonies, 139
Etui, 202
Eves, Miss Sarah, journal of, 241

Falbalas, 143
Falling bands, 61, 96
Falling collars, 61, 96
Fans, 68, 189, 214
Farthingale, 47, 193
Farthingale breeches, 44
Fashion dolls, 178, 181, 256
Feathers in the hair, 195, 214
Fenwick, Lady Mary, 108
First Troop City Cavalry, uniform of, 349
Fithian, Philip, diary of, 230, 234
Flounces, 143
Fob pockets, 318
Forrest, Mrs., 47
Franks, Miss, 256
French curls, 196
French falls, 64
French settlers, dress of, 33, 34
French taste prevalent in America, 256
Frocks or overshirts, 263
Full dress in New England (middle of 18th century), 214, 217
Funeral of Lady Andros, 107
Furbelows, 143
Fur caps, 130
Fur-trimmed jackets, 130

Galloon, 68
Gauntlets, 99
Geneva gown, 56, 114
George III, dress in the reign of, 202, 316
German settlers, 160, 163
Gipsy hats, 101, 196, 214
Gloves, 67, 96, 99, 100, 256, 323
Gold beads, 217
Gold lace, 99
Gorget, 60
Gray hair fashionable, 307
Great-coats for men, 316, 319, 320, 332
Great-coats for women, 257, 258
Green aprons worn by Quakers, 140
Gumbos, 35
Guns, 99, 100

Hair-dressing, 217, 218, 230, 252
Hair powder, 143, 193, 331
Half-Moon, The, 121
Hampshire kerseys, 96
Hatchments, 107
Hats, 95, 135, 140, 143, 332
Head-dresses, 143, 194
Helmets, 59
Herrisons, 268
Hibbins, Mistress Anne, 110
Higginson, letter from, 84
High heels, 139
High prices during the Revolution, 256
Hogarth, 307
Holland, dress of the women, 89
Holland shirts, 51, 61, 64
Hollar, Wenceslaus, 86
Home Life in New England, 18th century, 263

Homespun parties, 252
Hoods, 34, 68, 100, 108, 152, 185, 186, 214
Hooks and eyes, 96
Hoop, the, 182, 193, 195, 217, 256
Hooped petticoats, 182, 193, 196, 199
Horn flasks, 99
Horse-blocks, 263
Horsehair bonnets, 222
Hose, 68
Household servants, 244
Hubbard store, contents of, 73
Hudson, Captain, 109
Hudson, Henry, 121
Huguenots, the, 122
Hunting shirts, 346, 354

INAUGURATION ball, description of, 267
Inauguration costumes of Washington, 267, 328
Irish stockings, 96
Isham, Sir Thomas, wedding suit of, 110
Italian curls, 196

JACKETS, 130
Jefferson, Thomas, suit worn by, 328
Jersey Blues, uniform of the, 349
Jerseys (the) settled, 136
Jesuit missionaries, 25, 26
Jewelry, 17th century, 72
Jockey coat, 311
Judges, costume of, 152
Jute-braids, 250

KEEPER of the Great Seal, 155
Kerchiefs, 34
Kitchen utensils, 74
Knit caps, 96

LABOURERS, 53, 133, 328
Labrador tea, 252
Lake, Mrs., 93; list of household articles, 93; fur mantle, 93
Lange, Dr. Jacob de, wardrobe of, 134
Lange, Mrs. de, wardrobe of, 133
Lappets, 195
La Salle, Robert Cavalier, Sieur, 32, 33
Law Courts in England, 17th century, 151
Lawyers' bags, 335
Lawyers in the Colonies, 17th century, 114, 115, 148; 18th century, 335
Leather breeches, 328, 332, 346
Legal costumes, 17th century, 148; 18th century, 335
Legal customs, 17th century, 148; 18th century, 335, 336
Leggings, 34, 332
Lemcke, Count, 167
Leverett, Sir John, Governor of the Massachusetts Colony, 100

Light Horse of Philadelphia, uniform of the, 349
Livery at Mt. Vernon, 245
Lolonais, Francis, 28
Long Island settled, 136
Long waistcoats, 303
Lynn, shoes made at, 95; worn by women, 217

MACARONI costume, 241
Macaronis, the, 241, 243
Maine settled in 1623, 113
Mandillion, 84, 85, 96
Manhattan, gay costumes in, 122
Manifesto against long hair, 89
Mantillas, 28
Mantles, 68
Marie Antoinette, Queen, makes a reform in dress of children, 292
Maryland settled, 56
Masks, 193
Mason, 53
Massachusetts Line, Orders for, 365
Massachusetts: Settled in 1620, 83; Order of the General Court of, 94, 95, 108; dress of women, 95; a religious commonwealth, 115
Menendez de Aviles, Pedro de, 25
Mennonites, 160
Militia, dress of the, 346
Mincing air, 312
Minuet, the, 234
Minuit, Peter, 121
Minute-men, dress of the, 346
Mischianza, 255
Mittens, 67, 100
Mitts, children's, 284
Moccasins, 34
Mocking birds, 73
Monmouth caps, 44, 64, 96
Moravian caps, 167
Moravians, 163, 164, 167
Morgan, Sir Henry, 28
Morions, 55
Moro (1500–1778), 25
Mourning dress and customs, 17th century, 104, 107, 108
Mourning dress, 18th century, 251
Mourning rings, 72, 107
Muff-dogs, 62
Muffs, 62, 143, 190
Murillo (1618–1682), 25
Musical instruments, 74
Musk-melon bonnet, 222

NECKCLOTHS, 64, 109, 143, 147, 324
Négligées, 199, 230
Net worn over a queue, 316
New England, 17th century, dress of the women, 100
New Hampshire settled in 1623, 113
New-market coat, 316
New Orleans, 35

Non-conformists, gowns of, 114
Normandy peasants, 36

OAK sticks, 312
Opera glasses, 241
Ordinary people, dress of, 18th century, 328
Ornatus Muliebris Anglicanus, 86
Orrices, 147, 186
Outfit of fashionable man, 331
Outfit of the Massachusetts Bay Colonists, 84
Outfit of the Virginia Colonists, 44
Overalls, 357
Overshoes, 335

PAMUNKEYS, King of the, 77
Pamunkeys, Queen of the, 77
Parasols, 214
Pastors, choosing, in the Massachusetts Colony, 114
Patch boxes, 189
Patches, 62, 189
Patriotic agreement, 251
Patroons, 122
Pattens, 130, 201, 217
Pearls, 52, 72
Peccadilles, 51
Peddlers, 74
Penn, William, 139; advice on dress, 140; blue sash, 139; wigs, 143
Pennsbury, 140
Pepys, 109
Percy, Sir George, Governor of Virginia Colony, 51
Perfumed powders, 68
Perfumes, 202, 205
Periwigs or wigs, 64, 109, 140, 143, 147, 159, 299, 300, 307, 312, 315, 319
Perriot, 267, 271
Perspective glasses, 193
Petticoat breeches, 61
Petticoats, 68, 130, 193, 202, 217
Pigtails, 312
Pikes, 99
Pillions, 263
Planters' wives, dress of, 17th century, 71
Plymouth pilgrims, 83
Pockets, 242
Points, 53, 54, 59, 85, 104
Political badges, 189
Pomander, 202
Pompadours, 200
Pompons, 195, 210
Posey dance, 28
Potpourri, 205
Pouncet box, 202
Powder, hair, 143, 193, 331
Preaching gown, 56, 114
Presbyterians, gown worn by, 114
Pritchard, Mrs. Frances, wardrobe of, 71
Provincials, uniforms of the, 346
Puritans of the Massachusetts Bay Co., 83, 84

QUAKER aprons, 140
Quaker bonnets, 225
Quaker hats, 140
Quaker settlers in Pennsylvania Province, 139
Quaker weddings, description of, 226, 258
Quakers, dress of the, 139, 140, 225, 226, 229, 258
Quakers, portraits of, 258
Queensbury, Duchess of, a wonderful gown of, 195
Queues, 316, 331
Quilted petticoats, 202, 257
Quitasols, 230

RAMILIE wig, 299, 304
Rapiers, 109
Restraining Acts of the Pilgrims, 96
Revere, Paul, a dentist, 248
Rhode Island settled 1636, 113
Richbell, Robert, 109
Riding dress, 17th century, 109
Riding suit, a lady's, 18th century, 186
Ringlets, 273
Rings, 72, 130
Robings, 196, 273
Roelas, Juan de Las, 1558–1625, 25
Rollers, 218
Roquelaures, 229, 303, 320
Rosettes, 96
Roundhead Puritans (old song), 89
Ruffled shirts, 332
Ruffles, 139, 147, 195, 202
Ruffs, 26, 44, 159
Russell, 222

SACQUE, 182, 187, 201, 202
Sailors, dress of, 328
Samare, 133
Sandys, George, 52
Sandys, Sir Edwin, 44
Sartori, Mrs., story of dress worn by, 274
Scarfs, 214
Scarlet cloaks worn by women, 263
Scarlet robes worn by Judges, 103, 152, 335
Scarlet stockings, 299
Scent bottles, 202
Sedan chairs, 182
Sergeant-at-law, reign of Charles II, 156; reign of James II, 159
Servants, 18th century, 244, 246, 268
Seventh Day Baptists, 168
Shoe-buckles, 64, 139
Shoemaking at Salem, 90
Shoes, 64, 68, 95, 96, 139, 143, 217, 328
Shifts, 130
Shirts, 51, 61, 64
Short-waists, 273, 274
Shoulder belts, 99
Silver lace, 99
Silverware (17th century), 74
Skimmer hat, 222
Slashed sleeves, 51, 96

Slaves, dress of, 245, 246
Sleeves, 94, 143, 202, 217
Slippers, 214
Smith, Captain John, 44
Snuff-boxes, 202, 311
Snuff, use of, 311
Spanish gentleman, dress of, 16th century, 26
Spanish painters, 25
Spanish point-lace, 143
Spanish settlers, 25
Spanish soldiers, 16th century, 27
Spanish women, dress of, 28
Spectacles, 193
Square toes, 139, 311
St. Augustine, 25, 26
Stays, 190, 217
Steinkirk, 147
Stock buckles, 300
Stockings, 64, 68, 143, 214, 217, 299
Stocks, 332
Stoffelsen, Vrouentje Ides, inventory of clothing, 130
Stomachers, 143, 182, 202
Store in the Virginia Colony, contents of a, 73
Striped silk, coats of, 273
Stuyvesant, Peter, Governor of New Amsterdam, 125
Sumptuous dress, 109
Surplices, 54

TABBY, 68
Tailors, 53, 249
Tanneries, 95
Tassetts, 59
Temple spectacles, 193
Tête moutonée, 196
Texas, 31
Theatre, first, in America, 238
Theatrical costumes, 238
Theatrum Mulierum, 89
Thrums, 53, 328
Tiffany hoods, 95
Tippets, 155, 193
Tow cloth, 263
Tower and commode, 181
Traders, 34
Tradesmen, dress of, 328
Training Day, 100
Treaty of Paris in 1764, 36
Tuilles, 59
Turbans, 214

UMBRELLAS, 214, 320
Undergirdle, 130
Uniforms, military, 1775–1800, 340
Uniforms, naval, 1775–1800, 340

VANDYKE collar, 52
Vandyke edging, 51
Vargas, Luis de (1502–1568), 25
Velasquez, Diego (1599–1660), 25
Vests, 34
Virginia ball, 230
Virginia Company, 43
Virginia Infantry, uniform of the, 349
Vos, Madame Cornelia de, 134

WAGON bonnet, 225
Waistcoats, 67, 143, 186, 303, 307, 324, 332
Walloons, the, 122
Walpole, Horace, 206
Wansey's, Mr., description of dress at the theatre in Philadelphia, 272, 273
Warren's, Mrs. Mercy, 271; verses on dress, 272
Washington, George, dress of, first inauguration, 267; second inauguration, 328; uniform of, 349
Washington, Mrs., 268
Watches, 320
Waterproof capes, 320
Watteau, the artist, 190
Watteau sacque, 182
West Point, Brigade Orders, 369
Whig colours, 349
White, Bishop, anecdote of, 307
White, Mrs., inventory of, 200
Wig makers, 250
Wigs and periwigs, 64, 109, 140, 143, 147, 159, 299, 300, 303, 307, 312, 315, 319
Willoughby, Mrs. Sarah, wardrobe of, 71
Winthrop, Margaret, 86
Wister, Sally, dress of, 257
Wooden heels, 68, 95
Wooden shoes, 68
Worked head, 194
Workingman, dress of, 17th century, 53, 54
Workingman, dress of, 18th century, 244, 328, 331

YANKEE Doodle, 242

ZINZENDORF, Count, dress of, 168

AUTHORITIES CONSULTED

Authorities Consulted

Calendar of Virginia State Papers, Richmond, 1875.

History of the Virginia Settlement, Captain John Smith, London, 1624.

First Discovery and Settlement of Virginia, William Stith, Williamsburg, 1747.

Virginia Vetusta, Edward D. Neill, Albany, 1885.

Virginia Carolorum, Edward D. Neill, Albany, 1886.

Economic History of Virginia in the Seventeenth Century, Philip Alexander Bruce, New York, 1896.

Old Virginia and Her Neighbors, John Fiske, Boston, 1897.

History of the Barbadoes, John Poyer, London, 1808.

A True and Exact Account of the Island of the Barbadoes, Richard Ligon, London, 1657.

Annals of the Swedes on the Delaware, John C. Clay, Philadelphia, 1835.

Economic and Social History of New England, 1620–1789, William B. Weeden, Boston, 1890.

History of Norwich, Connecticut, Frances Mainwaring Caulkins, Norwich, 1866.

History and Antiquities of Boston, Samuel Drake, Boston, 1856.

History of Lynn, Massachusetts, Alonzo Lewis and James R. Newhall, Boston, 1865.

Life of William Penn, Samuel M. Janney, Philadelphia, 1852.

The Germans in Pennsylvania, William Beidelman, Easton, 1898.

The Story of Louisiana, Maurice Thompson, Boston, 1889.

Colonial Days and Ways, Helen Evertson Smith, New York, 1900.

Dutch and Quaker Colonies in America, John Fiske, Boston, 1899.

New Jersey as a Colony and as a State, Francis Bagley Lee, New York, 1902.

Social History of Flatbush, Mrs. Vanderbilt, New York, 1881.

History of New York, M. J. Lamb, New York, 1877.

A Short History of the English Colonies in America, Henry Cabot Lodge, New York, 1881.

A Story of the City of New York, Charles Burr Todd, New York, 1888.

Goode Vrow of Manahatta, Mrs. John King Van Rensselaer, New York, 1898.

Discovery of the Great Northwest, James Baldwin, New York, 1901.

History of the Antiquities of St. Augustine, Florida, George R. Fairbanks, New York, 1858.

Description of Louisiana in 1683, Father Hennepin, New York, 1888.

Men, Women and Manners in Colonial Times, Sidney G. Fisher, Philadelphia, 1898.

Annals of Philadelphia, John Watson, Philadelphia, 1829.

Annals of New York, John Watson, Philadelphia, 1846.

Letters to Franklin by his Family and Friends, 1751–1790, New York, 1859.

Child Life in Colonial Days, Mrs. Alice Morse Earle, New York, 1899.

Costume of Colonial Times, Mrs. Alice Morse Earle, New York, 1894.

Life of Margaret Winthrop, Mrs. Alice Morse Earle, New York, 1895.

Dolly Madison, Mrs. Goodwin, New York, 1896.

The Writings of George Washington, edited by Wm. Chauncey Ford, New York, 1889.

Martha Washington, Anne Hollingsworth Wharton, New York, 1896.

The Quaker, a Study in Costume, Mrs. Francis Gummere, Philadelphia, 1902.

Colonial Days and Dames, Anne Hollingsworth Wharton, Philadelphia, 1898.

Journal and Correspondence of Abigail Adams, New York, 1841.

Diary of Sally Wister, Philadelphia, 1902.

L'Evantail, Octave Uzanne, Paris, 1882.

L'Ombrelle; le gant; et le Mouchoir, Octave Uzanne, Paris, 1883.

Son Altesse, la Femme, Octave Uzanne, Paris, 1885.

Autobiography and Correspondence of Mrs. Delaney, Boston, 1880.

Diary of Madame D'Arblay, London, 1842.

History of the United States, Thomas Higginson, Boston, 1875.

The Republican Court, Rufus W. Griswold, New York, 1855.

Pioneers of France in the New World, Francis Parkman, Boston, 1865.

Discovery of the Great West, Francis Parkman, Boston, 1869.

The Spectator, London, 1712.

Pepys' Diary, edited by H. B. Wheatley, London, 1896.

Evelyn's Diary, edited by H. B. Wheatley, London, 1879.

Table Talk of Samuel Rogers, New York, 1856.

Nollekins and His Times, John T. Smith, London, 1895.

Trachten der Völker, A. Kretchmer, Leipzig, 1864.

Cyclopædia of Costume, J. R. Planché, London, 1876.

Pictorial History of England, Charles Knight, London, 1841.

History of English Dress, Mrs. Hill, London, 1893.

Annals of Fashion by a Lady of Rank, London, 1847.

Yester-year, Ten Centuries of Toilette, A. Robida, London, 1892.

History of Fashion in France, Augustin Challamel, London, 1882.

Institutions, Usages et Costumes du 17ieme siecle, Paul Lacroix, Paris, 1880.

Institutions, Usages et Costumes du 18ieme siecle, Paul Lacroix, Paris, 1878.

Costume in England, F. W. Fairholt, London, 1846.

England in the Eighteenth Century, William Connor Sydney, New York, 1891.

Notes on Civil Costume in England, Hon. Lewis Wingfield, London, 1889.

Le Costume Historique, A. Racinet, Paris, 1891.

Memoirs of Lady Sarah Lennox, London, 1902.

Civil Costume in England, Charles Martin, London, 1842.

Men, Maidens and Manners a Hundred Years Ago, John Ashton, London, 1888.

Brides and Bridals, John Cordy Jeffreson, London, 1872.

Mundus Muliebris and *The Fop's Dictionary*, Mary Evelyn, edited by her father, London, 1690.

Percy Society Publications, London, 1849.

Their Majesties' Servants, or Annals of the English Stage, Dr. Doran, London, 1865.

Glossary of Words, Phrases, Names and Allusions, Robert Nares, London, 1828.

Chronicles of Fashion, Mrs. Stone, London, 1848.

Gainsborough, Sir Walter Armstrong, London, 1898.

Sir Joshua Reynolds, Sir Walter Armstrong, London, 1900.

Hogarth, John and Joshua Boydell, London, 1798.

Romney, Sir Herbert Maxwell, London, 1902.

The Every Day Book, William Hone, London, 1826.

The King's Peace, a historical sketch of the English Law Courts, F. A. Inderwick, Q. C., London, 1895.

A Book about Lawyers, John Cordy Jeffreson, Barrister at Law, London, 1867.

Bench and Bar of Philadelphia, John Hill Martin, Philadelphia, 1883.

Sketches of the Judicial History of Massachusetts, 1630-1775, Emory Washburn, Boston, 1840.

A History of the American Church, Rt. Rev. Leighton Coleman, D.D., Bishop of Delaware, New York, 1903.

History of the American Episcopal Church, Rt. Rev. William Stevens Perry, D.D., Bishop of Iowa.

A Book about the Clergy, John Cordy Jeffreson, London, 1870.

A Book about Doctors, John Cordy Jeffreson, New York, 1861.

Diary of Samuel Sewall, Massachusetts Historical Collections, Boston, 1878.

Literary Diary of Ezra Stiles, D.D., LL.D., New York, 1901.

Diary of Manasseh Cutler, Cincinnati, 1888.

History of the British Army, Hon. J. W. Fortescue, London, 1902.

History of Our Navy, John R. Spears, New York, 1897.

Uniforms of the United States Army, 1775-1900, Published by the United States Government, Washington, 1900.

74
76
77